Studies in Economic History

Aims and Scope

This series from Springer provides a platform for works in economic history that truly integrate economics and history. Books on a wide range of related topics are welcomed and encouraged, including those in macro-economic history, financial history, labor history, industrial history, agricultural history, the history of institutions and organizations, spatial economic history, law and economic history, political economic history, historical demography, and environmental history.

Economic history studies have greatly developed over the past several decades through application of economics and econometrics. Particularly in recent years, a variety of new economic theories and sophisticated econometric techniques—including game theory, spatial economics, and generalized method of moment (GMM)—have been introduced for the great benefit of economic historians and the research community.

At the same time, a good economic history study should contribute more than just an application of economics and econometrics to past data. It raises novel research questions, proposes a new view of history, and/or provides rich documentation. This series is intended to integrate data analysis, close examination of archival works, and application of theoretical frameworks to offer new insights and even provide opportunities to rethink theories.

The purview of this new Springer series is truly global, encompassing all nations and areas of the world as well as all eras from ancient times to the present. The editorial board, who are internationally renowned leaders among economic historians, carefully evaluate and judge each manuscript, referring to reports from expert reviewers. The series publishes contributions by university professors and others well established in the academic community, as well as work deemed to be of equivalent merit.

More information about this series at http://www.springer.com/series/13279

Tomoko Hashino • Keijiro Otsuka
Editors

Industrial Districts in History and the Developing World

Springer

Editors
Tomoko Hashino
Kobe University
Kobe, Japan

Keijiro Otsuka
Kobe University
Kobe, Japan

ISSN 2364-1797 ISSN 2364-1800 (electronic)
Studies in Economic History
ISBN 978-981-10-9097-4 ISBN 978-981-10-0182-6 (eBook)
DOI 10.1007/978-981-10-0182-6

Softcover reprint of the hardcover 1st edition 2016

Printed on acid-free paper

This Springer imprint is published by Springer Nature
The registered company is Springer Science+Business Media Singapore Pte Ltd.

Preface

This book attempts to shed new light on the development of industrial districts in the past and at present. The industrial district, which refers to the geographical concentration of enterprises producing similar or closely related commodities in a small area, plays a significant role in the development of manufacturing industries not only historically in Europe and Japan but also at present in emerging East Asian economies and low-income countries in sub-Saharan Africa. The book identifies similarities and dissimilarities in the development patterns of a variety of industrial districts and explores the reasons for them. More specifically, the book examines whether Marshallian agglomeration economies provide sufficient explanations for the development patterns of industrial districts and seeks to discover common key factors that support the sustainable development of industrial districts but which did not receive enough attention in the literature. We are proud to say that this is the first systematic study that addresses the issue of these missing key factors.

In spite of the common issues studied by economic historians and development economists regarding the role of industrial districts, the dialogue between the two groups of researchers has been largely absent or at best weak. Thus, the editors of this volume organized a session entitled "Visiting Industrial Districts in History and the Developing World" at the 17th World Economic History Congress in Kyoto, Japan, in August 2015 by inviting both economic historians and development economists. Many authors of this volume, including Tetshushi Sonobe, Jordi Domenech, Jianqing Ruan, and the two of us, were presenters in this session. Pierre Vernus also participated. Through active discussions and mutual learning in Kyoto, we all agreed to publish a collected volume of case studies on industrial districts in history and the developing world. To enrich this volume, we invited Hubert Schmitz and Bernard Musyck to contribute their study on the postwar development of four industrial districts in Europe. We appreciate their positive response to our request.

The ultimate purpose of this book is to synthesize the results of all the case studies by economic historians interested in Spain, France, and other European countries and Japan and those by development economists interested in China, Vietnam, Bangladesh, Tanzania, and other countries in sub-Saharan Africa. Because, to our knowledge, collaboration between economic historians and development economists is rare, all the authors in this volume are hoping to prove that this type of collaboration is exceedingly fruitful.

In the course of preparing this volume, we have received useful support and comments from a large number of researchers. In particular, we would like to thank Takeshi Abe, Steve Broadberry, Janet Hunter, Debin Ma, Tetsuji Okazaki, Maarten Prak, Izumi Shirai, and Masayuki Tanimoto. We also benefited from valuable comments given by Osamu Saito, Yukihiko Kiyokawa, Ryoshin Minami, Konosuke Odaka, and Mataji Umemura, who have built the academic tradition at the Institute of Economic Research in Hitotsubashi University, in which economic development is properly regarded as a long-term historical process. We would also like to thank Yasuko Maeshima, Megumi Nishino, and Kumi Ogata for their editorial assistance. Finally, we are grateful for the financial support from the Japan Society for the Promotion of Science (JSPS KAKENHI Grant numbers (C) 25380425 and 25101002).

Kobe, Japan

Tomoko Hashino
Keijiro Otsuka

Contents

Contributors

Jordi Domenech Department of Social Sciences, Universidad Carlos III de Madrid, Getafe, Madrid, Spain

Tomoko Hashino Graduate School of Economics, Kobe University, Kobe, Japan

Bernard Musyck School of Economic Sciences and Administration, Frederick University, Nicosia, Cyprus

Keijiro Otsuka Graduate School of Economics, Kobe University, Kobe, Japan

Joan Ramon Rosés Department of Economic History, London School of Economics, London, UK

Jianqing Ruan China Academy for Rural Development, Zhejiang University, Zhejiang, China

Hubert Schmitz Institute of Development Studies, University of Sussex, Brighton, UK

Tetsushi Sonobe National Graduate Institute for Policy Studies, Tokyo, Japan

Pierre Vernus Rhône-Alpes Historical Research Unit (LARHRA), Lyon University, Lyon, France

Xiaobo Zhang International Food Policy Research Institute, Washington, DC, USA

About the Editors

Tomoko Hashino is a professor of economic history at Kobe University. Her research interests are in the evolutionary process of the textile industry in Japan as well as the development history of weaving districts in modern Japan. Her recent articles have appeared in the *Economic History Review*, *Business History Review*, *Australian Economic History Review*, and *Journal of the Japanese and International Economies*. Professor Hashino received her Ph.D. in economics from Hitotsubashi University in 2002. She has been a visiting fellow at the University of New South Wales, the London School of Economics and Political Science, and George Washington University.

Keijiro Otsuka is a professor of development economics at the Graduate School of Economics, Kobe University. After receiving a Ph.D. in economics from the University of Chicago in 1979, he served as an associate professor and a professor of economics at Tokyo Metropolitan University until 2001, when he joined GRIPS, where he was professor until March 2016.

He has been working extensively on the Green Revolution, land tenancy, property rights and natural resource management, cluster-based industrial development, and poverty dynamics. His studies are primarily survey-based with comparative perspectives between Asia and sub-Saharan Africa.

He received the Purple Ribbon Medal from the Japanese government in 2010 and was selected as an honorary life member of the International Association of Agricultural Economists in 2012, fellow of the Agricultural and Applied Economics Association (formerly the American Agricultural Economics Association) in 2013, and a distinguished fellow of the African Association of Agricultural Economists in 2013. He is the coauthor or coeditor of 23 books.

List of Figures

List of Tables

Part I
Introduction

Chapter 1
Beyond Marshallian Agglomeration Economies

Tomoko Hashino and Keijiro Otsuka

Abstract Most, if not all, industrial development in the history of advanced countries and in the developing world is based on the development of industrial districts. A unique feature of this edited volume is to compare the development of industrial districts in the history of Japan, Spain, France, other European countries as well as contemporary developing countries, including China, Bangladesh, and Tanzania. More similarities than dissimilarities are found in the role played by international technology transfer in stimulating innovation, which is an engine of development for industrial districts across a large number of cases. Also commonly found are critical roles played by producer cooperatives and local as well as central governments in internalizing benefits of Marshallian agglomeration economies. After all, this volume demonstrates the importance of collaboration between economic historians and development economists for a deeper understanding of the development process of industrial districts.

Keywords Industrial districts • International technology transfer • Producer cooperatives • Local and central governments • Marshallian agglomeration economies

1.1 Introduction

While economic historians in general are interested in the long-term development process of economies or economic sectors from low-income to higher income stages, development economists are concerned primarily with the development of low-income economies or their economic sectors compared with middle- and high-income economies. Obviously, there is a great deal of overlap between the interests of these two groups of economists. In fact, *The Second Industrial Divide* by Piore and Sabel (1984), which analyzed the postwar development of industrial districts in northern Italy, attracted a lot of attention from both economic historians and development economists.

T. Hashino (✉) • K. Otsuka
Graduate School of Economics, Kobe University, Kobe, Japan
e-mail: hashino@econ.kobe-u.ac.jp

T. Hashino, K. Otsuka (eds.), *Industrial Districts in History and the Developing World*, Studies in Economic History, DOI 10.1007/978-981-10-0182-6_1

At the outset, it is important to emphasize that, more often than not, the development of manufacturing industries is led by industrial district or cluster,[1] which is defined as "a geographical concentration or localization of enterprises producing similar or closely related goods in a small area" (Sonobe and Otsuka 2006, p. 4). Obviously, the Industrial Revolution in seventeenth and eighteenth century U.K. was based on a number of industrial districts in different major cities (Pollard 1981). The Silicon Valley in the U.S. is an outstanding example of a successful industrial district at present. It is also well-known that the development of indigenous manufacturing sectors in prewar Japan since the Meiji Restoration—e.g., the cotton- and silk-weaving industries—was based on industrial districts (Abe 1992, 2003; Abe and Saito 1988; Hashino 2012; Hashino and Kurosawa 2013; Hashino and Saito 2004).[2] Moreover, industrial development in China and in almost all developing countries in Asia and Africa is also led by the development of industrial districts (Long and Zhang 2011; Sonobe and Otsuka 2006, 2011). Therefore, both economic historians and development economists are strongly interested in the development of industrial districts.

In spite of similarities of interest in industrial districts, there has been little dialogue between economic historians and development economists about the development of industrial districts.[3] Is the mechanism behind the development of industrial districts in history qualitatively different from that in a contemporary developing world? If there are similarities, what are they? If there are not many similarities, how different are they and why is it the case? More deeply, what lessons can we learn from historical studies of the long-term development process of industrial districts in order to formulate policies that support the rise of such districts in developing countries? The first and fundamental purpose of this edited volume is to demonstrate that lessons from history are useful to achieve a greater understanding of factors that currently enhance the growth of industrial districts in developing countries.

Alfred Marshall (1920) was the first economist to theoretically characterize the advantages of industrial districts. These are (1) the ease of division and specialization of labor among enterprises producing various parts and components and assemblers, (2) information spillover or imitation, and (3) the development of skilled labor markets. If an enterprise is located in an isolated place without any part-suppliers or assemblers, this enterprise has to incur a large cost in transacting with this group of suppliers or assemblers based in a distant place; it would not know the development of new products, the introduction of new production methods, and the availability of

[1] While economic historians usually use the term "industrial districts," development economists generally use the term "industrial cluster." In our view, there is no essential difference between the two.

[2] The development of such indigenous sectors was more important than the development of modern sectors in terms of employment generation during the Meiji era in Japan (Nakamura 1983).

[3] Zeitlin (2008) points out that, although there has been burgeoning literature on industrial districts or regional clusters by historians and contemporary social scientists, a mutually productive dialogue has not been conducted mainly due to a disciplinary divide.

workers with a variety of skills elsewhere. Thus, a new enterprise prefers to be located in an industrial district, where transactions with other enterprises are easy, useful information is readily available, and workers with the desired skills can be easily found. Marshall's argument of agglomeration economies is highly convincing in explaining why industrial districts abound.

The death of distance or the huge fall in communication cost facilitates the formation of large industrial districts because it is primarily production cost rather than transport cost that determines the competitiveness of industrial districts. Thus, efficient industrial districts can dominate the world markets, as may be seen in the discussion of giant industrial districts in Zhejiang Province in China (see Chap. 10). On the other hand, the death of distance facilitates the dispersion of industrial locations if agglomeration economies are weak or non-existent. This is likely to be the case in computer-based business-processing service industries that are moving to small towns and distant countries, where quality of service is high and input cost is low.

The defect in Marshall's argument of agglomeration economies is the absence of the "theory of innovation." Since the time of Joseph Schumpeter (1912), economists have known that innovation is an engine of growth. What shall entrepreneurs in the industrial district imitate if there is no mechanism of generating innovations in the districts in the first place? Actually, innovation is an engine of growth in many industrial districts, as will be demonstrated in this volume.[4] Thus, the theory of agglomeration economies of the industrial district is incomplete, unless it furnishes the mechanism that generates the innovations. If the industrial district has inherent forces to generate innovations, it tends to expand production continuously and maintain prominence over an extended period. Thus, a technology gap is created between the central district and peripheral districts in other countries, but the latter may be protected from competition from the former by large transport costs. In the longer run, however, the technology gap may create opportunities that peripheral districts can take advantage of and they may begin to develop on the basis of international technology transfer. Although this volume fails to provide concrete evidence, it suggests the importance of technological innovations and international technology transfer in explaining the historical rise and fall of world economic inequalities, as argued by Brandt et al. (2014), Mokyr (1990), and Murmann (2003), among others.

The second major purpose of this study is to explore how innovation takes place in the industrial district, which is universally an engine of growth. We postulate that a pivotal role is played by technology transfer from advanced to less advanced districts in the same country or, more importantly, across countries. Transferred technology, however, will be imitated quickly within an industrial district, as is aptly pointed out by Marshall. Because of such imitation, a gap is created between private and social returns to innovation, which implies that private incentive to innovate is likely to be suboptimal. Consequently, innovation activities are likely to be inactive

[4] See, for example, Sonobe and Otsuka (2006, 2011, 2014) for the role of innovations in the development of industrial districts in developing countries in Asia and Africa.

or even absent in the industrial districts, unless institutions are developed to internalize the externalities or benefit of knowledge spillovers. Our hypothesis is that, in order to internalize the external benefits of innovation, collective action is taken by entrepreneurs in the industrial districts, taking advantage of low transaction costs among them, which arise from close geographical proximities. In other words, we postulate that a trade association, a producer cooperative, or any other collective organization plays a central role in generating innovations in successfully developed industrial districts. Schmitz (1995) aptly argues that the "collective efficiency" of an industrial district is enhanced by such a collective action.[5]

It must be clearly recognized that innovation usually entails upgrading of product quality. Since buyers, retailers, and consumers of products cannot accurately assess the quality of improved products, the problem of information asymmetry arises. Thus, to be successful, not only must new innovative technologies be introduced but improved marketing methods as well. Establishing the reputation of the industrial district as the home of dependable, high-quality producers is often a key marketing strategy. To do so, the producers' group must undertake quality inspections to ensure the supply of high-quality products from the district. Hence, collective action by the producers' group is critically important in both technological and marketing innovations.

Similar to industrial districts in the manufacturing sector, the geographical concentration of production of such high-quality agricultural products as fresh fruits, vegetables, and livestock is widely observed historically in developed countries and in contemporary developing countries.[6] Since information spillovers, which tend to suppress private incentives to innovate, and quality control, which is designed to reduce information asymmetry, are essential issues in the development of these "agricultural districts," as in the case of industrial districts, it will be of interest to compare the development of the two types of districts.[7] A unique feature of this edited volume is the analysis of how "agricultural districts" have developed in comparison with "industrial districts."

While "local" spillover effects may be effectively internalized by the producer cooperatives, there are cases in which support for them by local and central government is in order. For example, Japanese consulates under the guidance of the central government reported the reputation of exported Japanese silk cloth in Europe to local industrial districts in Japan (Hashino 2010). The local government can endorse the function of trade associations, determine the grade of products, and legally

[5] In his literature review, Zeitlin (2008) points out the prevalence of vocational education and training systems and research and technology transfer institutions organized by producer cooperatives, particularly in Europe.

[6] In the case of districts growing agricultural products, information spillovers and assurance of product quality are critically important but not division of labor and the development of labor market.

[7] Similar to the lack of dialogue between economic historians and development economists, there has been absence of interactions between agricultural economists interested in the production of high-value products under contract farming and other economists interested in the development of industrial districts. See Otsuka et al. (2016) for a recent review of literature on contract farming.

punish enterprises that violate collective agreements. We therefore hypothesize that government plays a supporting role in generating innovations in industrial districts.

Based on the preceding discussion, this volume consists of four parts. Part I discusses the main themes of this volume—i.e., drawing insights beyond Marshallian agglomeration economies and establishing a new paradigm of the long-term development of industrial districts, which may be referred to as the SOH model (after Sonobe, Otsuka, and Hashino) and will be discussed in Chap. 2. Part II tackles the pivotal role of technology transfer, Part III focuses on the central role of producer cooperatives, and Part IV deals with the supporting role of governments. Part II to Part IV consist of two to three chapters: the first one is about the historical case of Europe; the second one, about the case of prewar or postwar Japan; and the third, about contemporary developing countries.[8] By comparing how innovations are generated through various case studies, we attempt to shed new light on hitherto neglected but critically important aspects of the development of industrial districts. In the remainder of this chapter, we briefly explain the essence of the three parts of the book.

1.2 Pivotal Role of Technology Transfer

More often than not, new industrial districts are established by technology imports from more advanced districts abroad or in the same country. Furthermore, the subsequent development of the industrial district is often governed by the pace of technology imports in the later stage of its development. Thus, Part I of this volume is devoted to an elucidation of the pivotal role played by technology transfer in the development of industrial districts.

The cotton textile industry complex in Spain, which is analyzed in Chap. 3, is an interesting example, as it was greatly influenced by imports of advanced technologies from the cotton-spinning and -weaving industries in the U.K. The chapter initially describes the role of domestic public and civil institutions in promoting the adoption of foreign technologies and the rapid upgrading of domestic capabilities since the late eighteenth century. The diffusion of spinning and weaving technologies in the first half of the nineteenth century met with the need to adapt foreign technologies to domestic capabilities, to local factor endowments (capital, sources of energy, and labor), and regional markets, a process, which, in turn, generated internal differentiation within the industrial district. This study depicts the changes in the competitive advantages of regions within the same district, the process of creative destruction, and the upgrading of capabilities and product quality in the nineteenth century. It also documents spillovers and backward and forward linkages (machinery production, mining, and transport, among others) in the booming period

[8] In Part III, Chap. 7 reviews the development of agricultural district in prewar Japan in comparison with that in contemporary developing countries.

of the industry. Finally, this chapter explores the maturation process of the district and its long-term transformation.

Chapter 4 analyzes the development of three silk-weaving districts in prewar Japan—Nishijin, Kiryu, and Fukui. Nishijin, located in Kyoto City, which was the capital of Japan until 1868, was the oldest and most advanced silk-weaving district in Japan. Nishijin specialized in the production of high-quality *kimono* by employing highly skilled workers. To modernize this industry, the Kyoto prefectural government sent a delegate to Lyon to learn about advanced weaving technologies in the late nineteenth century. Kiryu, located 150 km north of Tokyo, imitated the technology from Nishijin and produced a somewhat lower quality *kimono* for mass consumption. Kiryu also produced simple plain silk cloth, called *habutae*, for export in the 1880s but discontinued its production thereafter. While the production of *habutae* used unskilled labor, Kiryu was not a low-wage area. The government of Fukui prefecture, which had no tradition of silk-weaving industries as well as other industries, invited an instructor from Kiryu to teach *habutae* production. Interestingly, the Fukui industrial district became most active in introducing power looms and most successful in exporting *habutae* to Europe and the U.S., unlike Nishijin and Kiryu, which largely specialized in silk production for domestic markets. Such differences are attributed to different endowments of skilled weaving workers among the three industrial districts. This comparative case study clearly attests to the importance of technology transfer from abroad and from advanced to less advanced industrial districts within Japan.

Technology transfer plays a critical role in the establishment of new industrial districts and in their subsequent development not only in the historical cases of Spain and Japan but also in developing countries. Chapter 5 reports the "miraculous" development of the garment district in Bangladesh and the less impressive but exceptionally successful development of the garment district in sub-Saharan Africa. In the case of Bangladesh, the garment industry now employs nearly 4 million workers and accounts for 80 % of the country's export. Its development began with the training of newly recruited and highly educated 130 workers in Korea for 8 months by Daewoo, which was interested in embarking on garment production in Bangladesh. Within a few years after their return to Bangladesh, all 130 workers quit their original job and initiated either garment enterprises or trading houses, which provided inputs, technological information, and export services to newly established enterprises. It is clear that the spectacular development of this industry would not have been possible without the intensive training of these newly recruited workers. Much less intensive short-term training in garment production was offered by the United Nations Industrial Development Organization for female entrepreneurs in Tanzania in the 1990s. This led to the establishment of hundreds of small-scale garment enterprises, majority of which are managed by female entrepreneurs. This case adds to the growing body of evidence that shows that technology transfer from abroad can contribute to the development of industrial districts in developing countries.

The three chapters in Part II demonstrate the utmost importance of technology transfer in the development of industrial districts. Furthermore, the cases of Fukui in Japan, Bangladesh, and Tanzania prove that training is an effective means to facilitate technology transfer.

1.3 Central Role of Producer Cooperatives

As mentioned earlier, producer cooperatives can play dual roles in internalizing information externalities among enterprises within the industrial district and in assuring product quality to resolve the information asymmetry problem associated with quality upgrading. Cases supporting such arguments abound in both history and in the developing world. Indeed, all chapters in Parts II and III deal with cases in which producer cooperatives or trade associations contributed to the development of industrial districts, including "agricultural districts" in Chap. 7. Three chapters included in Part IV touch not only on the contribution of producer cooperatives but also on the supportive role played by governments.

External and adverse shocks often trigger institutional innovations by a group of producers in the industrial district. The analysis of the development of a silk-weaving district in Lyon (Chap. 6) as well as the case studies of a number of industrial districts in Zhejang Province, China (Chap. 10) addresses this issue. Lyon traditionally depended on high-quality raw silk produced in Europe, particularly in Italy. However, silkworm diseases broke out, destroying the supply capacity of high-quality raw silk in Europe in the middle of the nineteenth century. Thus, producers of high-quality silk fabrics in Lyon were forced to use imported silk of unknown and varying quality from China and Japan. As a result, the quality of silk fabrics produced in Lyon not only declined generally but also varied from enterprise to enterprise, which has created information asymmetry among consumers. There was obviously a need to improve product quality in Lyon to restore its reputation as an excellent silk producer. It was the trade associations in Lyon that undertook inspection of the quality of raw silk imported from Asia, assuring the quality of the products. The author concludes that were it not for this collective action, Lyon would have lost its reputation as an industrial district that produces high-quality silk fabrics.

A producer cooperative is expected to introduce new technologies, acquire and disseminate marketing information, and assure product quality in the industrial district. These are exactly the activities that led to the successful production of apples and tangerine oranges in small districts in Japan (Chap. 6). The apple-growing district was newly established in Aomori prefecture, owing to the collective actions of producer cooperatives in prewar Japan. In the postwar period, some orange-growing district attempted to upgrade the quality of the products, assure their quality, and establish regional brands. Here, too, the producer cooperatives played a key role in promoting high-quality products in the market by providing production instructions and engaging in quality assurance.

In developing countries, the export of fresh fruits and vegetables to high-income countries has sharply increased in the last few decades. To ensure quality and safety of products, contract farming emerged. Agents of supermarkets in high-income countries and farmers in developing countries discuss not only volume, quality, product price, and time of delivery but also the use of high-quality inputs and improved production methods. This is similar to 'putting-out' contracts in manufacturing. While it is expected that contract farming brings about modern improved production technologies and marketing systems, there is fear of a big income gap between the rich large farmers and the poor small-scale farmers because it is much cheaper for purchasing agents to make a small number of contracts with large farmers than a large number of contracts with small farmers. To avoid the exclusion of small farmers, producer cooperatives, consisting of small-scale farmers, play a critical role. Chapter 7 provides a comprehensive review of the literature on contract farming, the role of producer cooperatives, and the inclusion of small farmers in developing countries. Although detailed descriptive analyses of each producer cooperative are lacking, many lessons can still be learned from the experience of these Japanese cooperatives that may prove crucial in replicating the approach to institutions in developing countries.

Thus, two chapters in Part III commonly elucidate on the critical role played by producer cooperatives in upgrading or maintaining the quality of products and establishing brand names, thereby contributing to the development of industrial districts. This finding deepens our understanding of the advantages of industrial districts beyond the Marshallian agglomeration economies.

1.4 Supporting Role of Local Government

Chapter 8 provides an interesting account of the four industrial districts in Europe—the Third Italy, Baden-Württemberg in Germany, West Jutland in Denmark, and South-West Flanders in Belgium. Despite hugely different historical backgrounds, cultures, and stages of development compared with Asia and developing countries, producer cooperatives play critical roles in the provision of training, credit, and miscellaneous services, which is consistent with our hypothesis that effective collective action is needed to internalize the externalities. This study finds that, although governments or government-sponsored institutions cannot create an effective industrial organization, including producer cooperatives, once private initiative has led to collective action, they can play an important part in helping industry to innovate and expand.

Surprisingly, similar phenomena are reported in the development of various industrial districts engaged in weaving of silk fabrics in prewar Japan (Chap. 9). Producer cooperatives set up training centers in order to introduce new technologies from more advanced industrial districts and abroad. As the level of technologies taught in the training centers became more advanced and complicated, producer cooperatives needed instructors from advanced institutions. At this stage, producer cooperatives requested the prefectural government as well as the central government to assist in the training program by sending qualified instructors. Gradually, the training centers initially created with private initiative were institutionalized, meaning that these centers have become vocational schools, which significantly contributed to the subsequent growth of the industrial districts.

The quality of products coming from newly developed industrial districts in Zhejiang Province in China was awfully low in the 1980s and the 1990s, which led to consumer boycott of products originating from this province. Consequently, the negative shocks posed a serious threat to the survival of many small enterprises in the industrial districts. Chapter 10 describes how such a crisis catalyzed collective action from entrepreneurs to enhance product quality and promote improved production methods. The local governments actively supported such collective actions by strengthening industrial associations, training workers, establishing quality inspection centers, and facilitating research and development activities. These efforts led to dramatic improvement of product quality in a large number of industrial districts in this province, which, in turn, resulted in a remarkable industrial district-based development in Zhejiang.

It is clear from the three studies in Part IV that government can play a critically important role in facilitating the development of industrial districts by providing public goods and services. One must also recall local government assistance in importing technology for the cotton textile industrial complex in Spain (Chap. 3) and the silk-weaving industrial districts in Japan (Chap. 4). This is a useful lesson for governments in developing countries, which have seldom taken any supportive policy measures to develop their industrial districts.

References

Abe T (1992) The development of the producing-center cotton textile industry in Japan between the two world wars. Jpn Yearb Bus His 9:4–27

Abe T (2003) The development of the putting-out system in modern Japan: the case of the cotton industry. In: Odaka K, Sawai M (eds) Small firms, large concerns: the development of small business in comparative perspective. Oxford University Press, Oxford

Abe T, Saito O (1988) From putting-out to the factory: a cotton weaving district in the late Meiji Japan. Text Hist 19(2):143–158

Brandt L, Ma D, Rawski TG (2014) From divergence to convergence: reevaluating the history behind China's economic growth. J Econ Lit 52(1):45–123

Hashino T (2010) The importance of consular reports for the export growth of Japanese silk fabric *Habutae* in the Late 19th century. In: Ulbert J, Prijac L (eds) Consulship in the 19th century. DOBU Verlag, Hamburg

Hashino T (2012) Institutionalising technical education: the case of weaving districts in Meiji Japan. Aust Econ Hist Rev 52(1):25–42

Hashino T, Kurosawa T (2013) Beyond Marshallian agglomeration economies: the roles of trade associations in Meiji Japan. Bus His Rev 87(3):489–513

Hashino T, Saito O (2004) Tradition and interaction: research trends in modern Japanese industrial history. Aust Econ Hist Rev 44(3):241–258

Long C, Zhang X (2011) Cluster-based industrialization in China: financing and performance. J Int Econ 84(1):112–123

Marshall A (1920) Principles of economics. Macmillan, London

Mokyr J (1990) The lever of riches: technological creativity and economic progress. Oxford University Press, Oxford
Murmann JP (2003) Knowledge and competitive advantage: the coevolution of firms, technology, and national institutions. Cambridge University Press, Cambridge
Nakamura T (1983) Economic growth in prewar Japan. Yale University Press, New Haven
Otsuka K, Nakano Y, Takahashi K (2016, forthcoming) Contract farming in developed and developing countries. Annual Review of Resource Economics
Piore MJ, Sabel CF (1984) The second industrial divide: possibilities for prosperity. Basic Books, New York
Pollard S (1981) Peaceful conquest: the industrialization of Europe, 1760–1970. Oxford University Press, Oxford
Schmitz H (1995) Collective efficiency: growth path for small-scale industry. J Dev Stud 31(4):529–566
Schumpeter JA (1912) The theory of economic development. Oxford University Press, New York
Sonobe T, Otsuka K (2006) Cluster-based industrial development: an East Asian model. Palgrave Macmillan, Basingstoke
Sonobe T, Otsuka K (2011) Cluster-based industrial development: a comparative study of Asia and Africa. Palgrave Macmillan, Basingstoke
Sonobe T, Otsuka K (2014) Cluster-based industrial development: *Kaizen* management for MSE growth in developing countries. Palgrave Macmillan, Basingstoke
Zeitlin J (2008) Industrial districts and regional clusters. In: Jones GG, Zeitlin J (eds) The Oxford handbook of business history. Oxford University Press, Oxford

Chapter 2
Toward a New Paradigm of the Long-Term Development of Industrial Districts

Tetsushi Sonobe, Keijiro Otsuka, and Tomoko Hashino

Abstract While the model of long-term development of industrial districts proposed by Sonobe and Otsuka (Cluster-based industrial development: an East Asian model. Palgrave Macmillan, Basingstoke 2006; Cluster-based industrial development: a comparative study of Asia and Africa. Palgrave Macmillan, Basingstoke, 2011) is useful for understanding the economic forces that lead to the formation of an industrial district, the low and declining profitability of continuing production of low-quality products and the inducement to innovation for quality improvement by innovative entrepreneurs, it is not sufficient to explain the diverse development paths of industrial districts throughout history and across the developing world. This chapter attempts to extend and elaborate the Sonobe-Otsuka model in the light of a variety of empirical findings reported in various chapters in this volume. A new comprehensive model, which may be termed the SOH (Sonobe-Otsuka-Hashino) model, takes into account the roles of technology transfer, producer cooperatives or trade associations, and governments in transforming "survival" clusters into "dynamic" ones by facilitating and sustaining "multi-faceted" innovations.

Keywords Quality crisis • Technology transfer • Trade association • Role of government • Sonobe-Otsuka model • SOH model

2.1 Introduction

While Marshallian agglomeration economies explain why many enterprises are clustered, they cannot explain why there are both static or survival clusters and dynamic clusters.[1] Sonobe and Otsuka (2006, 2011, 2014) strongly argue that the key to understanding the long-term development process of industrial district is to

[1] As was pointed out in Chap. 1, we use the terms "cluster" and "district" interchangeably.

T. Sonobe
National Graduate Institute for Policy Studies, Tokyo, Japan

K. Otsuka (✉) • T. Hashino
Graduate School of Economics, Kobe University, Kobe, Japan
e-mail: otsuka@econ.kobe-u.ac.jp

T. Hashino, K. Otsuka (eds.), *Industrial Districts in History and the Developing World*, Studies in Economic History, DOI 10.1007/978-981-10-0182-6_2

identify the economic forces that lead to innovations. While their model is useful in understanding why such forces are conducive to the long-term development of industrial districts, it cannot sufficiently explain the diverse development paths of industrial clusters reported in this volume.

The purpose of this chapter is to synthesize major findings reported in this volume in the light of an extended and enriched version of the Sonobe-Otsuka model of long-term development of industrial districts, which may be termed the SOH (Sonobe, Otsuka, and Hashino) model. The rest of this chapter is structured as follows. Section 2.2 briefly reviews the original Sonobe-Otsuka model. Section 2.3 highlights the importance of technology transfer in stimulating innovations, whereas Section 2.4 discusses the role of quality crisis in inducing innovations. Sections 2.5 and 2.6 examine the roles of producer cooperatives or trade associations and local and central governments in internalizing external economies so as to realize innovations. Section 2.7 summarizes the essence of the SOH model of long-term development of industrial districts.

2.2 The Sonobe-Otsuka Model Revisited

The Sonobe-Otsuka model consists of three stages of development of industrial clusters (Sonobe and Otsuka 2006, pp. 27–33): (1) initiation stage, (2) quantity expansion stage, and (3) quality improvement stage. An entrepreneur or a group of entrepreneurs initiates a new business often by imitating an imported good from more advanced countries. If the product is easy to produce but difficult to sell, as is the case with garments and leather shoes, it is usually traders who initiate the new business. On the other hand, if the product is difficult to produce but easy to sell, as is the case with machinery, it is often engineers who initiate the new business. The quality of products at the initiation stage is low because entrepreneurs may be inexperienced and because some materials and parts as well as skilled workers available in more advanced countries may be unavailable in a developing country. Yet, profitability tends to be high because of the high demand of low-income consumers who prefer the low-quality but low-priced products to the high-quality but high-priced imported good. This situation is depicted by the left part of Fig. 2.1, which is adopted from Sonobe and Otsuka (2011, p. 6).

The high profit attracts the entry of imitators into the industry, as seen in the model of Schumpeter (1912). They are often spin-offs—i.e., employees working for the pioneer of the new industry. They use the same inputs and adopt the same production processes and sell the same kind of products in the same markets where the pioneer operates. In this way, an industrial district or cluster is formed without exception, as reported in a number of studies included in this volume.[2] Sonobe and Otsuka (2006, 2011) call this stage the "quantity expansion stage" because the industrial cluster expands due to the entry of new firms without qualitative upgrad-

[2]Also, see a series of studies by Sonobe and Otsuka (2006, 2011, 2014).

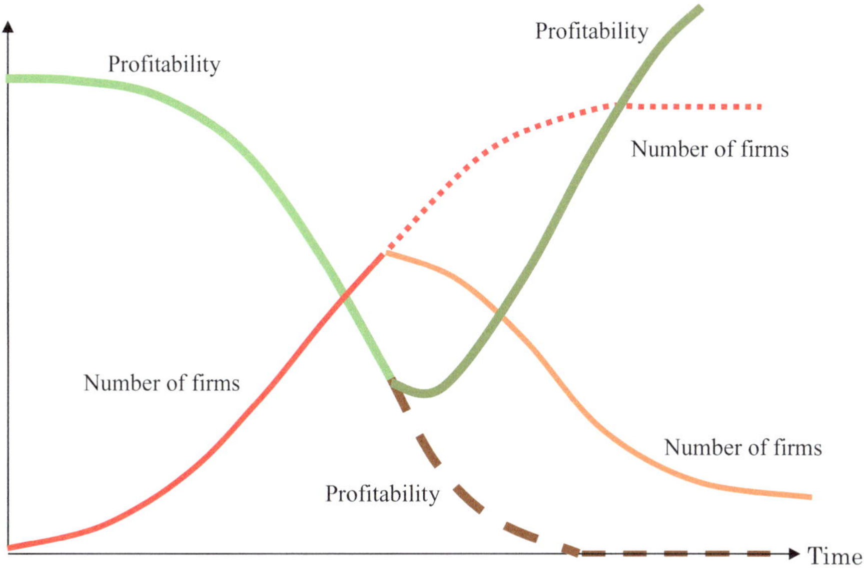

Fig. 2.1 An illustration of the development paths of survival and dynamic industrial clusters

ing, such as improvements in productivity and product quality. At this stage, the quality of the product is low and, hence, it can be sold only in the domestic market or in an even narrower local market in a developing country. Due to the adoption of simple labor-using technologies that do not exhibit increasing returns to scale, firm size tends to be small. Since the market supply of the homogenous product increases due to the massive new entry, while the demand does not grow concomitantly, the price of the product decreases and, hence, the profitability of continuing the production of low-quality products declines (see the declining portion of profitability curve in Fig. 2.1).[3]

Two types of industrial clusters emerge thereafter: survival cluster and dynamic cluster. While survival clusters are often found in sub-Saharan Africa, dynamic clusters are commonly found in East Asia. In survival clusters, the number of firms increases until the profit approaches zero, thereby making firms struggle for survival (see dotted red curve for the increasing number of firms and dotted brown curve for declining profitability in Fig. 2.1). In dynamic clusters, "innovations," the meaning of which will be explained shortly, take place and restore the profitability of "innovators" and those firms that imitate the innovations soon, but those firms which cannot imitate innovations are forced to exit or are merged by the innovators or early followers (see solid rising green profitability curve and solid declining orange curve for the number of firms). Innovations here do not mean large breakthroughs envisaged by Schumpeter (1912), which leads to "constructive destruc-

[3] Prices of inputs, which are inelastically supplied (e.g., land), may also increase, thereby reducing profitability.

tion," but refers to incremental improvements of technology, marketing, and management. Because of such innovations, the total value of production and the total number of workers in the industrial cluster expand even though the number of firms is likely to decrease.

Innovative entrepreneurs recognize that the reason for the decreased profitability toward the end of the quantity expansion stage was the low quality of their products. Thus, to restore profitability, the entrepreneur must improve quality by installing high-quality machines, using high-quality materials and parts, and employing highly skilled workers, such as engineers, designers, and accountants. In this way, both product and process innovations take place. This is, however, not enough to restore profitability because consumers do not immediately perceive the quality improvement. Thus, an entrepreneur must improve the marketing, including the establishment of brand names and direct sales to retailers and consumers instead of relying on traders. To produce high-quality products efficiently, production management, quality control, and labor management become major issues. Furthermore, to produce high-quality and differentiated products, an entrepreneur must procure newly designed, differentiated high-quality parts that embody innovative ideas from parts-suppliers without allowing the leakage of such ideas. Thus, Sonobe and Otsuka (2006, 2011) call these changes "multifaceted innovations" and designate a new stage of cluster-based industrial development—the "quality-improvement stage."

Sonobe and Otsuka (2006, 2011) recognize that innovations are accompanied by imitations and, hence, the social rate of return to innovations is higher than the private rate of return. Therefore, they argue that support for innovations by public sectors, international organizations, and donor countries can be justified from the social welfare point of view. Sonobe and Otsuka (2014) confirm, based on randomized control trials, that the social benefit of providing a management training program to stimulate innovations is sizable and exceeds the private benefit as well as the costs of providing and attending the program. They also suggest that transformative innovations take place in dynamic clusters in East Asia partly because of the ample supply of entrepreneurs in this region and partly because of the ease of learning from high-performing neighboring countries, which is not possible in sub-Saharan Africa.

2.3 Role of Technology Transfer

The role of technology transfer, both international and domestic, seems far more important than that assumed by Sonobe and Otsuka. Obviously, technology import from the U.K. had been an engine of development of the cotton textile district in Spain discussed by Domenech and Rosés (Chap. 3). Nishijin, a leading silk-weaving cluster in Japan, introduced new technologies from Lyon and they were later imitated by Kiryu (Chap. 4 by Hashino). As a result, both Nishijin and Kiryu became silk-weaving centers in the modern history of the Japanese economy. Furthermore,

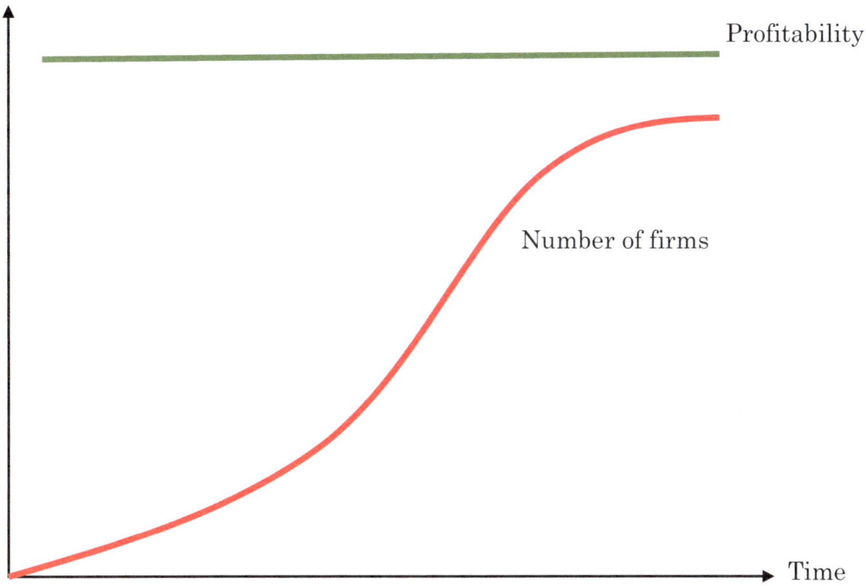

Fig. 2.2 An illustration of the development path of a jump-start industrial cluster

industrial clusters in developing countries, which learned foreign technologies, generally grew faster and became larger than those without learnings from abroad, according to a review of several case studies conducted by Sonobe (see Chap. 5).

Furthermore, successful technology transfers can make it possible to "jump-start" the development of industrial districts and enable them to enter immediately into the "quality improvement" stage, rather than pass through the quantity expansion stage. A historical example is the Fukui silk-weaving district in Japan, which began silk fabric production by learning technologies from Kiryu through a training program (Chap. 4 by Hashino). Also, intensive training programs provided by firms in newly industrialized countries in East Asia led to the development of the new and gigantic garment industry in Bangladesh as well as the new and modestly growing garment industry in Tanzania (Chap. 5 by Sonobe). Interestingly, both Fukui and Bangladesh exported their products from the beginning, suggesting that product quality had been high since inception. Figure 2.2 illustrates the development path of such "jump-start" clusters, in which profitability is always high. Although the number of firms increases, profitability does not decline appreciably because firms supply their products to the international market, which is so large that the increased supply of products from a particular industrial district does not affect product price and profitability.[4] Also, it is worth mentioning that the contract farming scheme of high-value agricultural products in developing countries resembles the initiation of

[4] Although export did not start from the beginning, the motorcycle industry in Chongqing in China began production with the establishment of joint ventures with Japanese motorcycle companies (Sonobe et al. 2006), which can be also regarded as a variant of "jump-start."

new business for export by introducing advanced technologies and marketing systems from abroad as discussed by Otsuka (Chap. 7).

Thus, the available evidence indicates that the jump-start of industrial clusters is possible if appropriate training is offered or if a joint venture is successfully formed. In practice, however, finding a new promising industry is a major challenge.

2.4 Quality Crisis and Innovation

The Sonobe-Otsuka model assumes that profitability declines due to the "excessive" production of low-quality products. The cause of the decline in profitability, however, may be the production of fake and inferior products, which damages the entire industrial district's reputation. In the Lyon silk-weaving cluster, the declining availability of high-quality raw silk produced in Europe forced producers to use lower quality Asian raw silk, which led not only to low-quality products but also to uncertainty regarding the quality of products (Chap. 6 by Vernus). This resulted in a quality crisis. The serious quality crisis occurred in a number of industrial clusters in Zhejiang Province in China, whose economic growth was almost exclusively cluster-led. Intentionally or unintentionally, counterfeits were shipped from various industrial clusters, which resulted in consumers' boycott and sometimes prohibition of sale from the clusters in Zhejiang Province through local policies as is pointed out by Ruan and Zhang (Chap. 10).[5] Similarly, the export of inferior-quality products from silk-weaving industrial districts to Europe in prewar Japan was a major issue (Chap. 9 by Hashino).

Clearly, the quality crisis inspired innovations. The introduction of quality control and standards, support for research and dissemination of improved technology, and exclusion of producers of inferior-quality products were measures taken by trade associations and governments. Such activities contributed to the quality improvement of the products and the enhancement of the image of the district brand.

2.5 Local Public Goods and Trade Associations

Innovative ideas and knowledge can be local public goods, as they can be used by all the producers in the industrial district. Similarly, marketing information—e.g., information about prices, demand structure, and reputation of products of a particular industrial district in urban markets—can be shared by all producers. To the extent that consumers care about the quality of products in a particular district rather than that of particular producers, the reputation of the quality of products

[5] In the context of Pakistan, a ban on the export of low-quality surgical instruments induced producers' associations to undertake various activities to improve the quality of products in cooperation with the government (Nadvi 1999).

manufactured in the district can be a local public good. Thus, to the extent that reputation is a local public good, collective action to control and maintain the quality of products of the entire industrial district is critical

Almost without exception, trade associations or producer cooperatives play a central role in introducing new useful ideas, providing training programs, conducting research activities, collecting marketing information, and controlling product quality in successfully developed industrial and agricultural districts. Examples include a number of silk-weaving districts in modern Japan (Chaps. 4 and 9 by Hashino), a silk-weaving district in Lyon (Chap. 6 by Vernus), apple-growing districts in modern Japan and a large number of agricultural districts producing high-value agricultural products in a large number of low-income countries (Chap. 7 by Otsuka), a variety of industrial districts in Europe after World War II (Chap. 8 by Schmitz and Musyck), and a number of explosively growing industrial districts in Zhejiang Province in China (Chap. 10 by Ruan and Zhang).[6]

Although our knowledge of conditions under which trade associations or producer cooperatives are formed and how they function effectively is far from adequate, many case studies in this volume point to the central roles played by these groups in successfully developed dynamic industrial districts. Such collective action leads to what Schmitz (1995) calls "collective efficiency" of industrial clusters.

2.6 Supportive Role of Governments

A trade association's attempts to control the quality of products produced in the industrial district may or may not succeed because it is difficult for the association to punish producers who manufacture fake and inferior products. The government can assist the trade association by setting quality standards and enforcing them (see Chap. 10 in the case of China discussed by Ruan and Zhang).

Local government should support research activities and training programs of trade associations, to the extent that they fall short of the social optimum. In Europe, local governments supported the research activities of trade associations (Chap. 8 by Schmitz and Musyck). In Japan, training programs organized by trade associations were later converted into technical schools by the prefectural governments (Chap. 9 by Hashino). In China, local governments implemented a variety of measures to improve the quality of products, including the facilitation of the firms' R&D, establishment of quality inspection centers, and even the creation of trade associations (Chap. 10 by Ruan and Zhang).

The Kyoto prefectural government sent a delegation of skilled workers of silk fabric production to Lyon to learn advanced technologies in the late nineteenth century (Chap. 4 by Hashino). The Fukui prefectural government invited an engineer from Kiryu to teach the production method of *habutae* (plain silk fabric), which led

[6]This is also the case in industrial districts in Europe according to an extensive review by Zeitlin (2008).

to the establishment of a new silk-weaving district (Chap. 4). The provincial government introduced potato production and processing and nurtured a huge agro-industrial complex in China (Zhang and Hu 2014).

Local governments in China invested in marketplaces to facilitate market transactions between small-scale producers and traders (Chap. 10 by Ruan and Zhang; Sonobe and Otsuka 2006). The central government in Japan collected information on the quality and reputation of Japanese products in Europe and sent these to the industrial districts in rural Japan (Chap. 9 by Hashino). These activities facilitated market transactions and improvement of product quality.

In short, governments often supported the investment in local public goods by the trade associations, which led to the successful and accelerated development of industrial districts in a number of cases.[7] Schmitz and Musyck (Chap. 8) aptly call this as "institutionally enhanced growth."

2.7 The Essence of the SOH Model

Learning from the historical development of industrial districts in developed countries and comparing the experience of diverse cases of industrial districts as well as agricultural districts in developing countries enable us to expand the scope of the Sonobe-Otsuka model so as to enhance its explanatory power. The essence of this extended model, which may be termed the SOH model, can be summarized as follows:

- International as well as domestic technology transfer is often a major reason for the establishment of new industrial districts and innovations, which enhance the quality orientation of industrial districts.
- The profitability of production declines not only because of increased supply from numerous producers in the industrial district, which is a pecuniary diseconomy of externality, but also because of the counterfeits and inferior products of rotten producers, which is a direct diseconomy of externality. In both cases, declining profitability triggers efforts to introduce innovations leading to product differentiation and quality improvement combined.
- Since innovative knowledge and ideas spill over to those who do not incur the cost of searching, finding, and generating them, the social return to innovations exceeds the private return. Herein lies the room for profitable collective action. To internalize the externality or to stimulate innovations, trade associations are formed. More often than not, they play a central role in the successful development of industrial districts in history and the developing world.
- Brand name or reputation of industrial district is local public good. Thus, in order to maintain this, the trade association plays a critical role in controlling the quality of products produced in a particular industrial district.

[7] See Abe (1999) and Hashino and Kurosawa (2013) for a number of such cases in Japan.

- There are limitations on the activities of trade associations as they do not possess coercive powers. Thus, local governments can be of assistance to trade associations in regulating the quality of products and in learning new technology from advanced areas and countries. The central government is also involved in the provision of information about reputation of products abroad and advanced scientific knowledge.

In short, the SOH model strengthens the explanatory power of the original Sonobe-Otsuka model by explicitly introducing the roles of technology transfer, trade associations, and governments, based on the historical experiences of Europe and Japan and the observation of a number of industrial districts in the contemporary developing world. The SOH model is perfectly consistent with the findings in Chap. 8 by Schmitz and Musyck that local and regional institutions become more important in later than in the earlier phase of growth of industrial districts, because, in our view, they are designed to stimulate multifaceted innovations.

References

Abe T (1999) The development of the putting-out system in modern Japan: the case of the cotton-weaving industry. In: Odaka K, Sawai M (eds) Small firms, large concerns: the development of small business in comparative perspective. Oxford University Press, New York

Hashino T, Kurosawa T (2013) Beyond Marshallian agglomeration economies: the roles of the trade association in a weaving district. Bus His Rev 87(3):489–513

Nadvi K (1999) Collective efficiency and collective failures: the response of Sialkot surgical instrument cluster to global quality pressure. World Dev 27(9):1605–1626

Schmitz H (1995) Collective efficiency: growth path for small-scale industry. J Dev Stud 31(4):529–566

Schumpeter JA (1912) The theory of economic development. Oxford University Press, New York

Sonobe T, Otsuka K (2006) Cluster-based industrial development: an East Asian model. Palgrave Macmillan, Basingstoke

Sonobe T, Otsuka K (2011) Cluster-based industrial development: a comparative study of Asia and Africa. Palgrave Macmillan, Basingstoke

Sonobe T, Otsuka K (2014) Cluster-based industrial development: *Kaizen* management for MSE growth in developing countries. Palgrave Macmillan, Basingstoke

Sonobe T, Hu D, Otsuka K (2006) Industrial development in the inland region of China: a case study of the motorcycle industry. J Comp Econ 34(4):818–838

Zeitlin J (2008) Industrial districts and regional clusters. In: Jones GG, Zeitlin J (eds) The Oxford handbook of business history. Oxford University Press, New York

Zhang X, Hu D (2014) Overcoming successive bottlenecks: the evolution of a potato cluster in China. World Dev 63(C):102–112

Part II
Pivotal Role of Technology Transfer

Chapter 3
Technology Transfer and the Early Development of the Cotton Textile Industry in Nineteenth Century Spain

Jordi Domenech and Joan Ramon Rosés

Abstract This chapter analyzes the transformation process of Catalonia into a major industrial district. Our analysis finds that the origins of industrial development can be traced back to the first decades of the eighteenth century with a calico-printing industry appearing with the support of a prohibitionist trade policy. This early development led to the diffusion of a cotton spinning and weaving industry in the same century. After severe crises in the first decades of the nineteenth century, the Catalan cotton textile industry was able to reestablish its lead position in the Mediterranean basin on the basis of two fundamental pillars: availability of skilled labor and capacity to import the latest technologies from abroad, especially from Great Britain. This cotton-based industrial district underwent an important crisis in the first decades of the twentieth century but its skilled workforce and entrepreneurial networks helped develop new industrial sectors that have survived until today.

Keywords Industrialization • Technology transfer • Cotton textile industry • Trade policy • Factor endowments

3.1 Introduction

Catalonia was one of the early adopters of the British industrialization model in the nineteenth century. Catalonia's lead in industrialization was already evident in 1860, when 21 % of the total Catalan workforce was employed in manufacturing, above Spain's average of 13 %. By 1930, the Catalan manufacturing sector employed 47 % of the Catalan workforce, exceeding Spain's other industrialized regions, such as the Basque country (36 %) and Madrid (31 %), and almost twice the Spanish average (26 %) (Rosés et al. 2010, p. 253). Although de-industrialization,

J. Domenech (✉)
Department of Social Sciences, Universidad Carlos III de Madrid, Getafe, Madrid, Spain
e-mail: jdomenec@clio.uc3m.es

J.R. Rosés
Department of Economic History, London School of Economics, London, UK

T. Hashino, K. Otsuka (eds.), *Industrial Districts in History and the Developing World*, Studies in Economic History, DOI 10.1007/978-981-10-0182-6_3

productivity growth, and the global crisis have reduced the contribution of manufacturing to Catalan employment and GDP, Catalonia retains a strong specialization in manufacturing. In 2014, manufacturing contributed 20.2 % of Catalan value added, above the means for Spain (17.5 %) and the European Union (19 %). In terms of employment, the manufacturing industry employed 18.4 % of the Catalan workforce (compared with 13.9 % in the rest of Spain) (Idescat).[1] The long-run evolution of a manufacturing district explains the visible historical continuities in manufacturing specialization in Catalonia from the late eighteenth century until our day.

The Catalan cotton industry was an early adopter of British technology, meaning that by 1878 Catalonia had one of the largest cotton industries (measured in millions of spindles) in the European periphery, albeit considerably smaller than that of England. Given Spain's limited domestic market and low per capita income, the rapid growth of the industry from 1830 to the late nineteenth century was a substantial achievement. However, we see signs of early maturation in the period when the number of spindles was growing fast in Japan, Italy, and the Habsburg Empire (Table 3.1).

In this chapter, we depict the main drivers of the evolution of the Catalan industrial district since the late eighteenth century. Our narrative stresses the role of foreign technology adoption, its adaptation to domestic factor endowments, and the importance of learning by doing, creative destruction, and internal differentiation within the district. We also stress the role of shocks caused by war, de-colonization, and changes in both domestic and foreign trade policy, as well as the role of technological change and creative destruction. However, because the cotton textile industry specialized in the domestic market and had to produce a large range of cotton products, it could not specialize along its comparative advantage. The result was that the cotton textile industry was never internationally competitive and started to decline in the early twentieth century. By this point, Catalonia already had mostly

Table 3.1 The Catalan cotton textile industry in comparative perspective (million spindles)

Country	1878	1890	1901	1912–1913
England	41.0	43.5	46.1	55.7
US	10.5	13.5	20.2	31.5
Germany	4.7	4.9	8.1	11.2
Russia	3.0	4.0	8.0	9.2
France	4.6	4.0	5.7	7.4
Austria-Hungary	1.6	2.7	3.5	4.9
Italy	0.8	1.3	2.4	4.6
Spain	**1.8**	**1.8**	**2.6**	**2.0**
Belgium	0.8	na	0.9	1.5
Switzerland	1.9	1.9	1.6	1.4
Japan	na	0.3	1.3	2.6

Sources: Calvo (2002), p. 95; Saxonhouse (1991), p. 84; Otsuka et al. (1988), p. 213

[1] http://www.idescat.cat/economia/inec?tc=3&id=5703, accessed April 20 2016.

completed its structural change into a predominantly urban society with a diversified industrial base. The Catalan case also shows how textile manufacturing, despite its limited sophistication, can put regions on a path toward full industrial development and structural change.

3.2 Origins of the Catalan Industrial District

The origins of Catalan industrialization go back to institutions, factor endowments, commercial networks, and financial markets created in the pre-industrial period (Rosés 2003). The early history of Catalan industrialization has been studied in detail by Catalan historians, who trace the origins of Catalan industry to the development of a calico-printing industry in Barcelona, which later expanded into the production of cotton yarn and cloth (Thomson 2005).

In the eighteenth century, the Spanish state adopted a series of policies to reduce dependence on imports of manufactured goods and promote domestic manufacturing. The greater integration of world markets and imports of calicoes by British and Dutch East India companies were harming the domestic Catalan woolen and silk industries. In 1746, a royal decree by King Ferdinand VI banned imports of Asian textiles; this was reinforced in 1752 and 1756 by prohibitions on imports of all foreign textiles (Delgado 1990, p. 162). Moreover, guild restrictions had weakened in Catalonia as a result of legal changes in the eighteenth century. In 1758, the Crown created the *Junta de Comercio* [Board of Trade] of Barcelona, an institution dedicated to the promotion of domestic industries and capabilities, which opened technical schools in chemistry, mechanical engineering, and political economy.

Institutional and policy changes did not directly benefit the local woolen and silk industries. Instead, changing tastes increased demand for calicoes in Spain and among economic elites in Spanish America. In an unanticipated effect of mercantilist trade politics, these changing tastes resulted in the appearance of a local calico printing industry in Barcelona. This industry rapidly grew and, by 1786, Barcelona had become one of the leading textile centers in Western Europe, with 113 calico-printing manufacturers supplying calicoes to domestic and colonial markets (Sánchez 2000, p. 491).

Furthermore, the growth of a domestic calico-printing industry had important backward linkages to promote the development of local cotton weaving and later the cotton spinning industry. As in the case of import bans, trade and colonial policies had knock-on effects on the growth of a domestic cotton textile industry. At that time, the industry was labor-intensive and non-mechanized and thus its main constraint was the supply of raw cotton. Since Catalonia grows no cotton, the cotton yarn woven there originated from the Mediterranean island of Malta. Yet, the Spanish Crown wished to promote the production of cotton in its colonies. In 1752, Catalan textile producers were allowed to import raw cotton from America, although Maltese yarns remained competitive through the 1760s to 1770s. In 1771 though, much to the dismay of Catalan calico producers, the Crown introduced a 20 % tariff on imported cotton yarn, the form of cotton generally imported from Malta, which translated into an increase in final prices of calicoes of about 12 % (Delgado 1990, p. 169). In 1772, the Royal Spinning Company was created. The company was a charter of calico manufacturers in Barcelona, created to influence trade policy and promote a domestic cotton-spinning sector, which would use raw cotton imported from the Spanish colonies (Thomson 2008). In 1802, a royal decree passed in 1802 to ban imports of foreign yarns reinforced the trend toward import substitution of foreign cotton yarns, most especially Maltese yarns.

The expansion of the local calico printing sector and its backward linkages with cotton-weaving and -spinning industries redefined the geographical boundaries of the Catalan textile industry. While woolen and silk fabric producers were concentrated in central and northern Catalonia, the growth of calicoes moved the center of gravity of the Catalan textile industry to the coast, especially Barcelona, where most calico-printing establishments were located. Okuno (1999, p. 48) argues that there were continuities between the woolen and cotton industries, especially as the Royal Spinning Company employed cotton spinners from central Catalonia on a putting-out basis, even in areas without a strong putting-out tradition. It is also argued that productive and managerial skills, commercial networks, and capital were mapped on existing networks created during the dominance of the wool sector. However, cotton altered the competitive advantages of towns, favoring coastal locations with ready access to raw cotton over interior locations with higher transport costs. Traditional weaving centers either took up cotton or declined, while Barcelona became the dominant cotton-weaving and -finishing center (Thomson 2005, p. 720). Although cotton spinning developed in the late eighteenth century, it has been shown that Catalan calico producers remained heavily dependent on spun cotton, with imports of spun yarn from Malta peaking in the mid-1790s. Only the war with England, by cutting the supply of Maltese yarn, forced Catalan producers to expand their own spinning to feed the growing demand for spun yarn from weaving and printing establishments.

The development of the calico printing industry and the subsequent development of cotton spinning and weaving led to the creation of the Employers' Association of Cotton Yarn and Cloth Manufacturers in 1799. In the same period, the Association of Cotton Printers was created, although the date of creation is not known. These associations were fundamentally devoted to influencing trade policy, always in a protectionist or prohibitionist direction, and to denouncing illegal trade in foreign yarns and cloths.

In 1820, the three employers' associations merged in the Catalan Association of Cotton Yarn Spinners, Cloth Weavers and Printers (*Comisión de Fábricas de Hilados, Tejidos y Estampados de Algodón del Principado de Cataluña*). In 1847, this Association changed its name to *Junta de Fábricas*, the Factory Owners' Association, which was the basis of the current Catalan Employers' Association created in 1889. As in the early Catalan employers' associations, the main aim was to influence the design of trade policy in a protectionist direction.

3.3 Technology Transfer, Crisis, and District Development

Foreign technologies were crucial to the geographical expansion of Spain's cotton textile industry. In its pre-mechanized phase, cotton-weaving and -printing establishments in coastal areas relied on a network of spinners employed on a putting-out basis in rural areas. The British spinning jenny diffused quickly in Catalonia as the technology had several characteristics that were well suited to the putting-out system. First, the machine was cheap and easy for local Catalan engineers to replicate, keeping capital costs low. Second, production using the spinning jenny was labor-intensive and did not require proximity to sources of energy, meaning it remained suitable for dispersed production. The first spinning jennies were used in Spain by the Royal Spinning Company, 20 years after the machine was patented by James Hargreaves in 1766. Britain had already banned exports of machinery by this time and spinning jennies reached Spain from France. According to a leading expert on the early history of the Catalan cotton textile industry, by 1791, there were already 108 spinning jennies in Catalonia, most of them used in small workshops and cottages (Sánchez 2000, p. 494; Garcia Balañà 2004, p. 210; Martínez-Galarraga and Prat 2016, p. 555). Imports of machinery required the adaptation of foreign expertise to local conditions. In 1792, factory owners in the town of Cardona hired an English engineer then working in France, who introduced the mechanical carding machine (with cylinders) and an improved spinning jenny with 78 spindles (Sánchez 2000, p. 493).

Early experiments with spinning workshops or rooms in a centralized factory context, generally with female spinners tending spinning jennies, were not successful. The Royal Spinning Company opened the first spinning workshops entirely equipped with spinning jennies in 1787. However, for most levels of cotton yarn quality, early experiments with the new machinery resulted in production costs higher than those of alternative putting-out systems of organization (Garcia Balañà 2004, p. 161). The company therefore asked two factory engineers (Pere Molet and Valentí Cisterna) to identify the problems, improve quality, and reduce costs. The engineers then produced a report identifying the main problems and suggesting solutions. First, the use of unginned cotton from America caused technical problems. In Spanish America, labor shortages did not allow for seed removal and proper cleaning of cotton or compression into bales (Thomson 2005, p. 715). Consequently, raw cotton from Spanish America was more difficult to card, broke more often when spun, and was not amenable to spinning high-quality yarn. Second, labor costs were too high. Molet and Cisterna suggested cutting wages, piece rates, increasing productivity, and regularity of work efforts. Finally, a related problem was high turnover and absenteeism, which made it difficult to monitor quantity, quality, and costs (Garcia Balañà 2004, p. 165). Despite their recommendations, Molet and Cisterna did not succeed in cutting costs in the factory in comparison with the tried and tested labor-intensive spinning processes. The factory still employed 21 spinners tending spinning jennies in 1790, but by 1795, the company had closed its spinning workshops and returned to outsourcing cotton spinning on a putting-out basis (Garcia Balañà 2004, p. 212; Thomson 2005, p. 725).

There were a few problems in reproducing British-designed spinning jennies in Catalonia, which strongly suggests the use of a large supply of domestic artisan skills existing there in the last quarter of the eighteenth century. Skilled Catalan carpenters, generally employed in the domestic shipbuilding industry, were quickly able to produce replicas of the wooden spinning jenny. The Royal Spinning Company purchased the first domestically produced spinning jenny in 1789, 3 years after its introduction to Catalonia (Garcia Balañà 2004, p. 167). A carding machine introduced in 1790 was reproduced in less than 5 months (Thomson 2005, p. 727). In the early 1790s, a local carpenter in Berga developed an improved version of the spinning jenny with 120 spindles (the so-called *bergadana*). Similarly, two English machine makers sponsored the introduction of Arkwright's water frame (patented in 1769), although this experiment proved unsuccessful. Later, several water frames originally purchased by the Royal Spinning Company of Ávila (in Castile) were installed in Tarragona. Moreover, water frames were successfully replicated in the town of Olot by a local silversmith in 1793 (Thomson 2003, p. 299). Water frames were important at that stage, thanks to the greater range of yarns that they could produce and their ability to apply added torsion to the fibers to produce stronger yarns suited for warp.

Although Catalan artisans were able to quickly replicate the first spinning and carding machines, they remained unable to push the technological frontier. New mechanical spinning technologies such as Crompton's spinning mule or Arkwright's water frame entered Spain from France with substantial delays. Crompton's spinning mule reached Catalonia in 1806, almost 30 years after its invention (Sánchez 2000, p. 497). These delays were caused by the British ban on exports of machinery, the lack of familiarity with new technologies among the Catalan workforce, and the suitability of manual spinning technologies to Catalan factor endowments (abundance of labor and scarcity of non-human energy). Experimentation showed that, given Catalan factor endowments, late eighteenth century cotton-spinning technologies were better suited to a diffused, putting-out system employing rural households, in which such work was complementary to the seasonal evolution of rural tasks. In contrast, weaving and printing of cotton fabrics remained mostly centralized in coastal locations, in close proximity to urban consumer markets or ports through which products could be shipped to Spanish America. Barcelona thus remained the most attractive location for weaving and printing. In this period, although cotton spinning grew, Catalan producers continued to rely on imports of spun yarn from Malta.

The war with England in 1797 and the 1802 ban on imports of foreign yarn triggered the rapid development of domestic cotton spinning, leading to its rudimentary mechanization using water power or horses. This period saw the first trial of the mule jenny in Catalonia and also the diffusion of Arkwright's water frame. Thomson reports several water frames found in Barcelona, Manresa, Sabadell, Ripoll, Sallent, Vic, and Martorell (Thomson 2003, p. 300). In this period, larger factories appeared, powered by horses or water. For example, in 1799, the company "Serra, Tornudella y Cía." in Barcelona, had 23 water frames, 35 mule jennies, 10 carding machines, and 10 roving frames, powered by six horses. In Manresa, where water power was available, the company "Codina, Dalmau, Martí, and Serrano" installed 19 water frames, 32 mule jennies, seven carding machines, and seven roving frames in one factory and 18 water frames, five carding machines, and six roving frames in a second factory (Sánchez 2000, p. 496). By 1807, only 13.5 % of all spindles in the Catalan cotton textile industry were mechanized, and spinning jennies dominated until the mid-1830s (the number of manual spindles peaked in 1836) (Sánchez 2000, p. 508).

Therefore, in this initial phase of Catalan industrialization, mechanization remained rudimentary and dependent on water or animal power until the take-off period in 1830–1860. Most probably, early steam engines were not suited to Catalan factor endowments, namely, still scarce technical capabilities and relatively abundant labor,[2] as well as usable water flows and very expensive coal (Catalonia lacks coal reserves, as does the rest of Spain, with the exception of low-quality coal deposits in Asturias in the north). Spain's earliest experiments with steam engines date from 1805 but these first test runs were unsuccessful as local engineers were unable to replicate Watt's steam engines. The Napoleonic Wars and British industrial secrecy slowed the rate of technological diffusion. The first serious attempts to introduce steam engines date from the early 1830s, by which time steam engines were more coal-efficient, better enabling their diffusion. By 1829, manual spinning remained dominant in the Catalan cotton textile industry, with 290,700 spindles from early technologies like the spinning jenny or *bergadanes*, and only 70,285 spindles from mule jennies, or 7028 spindles from water frames and throstles.

3.4 The Revolutionary Period (1830–1860): Mechanization and Internal Differentiation

The first steam-powered factory in Catalonia was established in Barcelona in 1832. Although this first factory was destroyed by arsonists in 1835, from this time, the number of steam-powered mechanical spindles quickly took off. The year 1843 marked a turning point, as Britain lifted its ban on machinery exports. By 1847, numerous, large steam-powered establishments had been erected, in some cases combining steam engines with water power. These establishments were located in coastal locations, such as Vilanova i la Geltrú, Sitges, Reus, and Barcelona (several cases) or in interior towns with sufficient water power from nearby rivers, such as Girona, Berga, Gironella, Ribes de Freser, Campdevànol, and Ripoll (Gutiérrez 1997, p. 30).

The experience of successful adoption of steam engines and self-acting mules at *La España Industrial* [Industrial Spain] in the 1840s provides an example of technology adoption and the role of both domestic and foreign engineers in the diffusion of foreign technologies. Historians have identified local skilled workers and

[2] This is similar to the persistent use of hand looms in traditional silk-weaving districts in modern Japan (see Chap. 4).

engineers with technical education from the *Junta de Comercio* in Barcelona, which became one of the largest establishments in the sector, some of whom travelled to France and England to learn the latest cotton techniques. Such local skilled personnel included the heads of the spinning or weaving workshops at *La España Industrial*, who had spent time at Sharp Brothers in Manchester and helped the owners of their company buy machinery in England (Gutiérrez 1997, pp. 100–103). There is even evidence of firms competing to attract valuable and scarce engineers (for example, the companies Güell and La España Industrial competed for Martorell). Initially, machinery installation and testing was done using engineers and technicians employed by English producers, with domestic mechanics and engineers later becoming more autonomous in the use and management of spinning and weaving machines. The person in charge of installing the steam engines was Michael de Berge, an Englishman who had lived in Barcelona for a number of years. The self-acting mules were installed by mechanics and engineers from Sharp Brothers, helped by local engineers. These mechanics and engineers installed 36 of the 54 self-acting mules bought initially by Muntades Brothers (Gutiérrez 1997, p. 103). Edwin Attenborough, an engineer of Platt Brothers, installed the looms.

In this initial phase of the take-off period, three main regions appeared within the district, each with different specializations and organizational forms. The Catalan interior was characterized by traditional, small workshops and domestic production that used spinning jennies and *bergadanes* and specialized in the coarsest yarns, with almost 90 % of spun yarn having counts ranging from 10 to 20. A second region was around Manresa, where production generally used water power with Akwright's water frames and throstles, as well as mule jennies, and specialized in coarser and slightly finer yarns with counts of 20–30, although half of production still had counts of 10–20. Finally, coastal factories in Barcelona, Garraf, or Maresme (like Arenys de Mar or Mataró) used steam power and mules and specialized in medium and finer yarns with counts of 20–30 as well as 30–45 (Ferrer 2004, p. 356).

Using data for 1841 from Pascual Madoz's *Diccionario Geográfico-Estadístico* [The Geographical and Statistical Dictionary], Ferrer (2004) shows that working conditions differed considerably among these areas. In the area of manual spinning, which was dominated by small establishments integrating spinning and weaving, child work was very common, with children representing 35–50 % of the workforce employed in cotton spinning (Ferrer 2004, pp. 363–364). In the water-powered establishments, the ratio of children in the workforce was slightly smaller but remained within the 28–39 % range in 1841. In coastal areas, in steam-powered establishments, children barely represented 20 % of the total workforce employed in cotton spinning. For weaving, these numbers were smaller. Coastal areas employed more adult men and women as a proportion of the overall workforce, with women predominant in spinning and men in weaving. Additionally, wages were much higher in coastal, steam-powered factories, especially for women and children. According to Madoz, a woman spinner in a mechanized workshop in Barcelona made more than twice the salary of a woman spinner in the highest paying town in the manual spinning area (Igualada) and almost three times the average salary for woman spinners in the same area. Compared with a woman spinner in the area dominated by water-powered establishments, a woman spinner in Barcelona made more than twice as much. Children also enjoyed salaries that were 50 % higher than those of child spinners in the manual spinning or water-frame areas. Similar differences also existed in the weaving workshops of Catalan factories in 1841 (Ferrer 2004, p. 364).

Eventually, cottage industry using manual spinning techniques, after peaking in 1836, quickly disappeared. Table 3.2 shows the number of spinners by technology type for the Catalan textile industry, which shows the rapid decline of manual spinning between 1836 and 1861, associated first with the rapid increase of mule jennies, and later with that of self-acting mules and ring frames.

This transition to mechanical spinning brought about the full adoption of the factory system, as a result of which the average size of establishments increased. Table 3.3 shows how in 1850, in establishments in which the spinning section had more than 50 workers, steam was the main energy source. Steam-powered establishments on average were larger than manual spinning establishments as well as water- or horse-powered establishments. Water power could sustain establishments with 50–200 workers. In comparison, establishments that used animal or human power

Table 3.2 Number of spindles in the Catalan cotton textile industry, by technology type

	Manual spindles	Mechanical spindles	Throstles and water frames	Mulejennies	Self-acting mules	Ring frames
1807	82,870	13,020	10,980	2040	0	0
1829	1,034,048	128,189	32,020	96,190	0	0
1841	725,787	316,320	34,680	281,640	0	0
1850	180,058	524,178	51,040	376,810	96,328	0
1860	7366	763,960	57,297	133,693	572,970	0
1913	0	1,842,000	0	na	760,000	1,082,000

Sources: Rosés (1998); Nadal et al. (2012)

Table 3.3 Establishment size and power source: cotton spinning in 1850

Establishment Size (number of workers)	Number of workers	% of total workers	Number of mills	% of total mills	Number of mills mainly powered by HAND	HORSES	WATER	STEAM
1–10	1804	9.9	191	35.4	180	7	1	3
11–49	5917	32.4	232	43	59	68	36	69
50–99	5406	29.6	81	15.1	3	3	22	53
100–199	3654	20.0	29	5.5	1	2	7	19
200–299	1166	6.4	5	0.9	0	0	0	5
300 or more	312	1.7	1	0.2	0	0	0	1
total	18,259	100	539	100	243	80	66	150

Source: Rosés (1998), p. 211

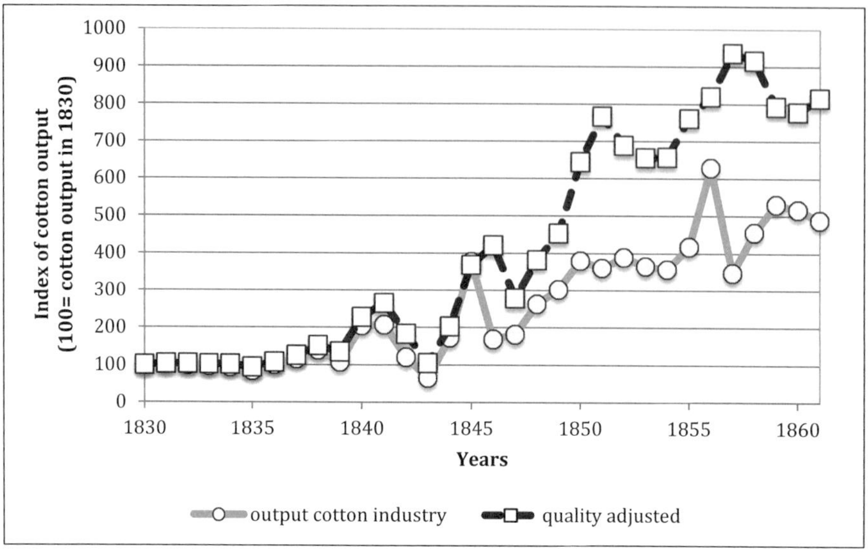

Fig. 3.1 Output of the Catalan cotton textile industry, 1830–1860 (1830 = 100) (Source: Rosés (2003), Appendix, p. 33

as the main source of energy rarely employed more than 50 workers. In 1850, around 60 % of workers were employed in establishments with 50 or more workers.

The adoption of mechanical spinning technologies and the factory system led to a large increase in the output of the cotton textile industry, in a typical take-off fashion. Joan R. Rosés calculated an average annual output growth rate for the cotton textile industry exceeding 5 % (Rosés 2003, p. 22). Figure 3.1 displays data from Rosés (2003) for two output indices of the industry from 1830 to 1861, with one index taking into account improvements in quality or at least specialization in higher counts (toward a mid-range count between 30 and 40).

This increase in average yarn count was important in the industry and can be interpreted as an improvement in quality. In fact, the Factory Owners' Association (*Junta de Fábricas*), boasted that technical change and skill improvement had increased cotton yarn counts to a median range of 30–40 (Garcia Balañà 2004, p. 278). What we know for sure is that higher yarn counts meant greater capital intensity as the thread needs greater stretching and twisting and must spend more time on the spindle. Additionally, production becomes more human-capital intensive, as the main skill in cotton spinning is the piecing of breaks in the thread (Wright 1981, p. 612). As a result, demand for labor shifted away from children and toward adult women and men. Figure 3.2 illustrates the evolution of quality from 1830 to 1860 based on the data from Rosés (2003) and shows that average quality almost doubled from 1830 to 1860. This quality upgrading process is consistent with the SOH model of the development of industrial districts discussed in Chap. 2.

Over time, technical change and learning by doing not only enabled an increase in average count numbers but also decreased prices of cotton products in relation to prices at the technological frontier (in Britain). In Fig. 3.3, we plot the evolution of yarn prices for comparable medium-range counts in Britain and Spain (expressed in Spanish cents), with British prices translated using exchange rates from Prados (1984). The figure shows a period in which cost and price converged rapidly to best practices, although the Catalan cotton textile industry never managed to fully close

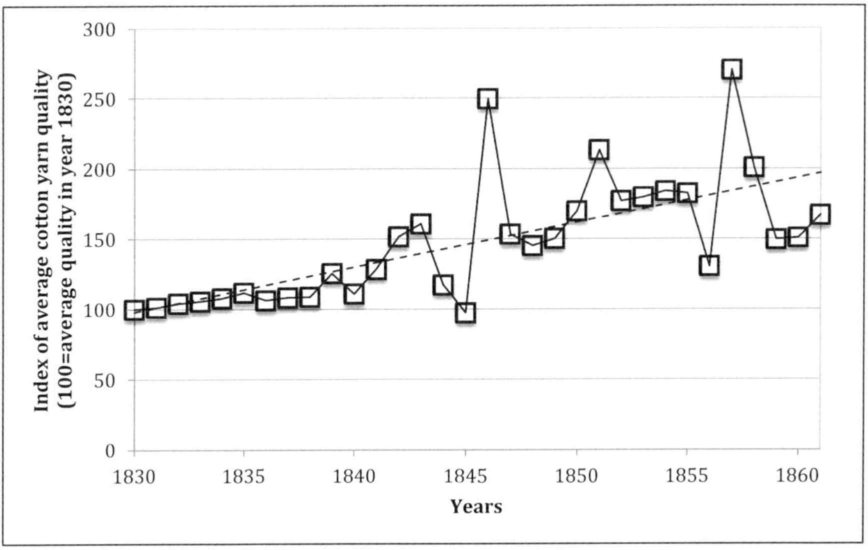

Fig. 3.2 Quality index of cotton output, 1830–1860 (1830 = 100) (Source: Rosés (2003), Appendix 1, p. 33)

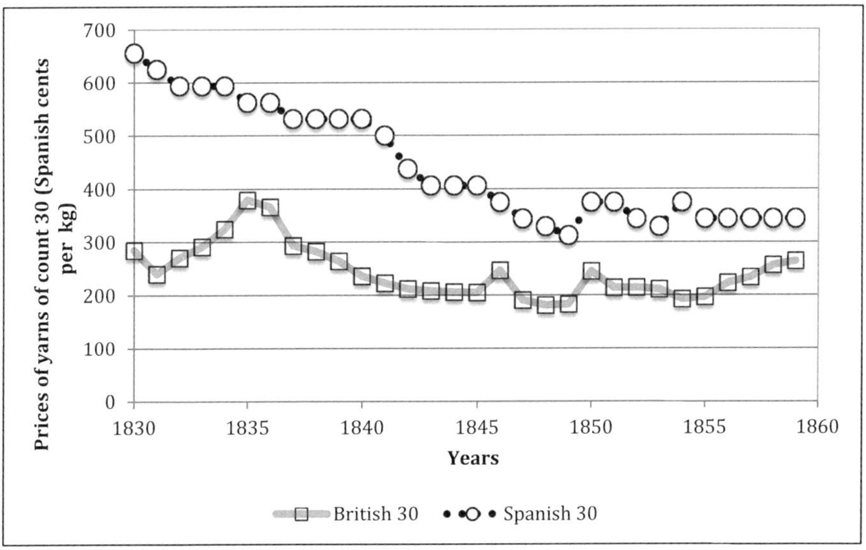

Fig. 3.3 Prices of British and Spanish cotton yarn, 1830–1860 (in Spanish cents per kg) (Sources: Rosés (1998), p. 283; Rosés (2001))

the gap with British producers. The fast reduction in costs and prices realized by Catalan producers was in itself a substantial success, yet Catalan cotton fabrics were never competitive in international markets (Rosés 2000).

3.5 Water-Powered Industrialization

The success of steam-powered industrialization in Catalonia depended crucially on the supply of cheap coal. In the 1850s and 1860s, the industry developed in parallel with that of coal mining in Catalonia and large investments were made in central and northern Catalonia to build railway connections to potential coal-mining areas (Carreras 1983, p. 43). Contemporaries believed Catalonia to possess untapped mineral resources, which would provide cheap and good-quality coal to the cotton textile industry and jump-start a domestic iron and steel industry (Pascual 1985, p. 49). After 1845, an investment boom, mostly financed by domestic Catalan capital, established 650 km of railways and other major infrastructure in Catalonia, such as the Canal d'Urgell. Unfortunately, the two most promising mining projects in Catalonia faltered. The mine near the town of Calaf turned out to deliver lignite, which was unsuitable for the most pressing industrial needs. Also, the railway built to access coal deposits in Sant Joan de les Abadesses could not be finished until 1881, after which the mine failed to live up to its promises, with neither quantity nor quality of coal mined being sufficient for the needs of Catalan industry (Nadal 1997, pp. 153–154; Pascual 1985, p. 68).

Technological change in water-using technologies came to the rescue of Catalan industry, with the transition from waterwheels to more energy-efficient Tourneyron-type water turbines. Several factors explain why owners of Catalan cotton textile factories opted for water power. First, the technological change mentioned above increased the viability of water power. Water turbines diffused quickly in countries where water power was efficient, such as France and the US, where turbines diffused quickly in the 1840s, and Catalonia, where similar diffusion occurred from 1857 onward. There is also evidence of domestic production of water turbines, for example, the firm Planas, Junoy, Barné y Cía in the city of Girona (Carreras 1983, p. 53). Second, by reducing transport costs, the opening of railway lines in the late 1850s and the 1860s allowed the Catalan textile industry to access untapped sources of water power. In 1859, the opening of the Barcelona-Manresa line reduced transportation costs for factories situated next to the Llobregat and Cardener rivers. Factories near the Ter River became fully viable as railways reached Vic in 1876 and Ripoll and Sant Joan de les Abadesses in 1881. The opening of railway connections between Manresa and Olvàn and Manresa and Sallent in 1884 and 1887 opened up the upper Llobregat valley (Carreras 1983, p. 54). Finally, river factories also benefitted from tax deductions and lower salaries.

These propitious circumstances meant that, from 1870 to 1911, energy use from water power increased by a factor of 20. Given geographical constraints, this fast growth meant all suitable water flows were quickly exploited. The evidence sug-

Table 3.4 Sources of energy in the Catalan cotton textile industry, 1841–1911

	Cotton spinning			Cotton industry	
	Horsepower from hydraulic power	Horsepower from steam engines	Animal power (horses)	Horse power hydraulic	Horsepower steam
1841	565	300	1229		
1846	1192	2149	427		
1848				2110	2414
1850	1660	1852	241		
1860				1800	6017
1861	1764				
1866	3197				
1870		9500			
1871	5138	na			
1876	9233	na			
1881	11,755	na			
1886	12,582	na			
1891	16,726	na			
1896	22,182	na			
1901	28,820	na			
1906	32,560	na			
1911	33,849	na			

Source: Carreras (1983), p. 42

gests that when suitable spots for water turbines were exhausted in the late nineteenth century, the growth of cotton textile industry slowed to a halt. Table 3.4 presents the breakdown of sources of energy in the industry, showing the rapid increase in water power. To a great extent, the paucity of data does not make it easy to assess the role of water power relative to steam, but the growth of horsepower from water was explosive.

The spread of water-powered factories reduced the attractiveness of coastal locations with access to cheaper coal, reducing the relative presence of spindles in the coastal regions of Maresme, Garraf, and Barcelona (Calvo 2002, p. 98). During the diffusion of water power, the industry thus spread to the Catalan interior, specifically the valleys of Llobregat, Cardoner, Freser, and Ter. This was the period of the company town adjacent to the river factory, an arrangement that benefited from lower wages, lower union control, and fiscal advantages. The center of the industry moved, with the interior gaining and several coastal locations seeing a relative decline. Figure 3.4 shows the lack of path dependency in the location of the industry, as local competitive advantages shifted with energy costs. For the subsample of Catalan towns with some existing cotton textile industry in 1861 or 1931, each dot on the graph represents a town, with horizontal and vertical axes representing the numbers of spindles per town in 1861 and 1931 (Fig. 3.4 does not display the observations for Barcelona, which had 261,000 spindles in 1861 and 241,000 in 1931). By 1919, about 80 % of spindles were located in the Catalan interior and powered by water turbines.

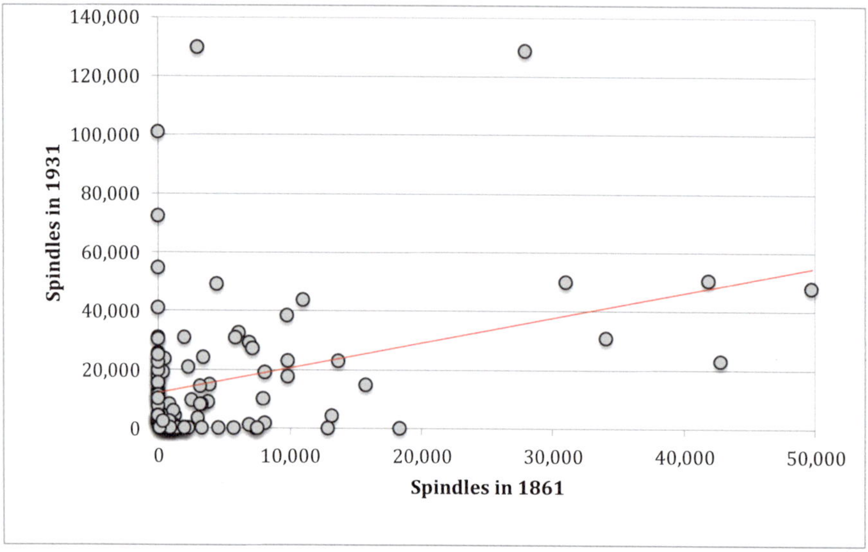

Fig. 3.4 Changes in the location of the Catalan cotton textile industry, 1861–1931 (Source: Own elaboration from data contained in Nadal et al. (2012))

3.6 Diversification

With auspicious beginnings in the first half of the nineteenth century, the Catalan cotton textile industry, by the early twentieth century, had reached only a modest size, its growth having been constrained by energy sources (no further spots for installation of water turbines remained available by the late nineteenth century), and it was unable to compete in international markets (Domenech 2008; Rosés 2000). The loss of its last remaining colonial market (Cuba) in 1898 dealt the industry a final blow. However, Catalonia became the most industrialized region of Spain and has remained so until today. From initial specialization in textiles and despite its lack of comparative advantage, a protected industry started to diversify into other sectors.

Given its factor endowments and especially the lack of natural resources like coal or iron, Catalonia did not have comparative advantages in heavy industry (iron and steel), but it did have sufficient artisanal and engineering skills for a machine-repair and production sector to appear alongside the cotton industry. Additionally, transport needs in textiles and agriculture also fomented the existence of a domestic metal and machinery-producing industry. Moreover, greater urbanization contributed to the growth of a food-processing industry catering to the needs of urban households. In Table 3.5, we present evidence of the level of diversification of the Catalan industrial sector, focusing on Barcelona as its most industrialized province. We use the population censuses of 1910, 1930, and 1970 to assess the long-term evolution of industrial diversification in Catalonia. Although Barcelona was

Table 3.5 Industrial specialization in the province of Barcelona, 1910–1970

	1910	1930	1970
Number of workers employed in manufacturing industries	155,899	472,717	717,360
% of workers employed in textile industry	54	34	na
% of workers employed in textile, knitting, and related industries (leather)	72	43	32
% of workers employed in the metal and mechanical industries	8.6	11.4	38.0
% of workers employed in chemical industries	1.5	3.9	11.0
% of workers employed in food processing industries	5.9	7.3	6.7

Sources: Censo de la Población de España (1913), tome IV; Censo de la Población de España (1932), tome III; Censo de la Población de España (1971), tome II

regarded a mature and diversified industrial economy by 1970, specialization in textiles and similar labor-intensive sectors remained evident, with 32 % of the industrial labor force working in textiles or related sectors. Yet, the 60 years from 1910 to 1970 witnessed a substantial diversification of the Catalan industrial base. In 1910, the industrial sector employed 156,000 workers, of which 54 % worked in textiles and 72 % in textiles and related sectors (such as knitting and leather). The period 1910–1930 saw fast growth and structural change, with the industrial labor force tripling in just two decades. By 1930, the share of workers employed in the textile industry was below 40 %. The metal and mechanical industries employed just 8.6 % of industrial workers in Catalonia in 1910, but by 1970, this ratio had reached almost 40 %. Between 1930 and 1970, the largest gains in percentage employment in the industrial sector occurred in the metal and mechanical industry and the chemical industry.

3.7 Conclusions

In this chapter, we have tracked the origins of the Catalan industrial district. Our narrative emphasizes foreign technology adoption and its adaptation to domestic factor endowments of natural resources, labor, and human capital. Successful adoption and posterior growth depended crucially on trade policy and its effects on import substitution, with coal-scarcity being the main physical constraint to industrial growth. The industrial take-off led to a wave of soil exploration and infrastructure construction and exploration that unexpectedly opened new possibilities for exploiting water power. As a result of this internal exploration and differentiation, district boundaries also kept changing. In this development process, which depends on technology import, several industrial districts were formed and each of them seems to have achieved the quantitative expansion in the early phase of development, followed by the quality improvement in the later stage, as predicted by the SOH model presented in Chap. 2.

With the limits of water utilization being reached in the late nineteenth century, industry started to diversify into other sectors. However, even today, the legacy of previous cotton textile specialization remains visible in terms of the importance of textiles and related industries in the Catalan industrial structure.

References

Calvo A (2002) La indústria cotonera catalana a començaments del segle XX (The Catalan cotton textile industry at the beginning of the twentieth century). Recerques 44:91–110

Carreras A (1983) El aprovechamiento de la energía hidráulica en Cataluña, 1840–1920. Un ensayo de interpretación (The exploitation of hydropower in Catalonia, 1840.1920. An interpretative essay) Revista de Historia Económica 1(2):31–63

Censo de la población de España según el empadronamiento hecho en la península e islas adyacentes el 31 de diciembre de 1910 (1910 Population Census of Spain) (1913). Imprenta de la Dirección General del Instituto Geográfico y Estadístico

Censo de la población de España según el empadronamiento hecho en la península e islas adyacentes y posesiones del norte y costa occidental de África el 31 de diciembre de 1930 (1930 Population Census of Spain) (1932). Talleres del Instituto Geográfico y Catastral, Madrid

Censo de la población de España. Año 1970 (1970 Population Census of Spain) (1971). Instituto Nacional de Estadística, Madrid

Delgado JM (1990) De la filatura manual a la mecànica: Un capítol del desenvolupament de la indústria cotonera a Catalunya (1749–1814) (From manual to mechanical spinning: a phase in the development of the Catalan cotton textile industry in Catalonia (1749–1810)). Recerques 23:161–179

Domenech J (2008) Labour market adjustment a hundred years ago: the case of the Catalan textile industry, 1880–1913. Econ His Rev 61(1):1–25

Ferrer L (2004) Bergadanas, continuas y mules. Tres geografías de la hilatura del algodón en Cataluña (1790–1830) (The three geographies of cotton spinning in Catalonia). Revista de Historia Económica 32(2):337–386

Garcia Balañà A (2004) La fabricació de la fàbrica: treball i política a la Catalunya cotonera (1784–1874) (The creation of the factory: labor and politics in the textile regions of Catalonia (1784–1874)). Publicacions de l'Abadia de Montserrat, Barcelona

Gutiérrez ML (1997) La España Industrial 1847–1853. Un model d'innovació tecnològica (La España Industrial 1847–1853. A model of technological innovation). Associació d'Enginyers Industrials de Catalunya, Barcelona

Martínez-Galarraga J, Prat M (2016) Wages, prices, and technology in early Catalan industrialization. Econ His Rev 69(2):548–574

Nadal J (1997) El fracaso de la Revolución Industrial en España, 18141913 (The failure of the Industrial Revolution in Spain, 1814–1913). Ariel, Barcelona

Nadal J, Benaul JM, Sudrià C (eds) (2012) Atles de la industrialització de Catalunya 1750–2010 (Atlas of Catalan industrialization, 1750–2010). Vicens Vives, Barcelona

Okuno Y (1999) Entre la llana i el cotó. Una nota sobre l'extensió de la indústria del cotó als pobles de Catalunya el darrer quart del segle XVIII (Between wool and cotton: a research note on the expansion of the cotton textile industry to the towns of Catalonia in the last quarter of the 18th century). Recerques 38:47–76

Otsuka K, Ranis G, Saxonhouse G (1988) Comparative technology choice in development: the Indian and Japanese cotton textile industries. Macmillan, Bakingstoke

Pascual P (1985) Ferrocarrils i industrialització a Catalunya (Railways and industrialization in Catalonia). Recerques 17:43–72

Prados de la Escosura L (1984) El comercio hispánico-británico en los siglos XVIII y XIX (The Spanish-British trade in the 18th and 19th centuries). Revista de Historia Económica 2(2):113–162

Rosés JR (1998) The Early Phase of Catalan Industrialization, 1830–1861. Unpublished PhD dissertation, European University Institute

Rosés JR (2000) The choice of technology in the Mediterranean Basin: British, Spanish, Italian, and US Mills compared. In: Pamuk S, Williamson JG (eds) The Mediterranean response to globalization before 1850. Routledge, London, pp 134–156

Rosés JR (2001) La competitividad internacional de la industria algodonera española (1830–1860) (The international competitiveness of the Spanish cotton industry (1830–1860)). Revista de Historia Económica 19:85–109

Rosés JR (2003) Regional industrialisation without national growth: the Catalan industrialisation and the growth of the Spanish economy (1830–1861). Working paper, Universidad Carlos III de Madrid

Rosés JR, Martínez-Galarraga J, Tirado D (2010) The upswing of regional income inequality in Spain (1860–1930). Explor Econ Hist 47(2):244–257

Sánchez A (2000) Crisis económica y respuesta empresarial. Los inicios del sistema fabril en la industria algodonera catalana, 1797–1839 (Economic crisis and firms' response: the origins of the factory system in the Catalan cotton textile industry, 1797–1839. Revista de Historia Económica 18(3):485–523

Saxonhouse G (1991) Mechanisms for technology transfer in Japanese economic history. Manag Decis Econ 12(2):83–92

Thomson JKJ (2003) Olot, Barcelona and Ávila and the introduction of the Arkwright technology to Catalonia. Revista de Historia Económica 11(2):297–334

Thomson JKJ (2005) Explaining the 'take-off' of the Catalan cotton industry. Econ His Rev 58(4):701–735

Thomson JKJ (2008) The Spanish trade in American cotton: Atlantic synergies in the age of enlightenment. Revista de Historia Económica/J Iber Lat Am Econ His 26(2):277–314

Wright G (1981) Cheap labor and southern textiles, 1880–1930. Q J Econ 96(4):605–629

Chapter 4
Contrasting Development Paths of Silk-Weaving Districts in Modern Japan

Tomoko Hashino

Abstract Many traditional industries prospered through the introduction of western technologies in the modernization process of Japanese economy. Nishijin, which was the most advanced silk-weaving district in Japan, played a leading role in technology transfer from the West in the silk-weaving industry. Kiryu District has been an 'imitator' of Nishijin, which developed by continuously introducing advanced technologies from Nishijin. Another imitating district was Fukui, which developed extremely rapidly after an engineer from Kiryu provided a 3-week training program. The development paths of the three major silk-weaving districts were contrasting: Nishijin was characterized by small-scale production organizations, use of hand looms, and production of traditional *kimono* for domestic markets, whereas Fukui was characterized by large-scale production organizations, more active adoption of power looms, and production of simple products for export. Kiryu lay in between. We argue that such contrasting patterns can be understood by differential endowment of skilled workers among the three districts.

Keywords Western technology • Traditional technology • Silk-weaving district • Technology transfer • Technology choice • Factor endowment

4.1 Introduction

Japan started learning from Western developed countries in the middle of the nineteenth century following the opening of its ports. At this time, the silk weaving industry in Japan had already 'developed' to a significant level despite depending on traditional technology such as hand-looms and natural dyestuffs. A survey by the Ministry of the Interior in the early Meiji period indicates that weaving was an important indigenous industry from the start of Japan's industrialization. While textile production comprised 27.7 % of total manufacturing production in the 1870s, fabric production accounted for 55.3 % of all textile production (Tanimoto 2006, p. 8).

T. Hashino (✉)
Graduate School of Economics, Kobe University, Kobe, Japan
e-mail: hashino@econ.kobe-u.ac.jp

T. Hashino, K. Otsuka (eds.), *Industrial Districts in History and the Developing World*, Studies in Economic History, DOI 10.1007/978-981-10-0182-6_4

One feature of indigenous industry in Japan was development based on the formation of industrial districts. As Abe (1992) explores in detail, many 'cotton-textile producing centers' or cotton-weaving districts, which consisted of small and medium-sized enterprises, prospered even after the establishment of large-scale modern weaving factories operated by large cotton-spinning firms. The districts resembled industrial districts as described by Sabel and Zeitlin (1985), who regard industrial districts as an alternative model of industrialization different from mass production systems. The silk-weaving industry in Lyon is presented as one of the most successful examples of an industrial district (Sabel and Zeitlin 1985, pp. 156–157). Rather than mass production, industrialists in Lyon chose the development path of flexible specialization based on division of labor (see Chap. 6 of this volume).

In the case of the silk-weaving industry in modern Japan, it is worth noting that different weaving districts followed contrasting development paths. In some weaving districts, process innovations introduced from Europe, such as flying-shuttle and power looms, dramatically increased labor productivity (Minami and Makino 1983; Hashino and Otsuka 2013a; Hashino and Otsuka 2013b). In other districts, the introduction of synthetic dyestuffs from Europe was effective for product innovation or the production of various upgraded fabrics as well as for reducing production costs (Tamura 2004; Hashino 2007a; Hashino 2012). Both cases indicate that technology transfer was an important engine for growth.

However, why did the extent of new technology introduction differ among districts? Interestingly, technology transfer flowed from the West to advanced weaving districts in Japan, and also from those advanced districts to less-developed districts. Nishijin in Kyoto, Japan's most advanced silk-weaving district, with a long tradition stretching back to the medieval period, played a leading role in technology transfer from the West. In the early Meiji Period, the local government of Kyoto sent students and craftsmen to Lyon to learn skills and introduce new technologies in weaving and dyeing. New technologies such as the flying shuttle and synthetic dyestuffs diffused rapidly to other weaving districts throughout Japan in various ways. An 'imitator' of Nishijin since the middle of the Tokugawa period was Kiryu, a weaving district that developed by continuously introducing advanced technologies from Nishijin. Another imitator district was Fukui, which developed extremely rapidly after an engineer from Kiryu provided a 3-week training program (Hashino and Otsuka 2013a). Fukui's growth depended on the export of *habutae*, an unfinished and plain silk fabric that was much easier to produce than the *kimono* that were the specialty of Nishijin and Kiryu. Figure 4.1 roughly sketches the location of the three silk-weaving districts discussed in this chapter.

The above three major silk-weaving districts played leading roles in the development of the weaving industry in modern Japan, although their modernization paths were quite different. Therefore, in this chapter, I wish to develop comparative historical perspectives on the different modernization paths of weaving districts in

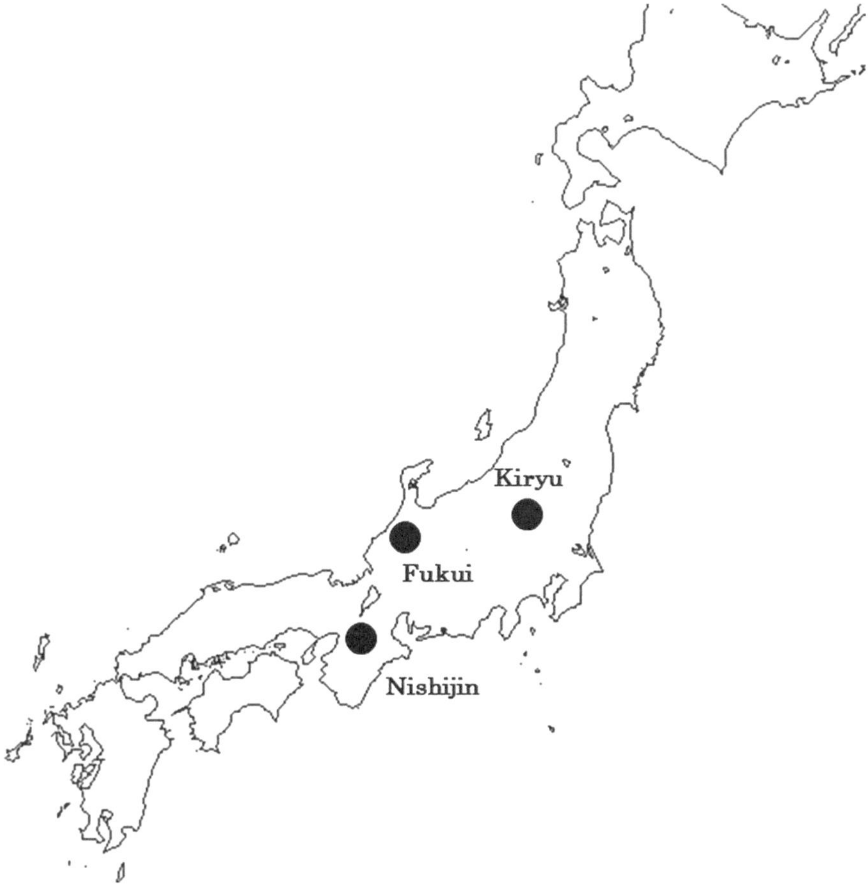

Fig. 4.1 The locations of Nishijin, Kiryu, and Fukui weaving districts

modern Japan, considering technology transfer, productivity, product quality, and endowment of skilled workers.

This chapter is organized as follows. Section 4.2 presents the long-term growth and short history of contrasting development in Nishijin, Kiryu, and Fukui districts. Section 4.3 compares the growth of the three districts in terms of production index, number of workers, and changes in labor productivity. Section 4.4 focuses on differences among the three districts in organization of production, skills, and wages. Section 4.5 concludes this chapter by summarizing the major findings and drawing implications for further research on comparative history of industrial districts.

4.2 The Long-Term Growth and History of Nishijin, Kiryu, and Fukui Silk-Weaving Districts

Figure 4.2 shows the changes in the real value of silk production in Nishijin, Kiryu, and Fukui from the last quarter of the nineteenth century to 1930. Several important observations can be made. First, Nishijin was the first giant, developing first and being followed by Kiryu. People often talked in terms of 'Nishijin in the west and Kiryu in the east', meaning Japan had two major silk-weaving districts in those days. Limited survey data from the Meiji government show that both districts produced numerous sophisticated fabrics (Hashino 2007a, pp. 30–31). Second, Fukui developed rapidly from the early 1890s. Its production exceeded that of Kiryu by the turn of the century and began to surpass that of Nishijin by the mid-1910s. Third, production in Fukui collapsed from the late 1910s. Note that Fukui's data in

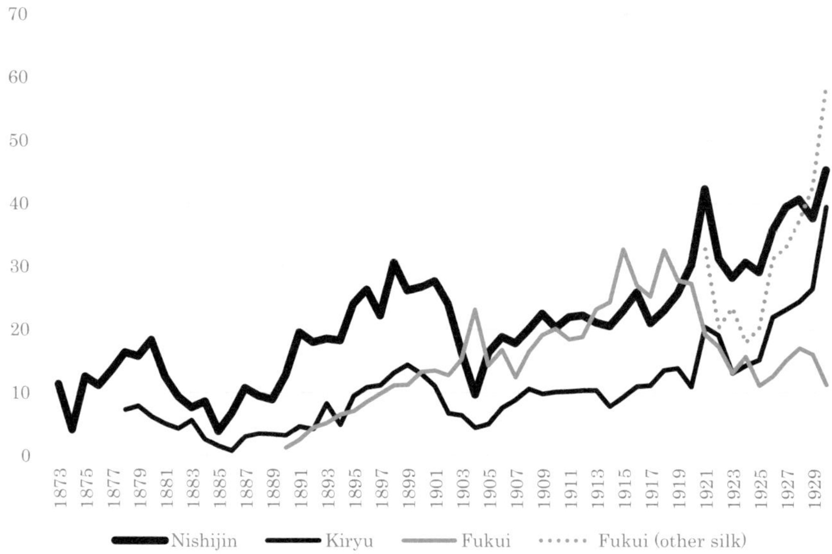

Fig. 4.2 Changes in the real value of production in Nishijin, Kiryu, and Fukui weaving districts from 1873 to 1930 (in unit of one million Yen) (Sources: Nishijin; Kyoto Prefecture ed. (1970) *Kyotofu tokei shiryo shu [Historical Materials of Kyoto Prefecture]* vol. 2. Kiryu; Gunma Prefecture ed. (1904) *Gunmaken Orimonogyo Enkaku Chosasho [History of the Weaving Industry in Gunma Prefecture]* (data for 1878–1901), *Gunmaken Tokeisho [Statistical Survey of Gunma Prefecture]* (after 1902). Figures from 1886 to 90 were estimated. Fukui; Fukui Prefecture ed. *Fukuiken Noshoko Nenpo [Annual Report on the Agriculture and Commerce of Fukui Prefecture]* (data for 1889–1901), *Fukuikenshi Shiryohen 17 [History of Fukui Prefecture 17, Data]* (data for 1902–1904), and *Fukuiken Tokeisho [Statistical Survey of Fukui Prefecture]* (data for 1905–1920). Notes: As a deflator, we used the price index for textile products from Ohkawa et al. (1967) *LTES: Price*, p.192. In the case of Fukui, the figures only show the value of *habutae* production. "Fukui (other silk)" refers to all silk products other than *habutae*)

Fig. 4.2 include only *habutae* production. In Fig. 4.2, 'Fukui (other silk)' (indicated by a broken line) shows the production of silk fabrics other than *habutae* in Fukui. In contrast to its declining *habutae* production, Fukui's production of other, probably sophisticated, fabrics for the export market increased rapidly in the mid-1920s. Finally, all districts saw production drop in the mid-1920s due to recession, but it quickly recovered and rapidly grew toward the end of the 1920s. During the recovery period, the growth of production in Fukui was especially remarkable.

Broadly speaking, the silk-weaving districts of early twentieth century Japan can be divided into two groups: domestic-market-oriented and export-market-oriented (Hashino and Kurosawa 2013, pp. 5–6). Whereas the former mainly produced a wider range of fabrics that were yarn-dyed and woven for traditional *kimono* and *obi* sash, the latter produced semi-finished materials such as *habutae* for piece dyeing. Fukui was the most popular *habutae*-producing district among Japan's export-market-oriented silk-weaving districts.

Nishijin had been the most advanced silk-weaving district in Japan, producing high-quality fabrics for the privileged classes since the medieval period. In the modern period, Nishijin continued to produce sophisticated and high-quality silk fabrics, mainly used for traditional *kimono* and *obi*. Silk weaving in Japan was originally started by Chinese and Korean immigrants. In 794, the Emperor moved the capital to Kyoto and established the Office of Textiles, or *Oribeshi*, which exclusively produced high-quality and sophisticated silk fabrics. In the medieval period, silk weaving was originally a government monopoly but gradually opened to the private sector. After the Onin War (1467–77), which devastated the Kyoto area and damaged the local weaving industry, people returned to an area called Nishijin to resume production of silk fabrics using textile technology introduced from China (Bank of Japan, Kyoto Branch 1914, p. 3). In those days, they produced silk fabrics for the wealthy, such as court nobles, the shogunate family, feudal lords, and priests.

Even after the capital was moved to Tokyo in 1868, Nishijin remained the leader in Japan's silk-weaving industry, despite bourgeoning numbers of local weaving districts developed by the introduction of advanced technology. After the Meiji Restoration, the local government of Kyoto prefecture aggressively sent students and craftsmen to Lyon to learn and introduce modern technologies such as jacquard, the flying-shuttle, and synthetic dyestuffs.[1] In 1873, these students and craftsmen introduced jacquard and flying-shuttle technologies to Japan. Thanks to them, 20 flying-shuttles were displayed at the exhibition held in Kyoto in 1873 (Ishii 1986, p. 109). This triggered the rapid diffusion of the flying-shuttle in Japan. Additionally, the Kyoto government established a model factory called *oridono* or Hall of Weaving (1877), which became critical in disseminating new technology to people from local weaving districts. Thus, the flying-shuttle was diffused to Fukui in 1877 and to Kiryu in 1883 (Ichikawa 1996, p.121). The Hall of Dyeing was also established in

[1] Before the arrival of jacquard machines, a 'human jacquard' system was used in Nishijin whereby a male weaver's wife or child sat on the second tier of the wooden draw loom and manipulated the warp by hand, selecting and batching the strands of the warp that had to be clustered in certain configurations to determine the design (Hareven 2002, p. 42).

Kyoto in 1880 under the supervision of a local craftsman who returned from Europe with the chemical dyeing method (Morris-Suzuki 1994, p.92).

Kiryu developed from the late eighteenth century through the introduction of advanced technologies in weaving and dyeing from Nishijin. Although Kiryu's long history of silk weaving dates back to ancient times, its rapid growth followed the introduction of yarn-dyed fabrics and draw looms for producing high-quality fabrics from Nishijin in the middle of the eighteenth century (Hashino and Kurosawa 2013, pp. 495–96). Kiryu specialized in imitating Nishijin's technology for producing high-quality fabrics and eventually started to produce fabrics more popular than those from Nishijin. Thereafter, fabric markets developed in both west and east Japan.

After the opening of Japan's ports in the middle of the nineteenth century, an influx of Western fabrics fascinated the Japanese with their vivid colors, designs, and textures. Kiryu and other districts near Edo (the former name of Tokyo) and the port of Yokohama developed methods to produce substitutes for Western fabrics by using imported dyestuffs, imitating their designs, and introducing thin, machine-made cotton yarns such as weft (Tamura 2004, chapter 1). The introduction of Jacquard to Nishijin through the import of technology from France and Austria was critical to the production of figured fabric. Kiryu also introduced Jacquard from the United States in 1886, and a loom carpenter produced a wooden jacquard machine by imitating French and American jacquards (Ichikawa 1996, p. 121). Kiryu attempted to develop production not only of popular figured fabrics for the domestic market but also of simple fabrics such as *habutae* for the larger export market. In fact, Kiryu was the first exporter of *habutae* in Japan.

In contrast to the above two traditional weaving districts, Fukui was a newly-emerging district and grew rapidly by focusing on *habutae* production (Hashino and Otsuka 2013b, p. 24). Before *habutae* production started, local people in Fukui City, especially ex-samurai, traditionally produced silk fabrics for *kimono* on a small scale for the domestic market. Demand for this fabric, called *hosho-tsumugi*, was limited however. Therefore, local people and the Fukui prefectural government made various attempts to promote new industries with larger market and export potential. The establishment of small factories to produce silk handkerchiefs for the export market in the early 1880s proved unsuccessful. However, the introduction of the flying-shuttle from Kyoto subsequently helped local weavers produce *habutae* introduced from Kiryu.

The *habutae* production that started in Fukui City in 1887 attracted the most interest. About 100 locals were taught basic methods of producing *habutae* by an engineer from Kiryu, whom the Fukui prefectural government invited to Fukui City for a 3-week training session (Harada 2002, pp.25–26). Using the flying-shuttle and knowledge acquired from the 3-week training program, production of *habutae* rapidly grew in Fukui City. More importantly, the method of producing *habutae* was sufficiently easy that rural people engaged in farming and other businesses were able to start *habutae* production. As a result, many people in both Fukai City itself as well as surrounding rural areas, became involved in production of *habutae* shortly after the industry arrived in Fukui City. According to Hashino and Otsuka (2015),

Fukui City accounted for 90 % of total production of silk fabric in Fukui Prefecture in 1890, declining to 40 % by 1908 (Hashino and Otsuka 2015, pp. 15–16). Small-scale cottage enterprises grew in clusters and the northern part of Fukui Prefecture became a *habutae*-weaving district. Surprisingly, shortly after *habutae* production started, Fukui prefecture became the top exporter of *habutae* in Japan (Hashino and Otsuka 2013b, 24). This rapid geographical expansion of production was a notable characteristic of Fukui weaving district, not found in other districts in Japan, including both Nishijin and Kiryu.

4.3 Contrasting Characteristics of Production in Three Silk-Weaving Districts

Figure 4.3 shows the changes in the number of silk-weaving enterprises in Nishijin, Kiryu, and Fukui districts. 'Enterprises' include factories (or workshops with more than 10 workers), family cottage workshops (with fewer than 10 workers), weaving manufacturers-cum-contractors, and out-weavers. The number of enterprises was highest in Nishijin and lowest in Fukui, with Kiryu lying in-between. Notably, these silk-weaving districts differ considerably in terms of numbers of enterprises. First, in both Nishijin and Kiryu, numbers of enterprises were increasing until the end of the 1910s. Nishijin in particular experienced a remarkable increase in its number of enterprises. The numbers of enterprises in both Nishijin and Kiryu remained almost constant in the second decade of the twentieth century, but decreased dramatically from the early 1920s, especially in Kiryu. Second, in contrast to the increasing trend in both Nishijin and Kiryu until the end of the 1910s, the number of enterprises in Fukui started declining sharply in the early 1910s and then stagnated. The broken line in Fig. 4.3, which shows the number of enterprises producing other silk fabrics, also shows the stagnation of the number of enterprises in Fukui in the 1920s.

How much did enterprise size differ among the three districts? Figure 4.4 compares enterprise size among the three districts in terms of the number of workers per district. Interestingly, enterprise size differed considerably among the three districts. Fukui displayed an increasing trend in enterprise size from the start of *habutae* production (Hashino and Otsuka 2015) with the peak occurring in the middle of the first decade of the twentieth century. Enterprise size subsequently started decreasing, only to increase again in the 1910s. Turning to the broken line that shows the average size of silk-fabric producing enterprises other than those producing *habutae*, their size reached 20 workers at the end of the 1920s. The average enterprise size in Nishijin also increased until the end of the nineteenth century, but never exceeded 10 workers and showed a decreasing trend toward the mid-1910s. Enterprise size in Kiryu increased slightly during the period for which data are available, but was much smaller than in Fukui. It can be said that silk fabrics in Nishijin and Kiryu were produced by small-scale enterprises, in contrast to *habutae* production in Fukui, which was dominated by larger-scale enterprises. Additionally, enterprise size was increasing in Fukui.

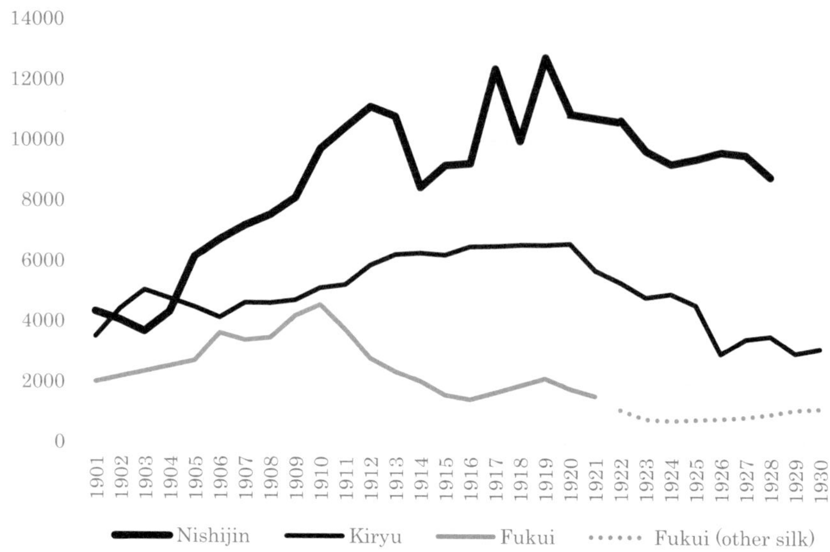

Fig. 4.3 Changes in the number of silk-weaving enterprises in Nishijin, Kiryu, and Fukui weaving districts from 1901 to 1930 (Sources: Nishijin and Kiryu; Same as Fig. 4.1, and Gunma Prefecture ed. *Statistical Survey of Gunma Prefecture*. Fukui; Mikami and Debuchi (1900) *Meiji 33 nen Fukui Ishikwa Ryokenka Kigyo Chosa Hokoku [A Report on the Weaving Industry in Fukui and Ishikawa Prefectures in 1900]* (data for 1890–1892), Fukui Prefecture ed. (1893–1900), *Fukuiken Kangyo Nenpo [Annual Report on the Promotion of Industry in Fukui Prefecture]* (data for 1893–1900), Fukui Prefecture ed. (1901) *Annual Report on the Agriculture and Commerce of Fukui Prefecture* (data for 1901), Fukui Prefecture ed. (1905–1921) *Statistical Survey of Fukui Prefecture* (data for 1905–1921). Notes: Linear interpolation was used for the data on the number of enterprises in Fukui in 1903 owing to data unavailability. The same method was also used for Nishijin in 1921 because of the abnormally low number of enterprises for which data was available in this year.)

How did such differences in enterprise size affect labor productivity? Figure 4.5 indicates the change in real labor productivity in the three districts (three-year average). Until the end of the first decade of the twentieth century, labor productivity differed little among three districts. However, from the mid-1910s the difference in labor productivity became far more marked. Labor productivity in *habutae* production in Fukui grew dramatically, more than doubling within several years. The broken line, which shows labor productivity for production of other silk fabrics in Fukui in 1920, also differs considerably relative to other weaving districts. However, labor productivity in Kiryu was stagnant and even decreasing in the 1910s. Yet, from the end of the 1910s, labor productivity started increasing and grew dramatically in the 1920s (Hashino and Otsuka 2013a). The trend in Nishijin lay between these two extremes. Though labor productivity in Nishijin increased during the boom period of WWI, it declined from the end of the 1910s. The trend of labor productivity in Nishijin appears opposite to the other two districts. The next section addresses why the three weaving districts display such a difference in labor productivity.

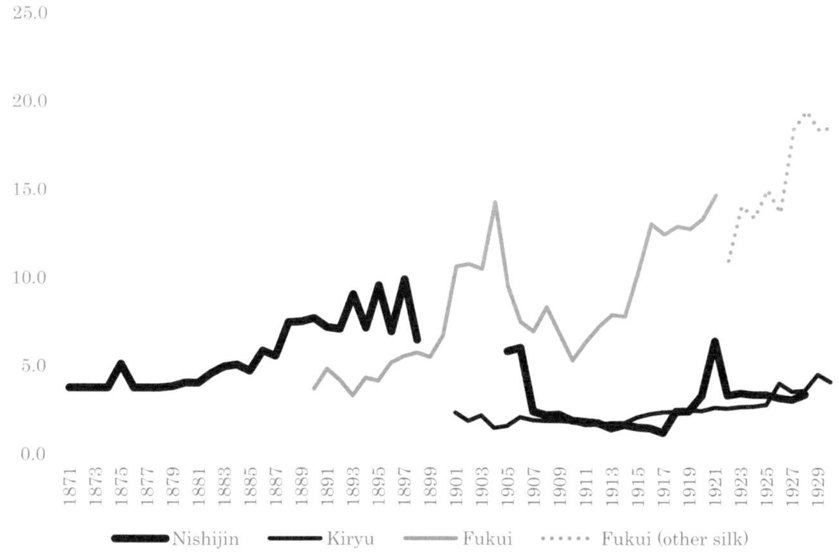

Fig. 4.4 Comparison of enterprise size measured in number of workers among Nishijin, Kiryu, and Fukui weaving districts (Sources: The same as for Figs. 4.2 and 4.3)

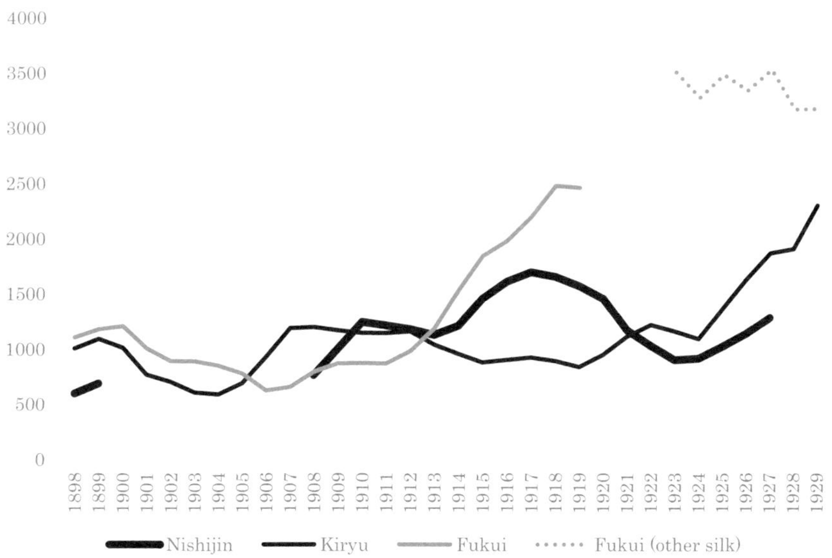

Fig. 4.5 Changes in real labor productivity in Nishijin, Kiryu, and Fukui weaving districts from 1898 to 1929 (three-year average, in Yen) (Sources: The same as for Figs. 4.2 and 4.3)

4.4 Different Organization of Production, Different Skills, and Wage Differentials

We hypothesize that difference in technology transfer or technology choice is the key factor that explains the difference in labor productivity shown in Fig. 4.5. According to Bessen (2012), a typical weaver in the early twentieth century United States could produce over 50 times as many yards of cloth in an hour as a weaver a century previously, indicating significant advancement in weaving technology (Bessen 2012, p. 44). Particularly, the introduction of power looms greatly boosted labor productivity in both the United States and Europe (Federico 1997, pp. 56–57). The power loom was introduced to Japan from Europe around 1860, but only after the 1910s did its adoption rate[2] increase rapidly in many weaving districts, beginning with cotton weaving districts (Minami and Makino, p. 3).

Figure 4.6 shows changes in the adoption rate of power looms in Nishijin, Kiryu, Fukui, and Tango. Tango, located in northern Kyoto prefecture, was a supplier of crape for Nishijin.[3] Adoption of power looms was fastest in Fukui and slowest in Nishijin. Tango was also a fast adopter. The adoption rate of power looms increased remarkably around 1910 in Fukui, precisely as labor productivity began increasing. In Kiryu, power looms were adopted widely in the 1920s, which again corresponds to the period when labor productivity increased. It can be conjectured that the major innovation in the early twentieth century was the introduction of power looms, which boosted silk fabric production and labor productivity. Since power looms had been available prior to their adoption, that adoption may have been the result, not of innovation, but of technology choices in response to increasing wages. In fact, imported power looms did not spread immediately even though the application of power looms to silk weaving started in Kiryu in 1872 and in Nishijin in 1882 (Minami and Makino 1983, p. 3). As Minami and Makino (1983) and Suzuki (1996) point out, the quality of domestically produced power looms gradually improved and their prices substantially declined.[4]

Interestingly, adoption of power looms was slowest in Nishijin, which was the most advanced silk-weaving district, and fastest in Fukui, which was the least advanced district. This difference can be explained by the difficulty in substituting skilled labor with advanced machines or by the ease of substituting unskilled labor with machines.[5] *Habutae* was a simple silk fabric that could be produced by

---

[2] The adoption rate of the power loom is calculated by dividing the number of power looms by the number of all types of looms.

[3] Crape made in Tango was dyed and printed in Nishijin for producing *kimono*. Crape and *habutae* were similar in that both were intermediate goods.

[4] Singleton (1997) points out that Japanese handloom makers were beginning to replicate the Western power loom by the mid-1870s. Toyoda and Kubota became prominent machine manufacturers in the 1890s, providing significantly lighter and cheaper power looms than Western manufacturers (Singleton 1997, p. 78).

[5] Minami and Makino (1983) point out that the adoption rate of power looms was relatively low in the weaving districts that produced figured and complex fabrics (Minami and Makino 1983, p. 13).

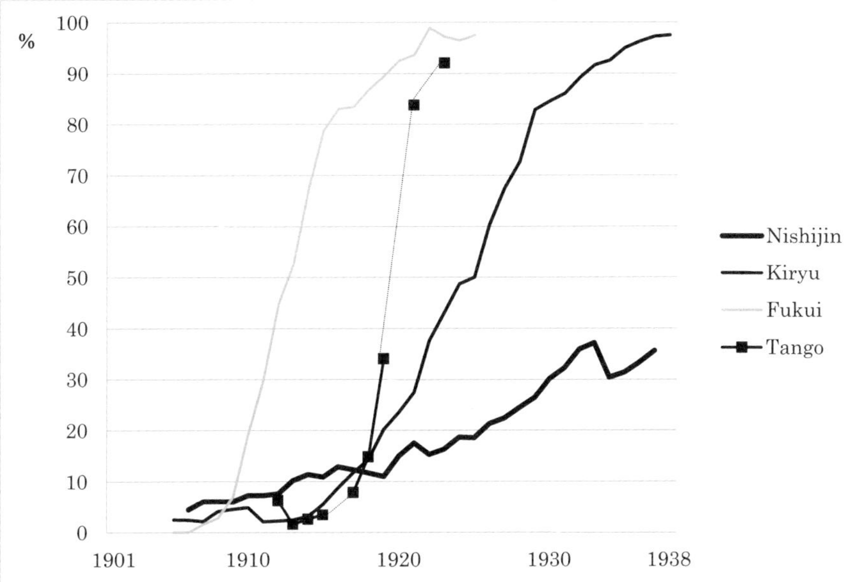

Fig. 4.6 Changes in the adoption rate of power looms in Nishiijn, Kiryu and Fukui weaving districts, as well as in Tango, which was a supplier of crape to the Nishijin weaving district (Sources: See Hashino and Otsuka (2013b, p. 25))

unskilled labor. Because Fukui lacked a strong traditional weaving industry, it also lacked skilled labor, implying a comparative advantage in unskilled labor-intensive *habutae* production. Meanwhile, Kiryu produced popular and cheap *kimono* and other products amenable to production by power looms. In contrast, the long tradition of silk weaving in Nishijin had resulted in a skilled labor force capable of producing such highly complicated and sophisticated products as *kimono*, which cannot be easily produced by power looms. Thus, Nishijin had a comparative advantage in the skilled production of high-quality domestic fabrics.

As shown in Fig. 4.4, there was a remarkable contrast in enterprise size and its changes between Fukui and the other two districts. Enterprise size was increasing in Fukui from the 1910s, but was stagnant in both Nishijin and Kiryu. The question arises of the impact of the introduction of new technology on the organization of production. According to Hashino (2007b, pp. 14–17), the factory system was not a prerequisite for the adoption of power looms as indicated by Minami and Makino (1983). Rather, there occurred simultaneous processes whereby the shift from hand looms to power looms accompanied the general transition from putting-out to the factory system (Saito 2013, p. 91). Thus, it is important to compare differences in the organization of production among the three districts under study.

Figure 4.7 indicates the changes in the percentages of factory workers and out-weavers in the three weaving districts. Here a factory is defined as a workshop with

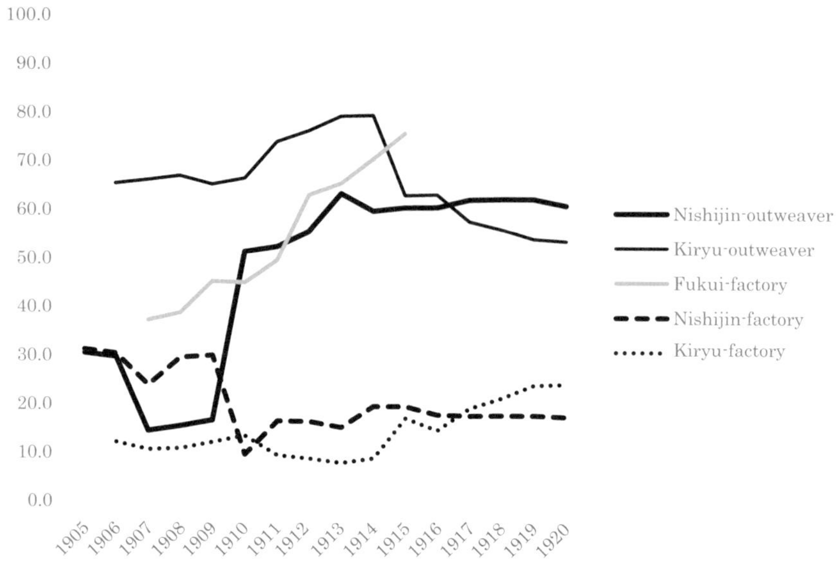

Fig. 4.7 Changes in the percentages of factory workers and out-weavers in Nishijin, Kiryu and Fukui weaving districts from 1905 to 1920 (%) (Sources: Nishijin; Kyoto Prefecture ed. *Statistical Survey of Kyoto Prefecture*. Kiryu; Gunma Prefecture ed. *Statistical Survey of Gunma Prefecture*. Fukui; Fukui Prefecture ed. *Statistical Survey of Fukui Prefecture* (data for 1905–21). Note: In the case of Fukui, the number of out-weavers involved in the production of *habutae* is negligible)

more than 10 workers. Interestingly, the percentage of factory workers increased rapidly and became dominant in Fukui from the late first decade of the twentieth century,[6] when the adoption rate of the power loom was increasing remarkably, as shown in Fig. 4.6. From the beginning of *habutae* production, almost all *habutae* was produced not by a putting-out system but by workshops such as small cottage-family enterprises (Hashino 2007a, p. 59). Therefore, it is reasonable to infer that adoption of power looms often accompanied the rise to prominence of factory production. In fact, the micro cottage industry disappeared as adoption rate of the power loom increased (Kandachi 1974).

In contrast, the percentage of factory workers was low in both Nishijin and Kiryu. In the case of Kiryu, the percentage of factory workers appears to start increasing from the end of the 1910s. However, the percentage of out-weavers was high in both districts, although the percentage of factory workers was high in Nishijin in the early years.[7] This occurs because both districts developed a putting-

[6] In Fig. 4.7, 'Fukui-factory' denotes the percentage of factory workers in *habutae*-producing factories.

[7] It seems that this reflects attempts to establish large modern factories in Nishijin. According to Hareven (2002), since the beginning of the twentieth century, family-based cottage industry has emerged as a characteristic production system in Japan (Hareven 2002, p. 55). Such production is smaller scale than factory production, with the latter involving more than 10 workers.

out system dependent on small-lot multi-production. The establishment of weaving workshops or factories was not suitable for such production. Especially in Nishijin, given its long tradition of producing high-quality luxury Japanese *kimono* and *obi* exclusively for the privileged, the market was relatively small and production was based on fine division of labor to deal with complicated production processes. Kiryu also developed a similar division of labor in which weaving manufacturers-cum-contractors organized many processes, including throwing, dyeing, designing, out-weaving, and finishing (Hashino and Kurosawa 2013, p. 504). In short, the organization of production was similar in Nishijin and Kiryu.

As is shown in Hashino and Otsuka (2013b), it seems that the adoption of power looms was critical in changing the organization of production to favor factories. The factory production system became dominant in Fukui and the putting-out system remained dominant in both Nishijin and Kiryu because *habutae* production was more amenable to power-loom production than traditional *kimono* and *obi*. Given that Nishijin and Kiryu were far more technically advanced than Fukui, they were capable of producing *habutae* as well as complex and sophisticated products such as *kimono* and *obi*. They simply chose not to produce *habutae*. Thus, it is hard to argue that the larger-scale factory production system involves more advanced organization of production than the out-weaving system. Restated, out-weavers using hand looms and skilled workers were the most efficient means of organization for the production of traditional fabrics when skilled labor was relatively cheap and power looms were not well adapted to the production of sophisticated silk products.

According to an interesting survey conducted by the Bank of Japan, Kyoto Branch (1914), Kiryu successfully imitated techniques from Nishijin for producing complex and sophisticated fabrics and began to produce fabrics that were more popular and lower priced than those from Nishijin (Bank of Japan, Kyoto Branch 1914, p. 33). The question is how Kiryu realized such low-cost production. Figure 4.8 shows the changes in the percentages of female workers at Nishijin, Kiryu, and Fukui, a metric based on the assumption that female workers were generally less skilled than male workers. The proportion of female workers differs markedly between Nishijin and the other two districts. That is, the percentage of female workers was high in both Kiryu and Fukui but low in Nishijin. Whereas weavers at Nishijin had traditionally been skilled male workers, at Fukui the workforce traditionally comprised unskilled female workers. Kiryu lay between these two extremes in terms of workforce composition. It can be conjectured that the declining percentages of female workers at both Fukui and Kiryu after the mid-1910s related to the introduction of power looms and the employment of relatively unskilled male workers (Hashino 2007a; Hashino 2007b). In both these districts, male workers primarily engaged in repairing and maintaining power looms. This is why the percentage of female workers was declining in the late 1910s, even though some female workers must have acquired skills over time. In the case of Nishijin, the proportion of male workers was high, because it was not possible to substitute highly skilled male workers and still produce high-quality and complicated fabrics from power looms. However, Kiryu relied on hand looms initially but gradually adopted power looms

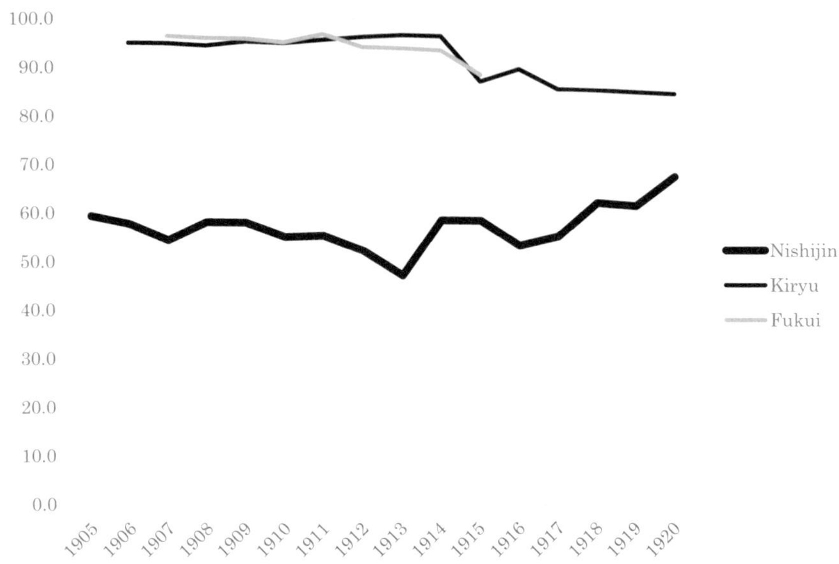

Fig. 4.8 Changes in percentages of female workers in Nishijin, Kiryu, and Fukui weaving districts from 1905 to 1920 (%) (Sources: The same as for Fig. 4.8)

worked by semi-skilled female workers to produce fabrics that were more popular and cheaper than those from Nishijin. By producing simple products, Fukui enjoyed a comparative advantage based on its abundant supply of unskilled low-wage female workers. Clearly, technology choice in the three weaving districts was affected by the availability of workers with different skills.

Worker's skill levels can be roughly measured by wage rates. Data limitations make it difficult to accurately compare wage rates among the three districts, but it is still possible to roughly picture the extent of wage differentials among the three weaving districts. Table 4.1 indicates the average nominal daily wage of weavers in Nishijin, Kiryu, and Fukui in the early twentieth century. The table shows the average wages of male weaving workers in Nishijin and of female weaving workers in both Kiryu and Fukui, and allows comparison of wage rates among these groups. Some important tendencies can be found from comparisons in Table 4.1. First, Nishijin had the highest average wages throughout the observation period, though fluctuations occurred. This seems to imply that the male weavers in Nishijin had higher skill levels than the weavers in the other two districts.[8] Wages in Fukui were far lower than those in Nishijin until 1910, indicating that the female weavers in Fukui were much less skilled than the male weavers in Nishijin. However, it seems that the demand for unskilled female workers increased in Fukui owing to the export boom of *habutae*, with the result that wages in Fukui almost caught up with Nishijin. Second, wage rates in Kiryu lay between those of the other two weaving districts in

[8] It is not clear why average wages in Nishijin decreased in both 1913 and 1916.

Table 4.1 Comparison of average wages of weavers in Nishijin, Kiryu, and Fukui weaving districts (nominal daily wage, in Yen, selected years)

Year	Nishijin (male worker)	Kiryu (female worker)	Fukui (female worker)
1904	0.69	n.a.	0.18
1907	1.03	n.a.	0.19
1910	1.20	n.a.	0.24
1913	0.55	n.a.	0.28
1916	0.48	0.32*	0.29
1919	1.18	0.79**	0.98

Sources: Nishijin, Editorial Board of 100 Year History of Kyoto Chamber of Commerce and Industry (1982), pp. 28–29. Kiryu, Gunma Prefectural Government (1916 and 1919) *Factory Survey*. Fukui, Fukui Prefectural Government (each year) *Statistical Survey of Fukui Prefecture*
Notes: * indicates data for 1915 and ** indicates data for 1918. In the case of Kiryu, I calculated the weighted average wage of female workers in factories with more than 10 workers, which appears in individual factory data from the *Factory Survey* (n=64 in 1915 and 88 in 1918). The figures for Fukui were calculated in the same way using data for individual workshops with more than 10 workers, which appeared in the *Statistical Survey* (n=6606 in 1904, 6520 in 1907, 8663 in 1910, 8627 in 1913, 9800 in 1916, and 14,413 in 1919)

1916, when wage data first became available, but became the lowest among the three districts in 1919. Owing to the lack of data, comparison among the three districts is quite difficult, but the substantially lower average wage in Kiryu relative to Nishijin suggests that weavers in the former district were less skilled than those in the latter. Finally, in 1919, the average wage rate increased markedly in Fukui in response to the economic boom, and surprisingly surpassed the average wage in Kiryu. Frankly, it is hard to explain why wage rates were almost identical in Kiryu and Fukui in 1916, yet became lower in the former by 1919. Possibly, in Fukui the increase in average wages accelerated the adoption of power looms and eroded the district's comparative advantage in relying on cheap unskilled workers to produce simple products (Hashino and Otsuka 2015, p.17).

To sum up, the differential endowments of the skilled, semi-skilled, and unskilled labor force, which had historically been accumulated under different production environments, resulted in different ways of organizing production, different production methods and products, and different labor productivities among the three silk-weaving districts.

4.5 Concluding Remarks

In this chapter, we examined the contrasting development paths of Nishijin, Kiryu, and Fukui silk-weaving districts. Modern technology was transferred from Nishijin to Kiryu, and later from Kiryu to Fukui. In terms of the extent of 'modernization' as measured by power loom adoption and factory production, Fukui was the most modern and Nishijin the least modern. Furthermore, power loom adoption boosted labor productivity first in Fukui, then Kiryu and only much later in Nishijin. This contrasting experience in the three major silk-weaving districts clearly suggests that successful technology transfer is far from simple, and involves appropriate choice of technology. The experience of Fukui and Kiryu weaving districts vividly shows that although both learned from Nishijin, they introduced very different technologies. Furthermore, Nishijin weaving district stuck to the most traditional technology.

Simultaneously, the critical role played by Nishijin as a center to all of Japan's weaving districts should be noted. As mentioned before, a delegation of craftsmen from Nishijin brought flying-shuttle and jacquard machines back from Lyon in the 1870s. This became the start of the development process that led to the spread of Western technology throughout Japan. However, the mission of the delegation had been to import power looms and steam engines to drive them, not flying-shuttle and jacquard machines (Nakaoka 2006, pp. 97–98). While the delegation were impressed by the power looms driven by steam engines they encountered in Lyon, they elected against choosing power looms partly because of their high cost and partly because they were thought inappropriate for Japan. It is truly remarkable that this delegation from Nishijin was insightful enough to find flying-shuttle and jacquard machines the most appropriate technologies for the Japanese weaving industry in the late nineteenth century. Because Nishijin had developed production technologies to a significant level before the early Meiji period, skilled craftsmen from Nishijin were qualified to make this appropriate decision regarding such an important matter. As Morris-Suzuki (1994) points out, small-scale silk- and cotton-weaving workshops were revolutionized as a result of innovative activities by the Kyoto local government and Nishijin. Thus, it is worth emphasizing that technology choices made by skilled craftsmen in the most advanced weaving district in Japan directed the development of many of the country's other weaving districts.

Technology choice, as discussed above, is relevant to the discussion on 'labor-intensive industrialization' proposed by Sugihara (2013). According to him, labor-intensive industries played a central role in the global diffusion of industrialization to East Asia (Sugihara 2013, p. 20). As discussed above, it is true that the silk-weaving industry was highly labor intensive and a newly-emerging weaving district such as Fukui enjoyed a comparative advantage arising from the availability of cheap labor. However, this study presented a good example to consider the critical role played by skilled workers in industrialization. Indeed, Saito (2013, pp. 99–100) argues that not only did a dichotomy exist between capital-intensive and labor-intensive industrialization but also that understanding the various paths of industrial development in the global economy requires considering degree of skill intensity (Saito 2013, p. 99–100). In this study, we proved that Nishijin was the most skill-intensive and the least capital-intensive among the three weaving districts. In contrast, Fukui was both labor-intensive and also the most capital-intensive. Kiryu was in-between, being moderately skill-intensive and also moderately capital-intensive. Restated, it is reasonable to conclude that skill intensity in the production process, which is critically determined by the history of skill accumulation, led to the different development paths of the three silk-weaving districts.

As was shown in this study, the local governments of Kyoto and Fukui played an important role in technology transfer in the early phase of industrialization. Further details on the role of local government will be discussed in Chap. 9, which focuses on the role of local government in the development of industrial districts in Japan.

References

Abe T (1992) The development of the producing-center cotton textile industry in Japan between the Two World Wars. Jpn Yearb Bus His 9:3–27

Bank of Japan, Kyoto Branch (ed) (1914) Nishijin kigyo gaikan (Overview of Nishijin weaving industry)

Bessen J (2012) More machines, better machines… or better workers? J Econ Hist 72(1):44–74

Federico G (1997) An economic history of the silk industry, 1830–1930. Cambridge University Press, Cambridge

Harada M (2002) Meiji-Taishoki habutae no ryutsu (Distribution of habutae in the Meiji and Taisho period). Public Policy Local Gov 6:25–36

Hareven TK (2002) The silk weavers of Kyoto: family and work in a changing traditional industry. University of California Press, Berkeley

Hashino T (2007a) Keizaihatten to sanchi shijo seido (Economic development, industrial districts, markets and institutions). Minerva, Kyoto

Hashino T (2007b) The rise of the power-loom factory in the traditional silk-weaving district: change in demand and labor market. In: Okazaki T (ed) Production organizations in Japanese economic development. Routledge, New York

Hashino T (2012) Institutionalising technical education: the case of weaving districts in Meiji Japan. Aust Econ Hist Rev 52(1):25–42

Hashino T, Kurosawa T (2013) Beyond marshallian agglomeration economies: the roles of the trade association in a weaving district. Bus His Rev 87(3):489–513

Hashino T, Otsuka K (2013a) Hand looms, power looms, and changing production organizations: the case of the Kiryu weaving district in early twentieth-century Japan. Econ Hist Rev 66(3):785–904

Hashino T, Otsuka K (2013b) Cluster-based industrial development in contemporary developing countries and modern Japanese economic history. J Jpn Int Econ 30:19–32

Hashino T, Otsuka K (2015) The rise and fall of industrialization and changing labor intensity: the case of export-oriented silk weaving district in modern Japan, Discussion paper No. 1501. Graduate School of Economics, Kobe University, Kobe

Ichikawa T (1996) Nihon noson kogyoshi kenkyu (Research on history of rural industry in Japan). Bunshindo, Tokyo

Ishii T (1986) Sen-i kikai gijutsu no hatten katei (Development process of technologies of textile machine). In: Nakaoka T, Isii T, Uchida H (eds) Kindai Nihon no gijutsu to gijutsu seisaku (Technology and technology policy in modern Japan). University of Tokyo Press, Tokyo

Kandachi H (1974) Meijiki noson orimonogyo no tenkai (Evolution of weaving industry in rural villages in the Meiji period). University of Tokyo Press, Tokyo

Minami R, Makino F (1983) Conditions for technological diffusion: case of power looms. Hitotsubashi J Econ 23(2):1–20

Morris-Suzuki T (1994) The technological transformation of Japan: from the seventeenth to the twenty-first century. Cambridge University Press, Cambridge

Nakaoka T (2006) Nihon kindai gijutsu no keisei: dento to kindai no dainamikusu (Formation of modern technology in Japan: dynamics between tradition and modern). Asahi Shinbunsha, Tokyo

Ohkawa K et al (1967) Choki keizai tokei: 8 bukka (Estimates of long-term economic statistics of Japan since 1868: 8 prices). Toyo Keizai Shinposha, Tokyo
Sabel C, Zeitlin J (1985) Historical alternatives to mass production: politics, markets and technology in nineteenth-century industrialization. Past Present 108:133–176
Saito O (2013) Proto-industrialization and labot-intensive industrialization: reflections on Smithian growth and the role of skill intensity. In: Austin G, Sugihara K (eds) Labor-intensive industrialization in global history. Roultedge, Oxon
Singleton J (1997) The world textile industry. Routledge, New York
Sugihara K (2013) Labor-intensive industrialization in global history: an interpretation of East Asian experiences. In: Austin G, Sugihara K (eds) Labor-intensive industrialization in global history. Routledge, Oxon
Suzuki J (1996) Meiji no kikai kogyo (The machine industry in Meiji Japan). Minerva, Kyoto
Tamura H (2004) Fasshon no shakai-keizaishi (The socio-economic history of fashon). Nihonhyoronsha, Tokyo
Tanimoto M (2006) The role of tradition in Japan's industrialization: another path to industrialization. In: Tanimoto M (ed) The role of tradition in Japan's industrialization. Oxford University Press, Oxford

Chapter 5
Emergence and Subsequent Development of Garment Clusters in Bangladesh and Tanzania

Tetsushi Sonobe

Abstract This chapter attempts to demonstrate the importance of technology transfer from abroad in the development of industrial clusters in developing countries by comparing the cases of cluster development with and without introducing technological and managerial knowledge from abroad. In particular, focus is placed on spectacular development of the garment cluster in Bangladesh, which initially learned technology and management by sending newly recruited workers to South Korea for intensive training. Although less spectacular than that in Bangladesh, the garment cluster in Tanzania also developed by learning from training programs offered by UNIDO. It is also found that, for successful development of industrial clusters, the entrepreneurial human capital plays a key role as successful technology transfer requires innovations in the improvement of product quality, production methods, and marketing.

Keywords Technology transfer • Industrial cluster • Garment cluster • Bangladesh • Tanzania • Training program • Entrepreneurial human capital

5.1 Introduction

The development of the export-oriented garment industry in Bangladesh began in 1978 with the intensive training program provided by Daewoo, a Korean garment firm, for 130 newly recruited workers of Desh Ltd., a newly established local firm (Rhee 1990; Easterly 2002). After receiving the 8-month training in Daewoo's factory in Korea, the Bangladeshi trainees returned to Desh's factory with Daewoo's skilled workers in 1980 to begin on-the-job training, which led to Desh's export of its first products. The successful start of exporting encouraged both the local business community and foreign firms to build garment factories in Chittagong, a port city, and Dhaka, the national capital.

T. Sonobe (✉)
National Graduate Institute for Policy Studies, Tokyo, Japan
e-mail: sonobete@grips.ac.jp

T. Hashino, K. Otsuka (eds.), *Industrial Districts in History and the Developing World*, Studies in Economic History, DOI 10.1007/978-981-10-0182-6_5

The total number of garment factories in Bangladesh reached 500 in 1985, 1000 in 1990, and 3200 in 2000. This impressive increase in numbers supports the hypothesis that technology transfer from abroad contributes to successful industrial cluster development. Moreover, the industry continued to grow rapidly for the last three decades, during which competition among producers in the world garment market has intensified substantially with the rapid increase in the number of low-wage countries able to supply garments, including former socialist countries. There was a pessimistic view that the garment industry in Bangladesh would not survive the ending of the Multi Fibre Arrangement in 2005 (e.g., Mlachila and Yang 2004; Siddiqi 2005), but in fact it has continued to grow to become the fourth largest supplier after China, Hong Kong, and Italy. This raises questions about whether the massive technology transfer in the early years is related to the sustained rapid growth in later years.

This chapter aims to address this and other questions about technology transfer and cluster-based development in relation to the garment industry. The first question involves the prevalence of technology transfer at the beginning of garment cluster development. The second question is how garment cluster formation can begin in a developing country without technology transfer from abroad. To answer these questions, we review the results of five case studies of garment clusters in Asia and Africa, including a historical case in Japan. These garment clusters were formed without the help of technology transfer from abroad, and instead relied on existing commercial networks and government assistance. These cases motivate us to ask what besides technology transfer helped the formation of the huge garment clusters in Dhaka and the smaller cluster in Chittagong.

After an industrial cluster forms, whether it will achieve sustained growth or become large is uncertain. These are different matters in principle, but how strongly the manner of cluster formation impacts its subsequent growth is an interesting question. To consider path dependence, we review the case of the garment industry in Tanzania and compare it with the Bangladesh case. Dar es Salaam, the de facto capital of Tanzania, has several hundred firms that produce and sell final products, as well as many subcontractors working for other producers or traders. This garment cluster started with the training programs offered by the United Nations Industrial Development Organization (UNIDO) and other development partners in the 1990s. As intended by these organizations, the training programs produced a number of entrepreneurs and led to the formation of an industrial cluster. However, the firms in this cluster are small, meaning generation of income and jobs has been less than one would expect based simply on the number of firms.

Compared with this cluster in Tanzania, the cluster in Bangladeshi is huge, has much more efficient production, and produces garments of much higher quality. It seems natural that a large garment cluster can more easily attract orders from overseas buyers than can a smaller cluster. Moreover, if buyers demand higher quality, faster delivery, and lower price, the larger cluster is more likely to have firms that can upgrade their capabilities to satisfy such demands. Hence it seems natural that the Bangladesh garment industry would grow and upgrade its capabilities faster than its Tanzanian counterpart. However, this logic alone cannot explain why

Bangladesh was able to overtake many previously larger garment supplying countries. To deepen our understanding of this phenomenon, this chapter draws on Mottaleb and Sonobe (2011), who conducted a random survey of knitwear manufacturers and garment traders in Dhaka. Data analysis clearly indicates that the behavior and performance of a trading or knitwear manufacturing firm is affected by whether its top manager (here called an entrepreneur) received formal training abroad, even if for a long time previously. We explore the implications of this finding below.

The rest of this chapter is organized as follows. Section 5.2 reviews the case studies of five garment clusters that did not receive technology transfer from abroad. Section 5.3 discusses the diffusion process of the knowledge transferred to Bangladesh and Tanzania. Section 5.4 examines the subsequent growth of the garment industry in Bangladesh. Section 5.5 presents conclusions.

5.2 Industrial Clusters Without Technology Transfer from Abroad

Almost any society has garment producers, and these producers may form clusters. A garment cluster typically forms when a new garment business model proves so profitable that imitators or followers start their own businesses near the pioneer. The new business model might be tailoring, vertically integrated mass-production, traders putting out to individual sewers, or subcontracting to factories. The contribution of a garment cluster to local job creation and income generation will probably be greatest if the cluster has numerous large factories that mass-produce ready-made garments (RMGs) to meet large demand in urban areas and foreign markets. This chapter focuses on such garment clusters.

Because garment production is labor-intensive and does not require large machinery or complex technology, one may wonder whether technology transfer matters to the development of a garment industry. Indeed, many garment clusters were established in developing countries without technology transfer from abroad. In this section, we review five case studies involving such clusters to understand why technology transfer from abroad can have impacts. Table 5.1 summarizes the information on these clusters.

5.2.1 Local Traders and Marketplace

The first cluster in Table 5.1 produces working clothes for farmers, factory workers, and construction workers in a remote rural area of Japan (Yamamura et al. 2003). This cluster was established soon after World War II. Before the war, the area had been known for special woven cloth used in traditional Japanese attire, and hence had numerous weavers and local traders who peddled the cloth across the country. Western-style clothes were also produced by a few factories to meet gradually

Table 5.1 Characteristics of the selected garment clusters

	Location	Time of initial cluster formation	Year of survey	Product lines	Source of knowledge & skills	Early markets	Role of (local) gov't /associations	Mean years of education of top managers	Total number of firms	Average number of workers per firm
1	A village in Hiroshima, Japan	Late 1940s	1998	Working clothes	-	Domestic through local traders	Association provided training	13.7	100 (excl. subcontractors)	na
2	A town in Zhejiang, China	Early 1980s	2000	Baby dresses	State-Owned Enterprises	Russia & domestic	Local govt. provided marketplace	7.5	5000 (incl. subcontractors)	15
3	A village near Hanoi, Vietnam	1980s	2006	Sweaters, trousers & caps	State-Owned Enterprises	Eastern Europe & domestic	-	7.9	143 (excluding subcontract-ors)	12.0
4	Three districts of Nairobi, Kenya	1974	2003	Dresses, shirts & bags	-	Domestic & trade fairs	Local govt. provided marketplace	8.6	1368 (excl. subcontractors)	4.8
5	Addis Ababa, Ethiopia	Mid-2000s	2007	Dresses, jackets & shirts	State-Owned Enterprises	Domestic & export samples	Govt. help via advantageous finance & land rents	10.1	700 (excl. subcontractors)	26.1
6	Greater Dhaka, Bangladesh	1979	2005	All kinds of woven/knitted clothes	Foreign firms	Europe & America	Gov't de- regulation of logistics & finance	15.0[a]	4107 (exporters only)	520
7	Dar es Salaam, Tanzania	1990s	2010	Dresses & homeware	Development partners	Domestic & trade fairs	Association Offers of training info & organizational fairs	10.7	700 (excl. subcontractors)	5.0

Note: [a] this is the mean number of years of schooling of the top managers of 92 knitwear manufacturing firms in the sample. The corresponding mean in the sample of 40 garment traders is 15.2 years increasing demand. Demand for Western-style clothes surged as soon as wartime rationing ended, and a number of weavers became sewers producing clothes. Although these new sewers offered only low-quality products, the surge in demand still meant many local traders were willing to take their products to retailers and marketplaces throughout the country.

However, once this boom ended, the prices of low-quality products swiftly and sharply declined. The long-established factories, which produced higher-quality products, were worried about reputational damage because both their products and the low-quality products produced by the new sewers were known by the name of the production area. Thus, the business association established by these factories invited a designer from a metropolitan area to give a seminar series on proper methods for clothes manufacture, with this seminar series being open at no cost to the non-member sewers. This collective action, together with the existence of numerous local traders, contributed to the formation of the working clothes cluster. This can be rephrased as follows: a cluster of weavers and traders changed their product to seize the profit opportunity arising from the sudden increase in demand resulting from knowledge spillovers, low transaction costs, and collective action, all of which are well-known benefits of belonging to a cluster.

The second cluster in Table 5.1 is located in a rural area of Zhejiang Province and began producing baby dresses in the early 1980s by adopting technology from state-owned enterprises (SOEs) in nearby urban areas (Sonobe et al. 2002; Fleisher et al. 2010). The development of this cluster benefited considerably from the local government's provision of marketplaces, in the form of buildings where products could be sold and materials procured, because such marketplaces attracted traders who took the products of cluster firms to remote markets, including those in Mongolia and Russia.

The third cluster is a village near Hanoi, Vietnam that produces knitwear, such as caps, sweaters, and trousers, for both the domestic and Eastern European markets (Nam et al. 2010; Suzuki et al. 2014). Many of the villagers used to work at a cooperative that subcontracted for an SOE exporting towels to Russia. After the collapse of the USSR destroyed this market, the cooperative was dissolved and its knitting machines given to the villagers. These villagers then began knitting simple products for the Hanoi market. Later, overseas Vietnamese traders with businesses in Russia and Eastern Europe who had originated from this village or its surrounding area began exporting village products to Russia and Eastern Europe.

The fourth cluster in Table 5.1 is located in Nairobi, Kenya. Like the baby dress cluster in China, it was established through the local government providing marketplaces (Akoten and Otsuka 2007). Most producers simply employ a few workers at small marketplace booths to sew a variety of shirts and dresses. Meanwhile, a few producers have small factories located outside marketplaces, produce larger quantities of a smaller variety of products, and earn greater profits. Akoten and Otsuka (2007) find that these miniature manufacturers established long-term relationships with traders from distant cities.

5.2.2 Common Pattern of Garment Cluster Development

The case studies mentioned above show that these four clusters share similar development paths. Their common development pattern also resembles the development paths of industrial clusters in different industries in Asia and Africa studied by Sonobe and Otsuka (2006, 2011). Table 5.2 is a modification of a table from Sonobe and Otsuka (2006, p. 29, Table 2.2). While the original table represented the common pattern of different industries in different countries, Table 5.2 represents the common development pattern of garment clusters in different countries.

The pioneer of the profitable business model that leads to cluster establishment may be a tailor, a former manager or engineer of an SOE or foreign firm, or a merchant. Meanwhile, the location where the pioneer develops their initial innovation is likely to be an urban area with strong demand for RMGs, but could be a rural area if the product is something unfashionable, like working clothes. A garment cluster is formed by imitators in the neighborhood of a pioneer. Workers employed by the pioneer who know the business model well are likely to be first imitators. As pro-

Table 5.2 An endogenous model of garment cluster development

Development phase	Prior experience of entrepreneurs	Education Level	Innovation, imitation, firm dynamics	Institutions
Initiation	Tailors, former SOE managers, merchants	Mixed	Discovery of a profitable combination of production and sales methods, such as mass-selling and factory production of RMGs	Co-existence of different business models (e.g., tailors, putting-out, household subcontractors)
Quantity Expansion	Spin-offs and entrants from various fields	Mixed	Proliferation of imitators, stagnation of productivity & product quality, increasing market supply, declining profitability	The formation of industrial clusters, associations, subcontracting to specialists.
Quality Improvement	Children of founders and newcomers with new ideas	High	Multi-faceted innovation upgrading production, QC, marketing, labor and financial management, exporting, emergence of large firms, exits	Merchandizing, reputation and brand names, direct sales, international procurement, vertical integration, emergence of large enterprises

duction expands, an increasing number of traders facilitate the business operations of the cluster by supplying it with raw materials and taking its products to distant markets. Thus, the entry of new firms from various sectors will begin to increase. Moreover, an association of garment producers, traders or both may be established to transfer business information and arrange collective actions. Division of labor may develop among producers, leading to the emergence of specialists.

During this stage of development, the production volume and value of the cluster increase primarily through an increase in the number of producers that results from massive entry of new firms rather than innovation. The product quality and production processes essentially remain the same. In this sense, this development phase may be called the quantity expansion phase. As long as positive profits are expected, entry of new firms continues and increases the output of the cluster as a whole, reducing product prices if market demand is limited relative to the cluster's capacity to supply. If the product price does not decline, input prices, including wage rates, may increase. In many cases, the profitability of the business model will eventually decline, in a process that will see profits driven to zero by new entrants.

Among the first four clusters in Table 5.2, the Nairobi cluster is stuck in the zero profit equilibrium described above, but the working clothes cluster in Japan and the baby dress cluster in China successfully escaped this phenomenon by replacing the old model with a new one.[1] The change began by improving quality control and production management, but branding and merchandizing, together with brand name protection devices, are indispensable to profiting from quality improvement. As these changes proceeded, production and employment increased. Because larger-scale operations complicate labor and financial management as well as procurement and inventory management, they require an overall upgrading of management capabilities. Clearly these changes are mutually complementary. The overall change may be called multi-faceted innovation.

The results of the comparative studies of 16 clusters in developing countries conducted by Sonobe and Otsuka (2006, 2011) indicate that upon completion of the multi-faceted innovation, industrial clusters enter a new stage of development in which firms differentiate their products and compete by developing new products and production processes. It seems that without achieving multi-faceted innovation, industrial clusters are doomed to zero profit equilibrium (Yoshino 2011). The next section will examine whether these findings apply to garment clusters started with technology transfer from abroad.

[1] The knitwear cluster near Hanoi escaped the zero profit equilibrium problem by increasing exports via overseas Vietnamese traders, but more recently its profitability has been declining (Higuchi et al. 2015).

5.2.3 A Failure to Replicate a Development Miracle without the Prime Mover

The fifth cluster in Table 5.2 is located in Addis Ababa, the capital of Ethiopia (Sonobe and Otsuka 2011, Ch.9). This city has a long-standing cluster of weavers of traditional attire as well as a cluster of more than 600 tailors of Western-style suits and dresses. A young tailor emerged from the latter of these clusters to become the owner/operator of RMG factories. He was the first in the national garment industry to use expensive imported materials and adopt both the two-shift system and merchandizing. His business model proved profitable and his business rapidly expanded. Following his lead, six tailors became factory owners/operators. These six factories plus that of the pioneer were not exporting when Sonobe and Otsuka (2011, Ch.9) surveyed garment firms in 2007.

Slightly before this survey was conducted, the central government adopted a new policy to promote garment production for export to the US market to take advantage of preferential US trade policy under the African Growth and Opportunity Act. Part of the policy was to provide land and finance at low rents and interest rates, respectively, which encouraged investors to establish 14 export-oriented firms. The survey data revealed that these 14 firms had much lower productivity than the factories established by tailors or even than micro-scale tailors. This low productivity was the result of low or negligible sales revenues. Few of these firms successfully obtained orders from buyers in the US.[2] In contrast, as we will see below, the Bangladeshi garment industry achieved considerable success from the very beginning.

The Ethiopian export-oriented garment firms failed to get export orders for the following reasons. The managers of the 14 export-oriented firms were highly educated, with most being former managers of SOEs, including producers of military uniforms and similar garments. However, none of the managers had experience in exporting garments to developed countries, and their knowledge of production management, quality control, and marketing was obsolete. Their potential buyers from the US, based on factory visits and received samples, concluded that few Ethiopian firms had sufficient capabilities to assure that a placed order would be adequately fulfilled via production and delivery.

5.2.4 Implications of the Five Cases

The five cases reviewed here all suggest that because garments are not a high-tech product, finding ways to sell garments rather than make them, such as through local traders, creation of marketplaces, and means of accessing distant traders, is important in the early phases of cluster development. However, selling ceases to be the

[2] The situation did not improve for at least a few years according to personal interviews the author conducted with the managers of two export-oriented firms in 2010.

issue as a cluster grows. The new problem then becomes the entry of new firms, which drives profits to zero. To restore profitability it is critical that firms upgrade their capabilities in production management, product development, marketing, and so on.

Capability upgrading is also needed to supply garment products to markets in developed countries. A producer cannot get an order without the capability to produce large quantities of products on time and exactly according to buyer specifications. Of course, wage rates are another important determinant of whether a country becomes an exporter of garment products. However, the comparative advantage of a labor-abundant country can be realized only if it has capable producers. An implication of these findings is that technology transfer from abroad will strongly impact garment cluster formation and growth if the transferred technology is relevant to the capabilities needed for multi-faceted innovation or to get export orders. In other words, entrepreneurial human capital plays a critical role in introducing, absorbing, and adapting new technologies from abroad.

5.3 Formation and Expansion of Clusters in Bangladesh and Tanzania

In this section, we examine how transferred technology was disseminated in Bangladesh and Tanzania, drawing on Rhee (1990), Easterly (2002), and Mottaleb and Sonobe (2011) for Bangladesh, and on Sonobe and Otsuka (2014, ch. 8) for Tanzania.

5.3.1 Cluster Formation in Bangladesh

The Desh-Daewoo training program was comprehensive and covered skills from sewing and machine maintenance through to quality control and international procurement and marketing. The 130 trainees were exceptionally highly educated relative to contemporary Bangladeshi standards because fluency in English was a requirement for the training in Korea. The trainees swiftly mastered production, managerial, and marketing expertise from Daewoo. Desh cancelled the collaboration agreement with Daewoo in the middle of 1981. By this stage, Desh could manage without Daewoo's help; it could not only find material procurement sources and export markets but also increase production and export value.

Soon after the cancellation of this agreement, these employees began leaving Desh for new firms, established either by themselves or by other business persons. According to Rhee (1990), within a few years, 115 of the 130 participants in the Desh-Daewoo training program left Desh. Column (1) of Table 5.3 shows the rapid growth in the number of export-oriented garment firms. The number increased from

Table 5.3 The growth of the Bangladesh export-oriented garment industry

Fiscal year[a]	(1) Number of export-oriented garment firms	(2) Employment (million workers)	(3) Export value in billion USD[b]			(4) % of total national export earnings
			Woven	Knit	Sum	
1983/84	134	0.04			0.03	3.9
1987/88	685	0.28			0.43	35.2
1991/92	1163	0.58			1.18	59.3
1995/96	2353	1.29	1.95	0.60	2.55	65.6
1999/00	3200	1.60	3.08	1.27	4.35	75.6
2003/04	3957	2.00	3.54	2.15	5.69	74.8
2007/08	4743	2.80	5.17	5.53	10.70	75.8
2011/12	5400	4.00	9.60	9.49	19.09	78.6
2014/15	4296	4.00	13.07	12.43	25.49	81.7

Sources: Webpage of the Bangladesh Garment Manufacturers and Exporters Association (BGMEA), http://bgmea.com.bd/home/pages/TradeInformation

Notes:

[a] The Bangladeshi fiscal year runs from July to June.

[b] The export value is in nominal USD, not deflated

1 to 134 after 4 years and reached 685 after 8 years. Some of these firms were joint ventures between Bangladeshi firms and firms from Korea and other newly industrialized economies (NIEs) in East Asia, but the vast majority were local. Firm size as measured in terms of number of employees was about 300 in fiscal year 1983/84 (see columns (1) and (2) of Table 5.3), which was large by the standards of low-income countries.

These investors found the garment business highly profitable because a previously missing resource, that is, a mass of experts, had become available. In those days, labor costs were much lower in Bangladesh than in other garment exporting countries, such the East Asian NIEs and the Philippines. Moreover, although not necessarily expected, labor costs remained low in the long run because women, who had few other places to work, could work at garment factories. Following the acquisition by Bangladesh of expertise comparable to that in competitor countries, its low labor costs made local garment production highly profitable.

Naturally, the investors invited the Desh-Daewoo trainees and those who had acquired knowledge and skills at foreign ventures to operate their newly established factories as managers. These managers then trained new recruits. Soon after training was complete, some of the new workers were poached to newer factories. According to Rhee (1990) and Easterly (2002), this high mobility of Bangladeshi workers was important in the rapid diffusion of knowledge and skills transferred from abroad.

According to Mottaleb and Sonobe (2011), the service that buying houses provided for relatively new factories was important in the rapid diffusion of technology transferred from abroad. Among the 130 Desh-Daewoo trainees, some became hired managers, others established their own garment factories, and the rest started buying houses. The service that buying houses provide for factories is not simply to match factories and foreign buyers but also to assure the delivery of products as per buyers' orders and the collection of money from buyers on behalf of factories. If a client factory had difficulty in production, the buying house would help in the short term by troubleshooting and in the long term by imparting necessary skills. After several years, the factory may master the production, managerial, and marketing knowhow and stop relying on the buying house to save costs. Buying houses thus act like elementary school teachers, who educate pupils for several years and then send them to the next stage of learning.

Another noteworthy feature of the garment export industry in Bangladesh is the high education level of its top managers, as shown in Table 5.1. Having observed the success of the 130 Desh-Daewoo trainees, highly educated youth realized that the garment export industry could open a window of opportunity, and so the industry began attracting not only rich investors but also highly educated youth.

Although our attention has been attracted to technology transfer, our earlier review of the five cases from other countries suggests that the government and the garment manufacturers association would also contribute to the rapid proliferation of garment factories in Bangladesh. Indeed, the Bangladeshi government offered a conducive environment for the garment export industry in the otherwise rigid system of trade and finance. Two notable examples were the introduction of a Special Bonded Warehouse system and a back-to-back usance import letter of credit (L/C) system (Rhee 1990, pp. 339–340). The Bangladesh Garment Manufacturers and Exporters Association was established in 1983 and immediately began facilitating information exchanges and making policy recommendations.

Thus, there is no doubt about the contribution of the government and the association to the development of the industry. Interestingly though, Rhee (1990) argues that the effective designs of the bonded warehouse system and the back-to-back L/C system were most likely created under the influence of Desh and Daewoo. This is a cogent argument because government officials in those days would have lacked a good understanding of the policies and regimes conducive to the development of the garment export industry.

The main causes of the enormous proliferation of garment firms throughout the 1980s and 1990s include the high profitability of using transferred technology, participation of educated youth, high worker mobility, buying houses which provide guidance and support for garment companies, and assistance from the government and industry associations. These findings amply support the hypothesis that technology transfer from abroad can contribute to industrial cluster formation.

5.3.2 *The Case of Tanzania*

We turn now to the last item in Table 5.1, namely the cluster in Dar es Salaam, Tanzania's largest city. Sonobe and Otsuka (2014, ch. 8) conducted a baseline survey of garment manufacturers in this cluster in 2010. The sample of 110 firms was randomly selected from about 240 members of the three major garment manufacturer associations. If self-employed workers without commercial premises were included, the total number of garment producers in the city reaches about 700.

According to the survey data, 67 % of the sample entrepreneurs have received business training from international organizations or other development partners or from the government and non-government organizations collaborating with development partners. The entrepreneurs of long-established firms in the sample and the leaders of the garment associations uniformly noted that UNIDO was the first to provide an impactful business training program. This program was successful in the sense that many training participants started garment businesses. Therefore similar training programs were planned and implemented, resulting in the further entry to the garment industry of new entrepreneurs. Those who participated in these training programs and then started their own workshops in the early years may be called pioneers in the Dar es Salaam garment industry.

According to the pioneers in the survey sample, the UNIDO training program aimed to nurture women entrepreneurs, and taught participants skills in sewing, sewing machine maintenance, and basic bookkeeping, as well as the importance of being proactive or entrepreneurial. In other words, UNIDO provided production skill training plus the common type of business development services provided by the international development community for micro and small enterprises in any kind of business in developing countries. The pioneers were housewives from relatively well-to-do families. They found that the dresses, bags, pillowcases, and other garment items available on the market in those days were either too expensive or poorly designed and sewn. The training program gave them the practical skills necessary to start their own businesses.

This cluster today has the following characteristics: firms are small, operated predominantly by female entrepreneurs, and spread across the city. As shown in Table 5.1, the average number of workers at the sample workshops is as low as five. Women entrepreneurs account for 85 % of the survey sample. The small size of firms and the female dominance are consistent with the purpose of the UNIDO training program. The geographically wide distribution may reflect that the training programs received participants from different parts of the city, and that training participants tended to operate home businesses.

These facts further support the hypothesis that technology transfer from abroad can contribute to industrial cluster formation. Moreover, the comparison of the Bangladesh and Tanzania cases suggests that cluster development path is affected by the kinds of knowledge and skills transferred. In Bangladesh, local firms obtained the technology needed to mass-produce and export garments, and this technology then attracted investors and educated youth. These local firms mobilize many workers and compete fiercely with foreign competitors on the global market. In Tanzania, local firms obtained the technology needed to operate small-scale businesses creating a small number of jobs, and this technology then attracted entrepreneurial housewives. To please members, garment industry associations frequently organize trade fairs in neighboring countries. Member entrepreneurs enjoy both making money during the trade fairs and conversations with other participants during associated bus tours. The comparison of the cases of Bangladesh and Tanzania demonstrates how different types of technology transfer from abroad led to different outcomes.

5.4 Long-Term Impacts of Technology Transfer

The rapid and sustained growth in the number of garment manufacturing firms in Bangladesh shown in column (1) of Table 5.3 is impressive, but note that employment in column (2) grew faster, and export value in column (3) grew faster again. That is, both average firm size and revenue per worker grew continuously. These facts indicate that the phenomenal growth performance of this industry was a result not just of firm proliferation but also of rapid and sustained firm growth. As mentioned in the introduction, the world garment market witnessed considerable intensification of competition throughout the 1990s and 2000s because of the dramatic increase in number of supplying countries after the end of the Cold War. Naturally the question arises as to what made firm growth possible despite the intensifying competition. Firm growth may be enabled by the manner in which the garment industry in Bangladesh got started, namely the massive technology transfer from abroad.

As mentioned in the introduction above, one may consider a larger cluster more advantageous than a smaller cluster in terms of capability upgrading. As buyers from developed countries, or global buyers, become increasingly demanding, suppliers in developing countries had to develop the ability to produce higher quality products in a shorter time and at lower cost. This is exactly what has happened in the world garment market since the 1990s, and to cope with such demand from buyers, suppliers had to learn more, whether from themselves or from abroad, according to the informants of Mottaleb and Sonobe (2011). Consider the following argument: the larger cluster is more likely than the smaller cluster to contain firms that upgrade their capabilities through learning from sources of useful knowledge, and that thus can better satisfy buyer demand. New know-how can then spill over within the cluster. Thus, the proliferation of garment firms was followed by an impressive upgrading of capabilities in Bangladesh. However, this argument fails to explain why Bangladesh caught up with and then overtook its larger competitors.

To better understand the impacts of technology transfer, this section looks at micro-level data collected by Mottaleb and Sonobe (2011) through surveys of 92 knitwear manufacturing firms and 40 buying houses. As shown in column (3) of Table 5.3, the manufacturing sector can be divided into woven and knitwear subsectors. White dress shirts, jackets, and other garments made of woven cloth belong to the former, while sweaters, polo-shirts, sweat-shirts, and socks belong to the latter. As observed from Table 5.3, the share of knitwear was initially small but increased throughout the 1990s and 2000s. Because of this increase, Mottaleb and Sonobe (2011) focused on knitwear manufacturers rather than woven manufacturers.

Table 5.4 Estimated functions explaining behaviors and performances of buying houses

	(1)	(2)	(3)
	Fraction of designs re-engineered	Sample making dummy	Ln (export revenue)
	Tobit	Probit	Random-effect
Years of schooling	−0.02	0.05	0.05
	(−0.46)	(0.34)	(0.35)
Prior formal training dummy	0.59**	1.58*	0.72**
	(2.58)	(1.75)	(1.98)
Age	−0.02	−0.04	−0.05
	(−1.16)	(−0.87)	(−1.36)
Years of prior experience in garment marketing	0.02	0.03	0.04
	(0.56)	(0.45)	(0.77)
Years of prior experience in garment production	−0.01	−0.07	0.03
	(−0.33)	(−1.03)	(0.85)
Years of operation	0.04*	0.13**	0.15**
	(1.82)	(2.74)	(3.34)
Foreign-owned dummy	1.67***	0.60	1.07***
	(6.35)	(1.04)	(2.77)
Foreign venture experience dummy	0.41**	−0.65	0.24
	(2.40)	(−1.40)	(0.70)
Year 2000 dummy	−0.03	0.01	−0.03
	(−0.67)	(−0.06)	(−0.15)
Year 2002 dummy	−0.02	−0.18	−0.02
	(−0.22)	(−0.56)	(−0.08)
Year 2004 dummy	0.04	−0.19	0.06
	(0.30)	(−0.46)	(0.16)
Year 2005 dummy	0.14	0.07	0.13
	(0.93)	(0.16)	(0.31)
Constant	0.19	0.52	14.2**
	(0.22)	(0.19)	(6.03)
Number of observations	176	176	176
Left censored	107		
Right censored	19		
Hausman test Chi-square and the *p*-value			6.80
			0.24

Numbers in parentheses are the *z*- or *t*-statistics based on standard errors that allow for intragroup correlation. ***, **, and * indicate significance at the 1 %, 5 %, and 10 % levels, respectively

Tables 5.4 and 5.5 summarize the information contained in the data. They present the estimates of the statistical association among relevant variables for buying houses and knitwear manufacturers, respectively. We are particularly interested in the association between training experience and business performance. Training experience is captured by the formal training dummy, which indicates whether the owner/operator of a firm has received intensive training overseas before starting

Table 5.5 Estimated functions explaining the size and growth of knitwear firms

Column	(1)	(2)	(3)	(4)
Dependent variable	ln (value added)	Fraction of revenue through buying house	International certificate	Foreign expert employment
Estimation method	Random-effect	Tobit	Probit	Probit
Years of schooling	0.15**	−0.16***	0.08***	0.07
	(2.07)	(−2.99)	(5.09)	(0.66)
Prior formal training dummy	0.10	−0.17	0.26***	0.93*
	(0.27)	(−0.50)	(2.86)	(1.91)
Age	−0.001	−0.01	−0.01*	−0.01
	(−0.09)	(−0.49)	(−1.72)	(−0.41)
Years of prior experience in garment marketing	0.03**	−0.01	0.01*	0.05
	(2.14)	(−0.81)	(1.67)	(1.43)
Years of prior experience in garment production	0.06***	0.001	0.011*	0.05
	(2.92)	(0.07)	(1.71)	(1.42)
Years of prior experience in other sectors	0.03*	0.01	0.014*	−0.01
	(1.65)	(0.48)	(1.81)	(−0.23)
Years of Operation	0.11***	−0.06***	0.03***	0.06
	(5.11)	(−2.83)	(3.13)	(1.40)
Producing sweater	0.76***	−0.67***	0.17*	0.95**
	(3.02)	(−4.01)	(1.93)	(20.2)
Year 2000 dummy	−0.19**	0.15	0.12**	0.12
	(−1.99)	(1.37)	(2.19)	(0.49)
Year 2002 dummy	−0.13	0.14	0.39***	0.44
	(−0.85)	(1.09)	(5.79)	(1.26)
Year 2004 dummy	0.03	0.13	0.48***	0.46
	(0.17)	(0.93)	(6.91)	(1.31)
Year 2005 dummy	0.29	0.12	0.47***	0.76**
	(1.59)	(0.78)	(6.15)	(2.09)
Constant	10.9***	3.45***	−1.2***	−3.46**
	(9.09)	(4.17)	(−4.23)	(−2.08)
Number of observations	341	341	341	341
Left censored		114		
Right censored		83		
Hausman test Chi-square	1.39	5.27	–	–
p-value	0.96	0.50		

Numbers in the parentheses are the *z*- or *t*-statistics based on standard errors that allow for intra-group correlation. ***, **, * indicate significance at the 1, 5, and 10 % level respectively their buying house. On-the-job training or short-term training (defined as less than two weeks) are not considered formal training here. In Table 5.4, the business performance of buying houses is measured by the following three dependent variables: (1) the fraction of their designs that are re-engineered, (2) a dummy variable indicating whether they provide a sample-making service, and (3) the logarithm of export value.

Design re-engineering and sample making are special services that only a limited number of buying houses can provide for their client manufacturers, and hence are more profitable than the services most buying houses provide. Common practice in international garment transactions is for product designs to come from a developed country buyer to a local supplier that then produces counter-samples as per the designs and sends them to the buyer for inspection. In this process, it may turn out that designs require modification to make them more attractive to consumers or more suitable for mass production. If the buyer allows a supplier to re-engineer a design but that supplier cannot do so satisfactorily, the supplier may ask a capable buying house for help. Sample-making services are provided for suppliers not yet able to make counter samples properly.

Toward the bottom of column (1) of Table 5.4, 176 observations of 40 buying houses can be seen for five data years (1998, 2000, 2002, 2004, and 2005).[3] Of these observations, 107 of the observed values of the fraction of designs re-engineered were zero, 19 were one (100 %), and remaining 50 were between zero and one. The estimated coefficients in column (1) indicate that buying houses whose founders participated in formal training before establishing their businesses, that have been operating longer, and that have work experience at foreign ventures, as well as foreign-owned buying houses, provide design re-engineering services more frequently.

Similarly, according to column (2), buying houses operated by traders who participated in formal training before starting their current businesses and who have operated buying houses for longer are more likely to provide sample-making services. Sample-making services are provided more frequently by buying houses than are design re-engineering services. Columns (1) and (2) indicate that among buying houses that provide sample-making services, foreign-owned buying houses and those with work experience at foreign ventures are likely to re-engineer designs. Column (3) characterizes the buying houses that handle exports on a larger scale. The coefficients indicate that larger-scale buying houses have founders with formal training experience, have been operating longer, and are foreign owned.

Note that the coefficients of the prior formal training dummy variable are positive and significant in all columns of Table 5.4. The average age of the owner-operators in the buying house sample was 43 years as of 2005. These owner-operators would have received formal training in their twenties, that is, in the 1980s. Thus, the estimation results indicate that the impact of the training given to traders in the

[3]The number of observations is less than 200 (40 sample firms multiplied by 5 years) because some of the 40 sample buying houses were not yet operating in the early years of data collection.

1980s, the early development stage of the garment industry, remained significant in the mid-2000s after the industry achieved its development miracle.

We turn now to Table 5.5, which characterizes knitwear manufacturers that are larger scale, rely less on buying houses, and are more likely to obtain international certifications and employ foreign experts. Operating size is measured by the logarithm of value added. According to column (1), larger firms tend to be operated by highly educated entrepreneurs with rich experience in garment marketing and manufacturing. Of course, the long established firms tend to have higher value added. The coefficient of the sweater-producing dummy implies that those firms producing sweaters are 76 % larger than other knitwear firms.[4] The coefficients of the year dummies indicate that while the average firm size in terms of added value declined 19 % in 2000 relative to 1998, it subsequently grew, and the average size in 2005 was 0.48 % (=0.29 % – (– 0.19 %)) greater than in 2000.

The coefficients in column (2) indicate that firms operated by less educated entrepreneurs are more dependent on the service provided by buying houses. Consistent with the story about teacher-like buying houses mentioned above, dependence on buying houses decreases as the manufacturer gains experience, as indicated by the coefficient of years of operation. Firms producing sweaters are less dependent on buying houses than non-sweater knitwear firms.

In these first two columns of Table 5.5, the coefficient on the prior formal training dummy variable is insignificant. Probably, the knowledge and skills the entrepreneurs acquired from the formal training program a decade or two previously are no longer vital to knitwear firm operations. While those buying houses are dealing with relatively inexperienced factories, most of the sample manufacturers graduated long ago from dependence on buying houses and are competing for orders from world-famous brands by using cutting-edge technologies. Moreover, they are large firms able to hire experts if needed. This is probably why the training experience of the top manager does not matter to the operation size of knitwear manufacturers.

By contrast, columns (3) and (4) have positive coefficients on the formal training variable, significant at the 1 % and nearly 5 % levels, respectively. According to Mottaleb and Sonobe's (2011) informants, obtaining certificates from international auditing bodies, such as the International Organization for Standardization (ISO), has been increasingly important to attracting buyers' attention as competition among suppliers in developing countries intensifies. Indeed the coefficients of the year dummies get larger and more significant. The positive and highly significant coefficient of the formal training variable in column (3) suggests that those entrepreneurs with formal training are more interested in new trends or challenges. Alternatively, the coefficient may be interpreted as indicating that formally trained entrepreneurs are more capable of successfully getting international certificates. However, the results in columns (1) and (2) suggest that the ability of the entrepreneur is less important than the ability of the firm to hire necessary talent. Thus, we are inclined

[4] Knitwear factories can be classified into circular- and flat-knit factories according to their machinery. While circular machines are used to produce T-shirts and polo-shirts, flat machines are used to produce sweaters.

to the interpretation that formally trained entrepreneurs are keener on new ideas and practices. The positive coefficient on the formal training variable in column (4) may be interpreted similarly. Formally trained entrepreneurs are more interested in the knowledge and skills possessed by foreign experts or more willing to learn from abroad.

5.5 Conclusions

In this chapter, we learned that saying knowledge spillovers contribute to localization can have two meanings. One meaning is that within an existing cluster, information flows easily and benefits numerous firms, which motivates firms to stay in the cluster. Among the five cases in this study, such a benefit of being in a cluster was experienced by weavers who became producers of Western-style clothes in the early postwar period in Japan. However, when garment clusters were formed in Dhaka and Chittagong, knowledge spillovers had another meaning: that is, without acquiring knowledge through poaching trained workers or the services of buying houses, manufacturing firms could not produce properly or export their products, and this is why they chose to build factories close to existing ones. The first meaning of knowledge spillovers concerns cluster maintenance while the second concerns cluster formation.

The comparison of the cases from Bangladesh, Tanzania, and Ethiopia has indicated the importance of learning from abroad. To export garments to developed country markets, firms require high-level expertise, which is nonexistent in developing countries. Thus, formation of a garment export cluster requires the acquisition from abroad of relevant knowledge and skills. Even for industrial clusters catering only to local markets, learning from abroad is important because profitability will eventually decline without sufficient upgrading of capabilities.

The cases of Bangladesh and Tanzania indicate that path dependence influences industrial development. Learning from abroad at the outset of cluster formation has long-term impacts on subsequent cluster development. The Bangladeshi garment industry presumably has enjoyed high sustained growth because it has continuously learned relevant knowledge, whether from abroad or elsewhere, to deal with ever more demanding requests from buyers. What drives continuous learning? In this chapter we have found path dependence at the firm level. That is, firms operated by top managers who received formal training long ago are more willing to adopt new business practices. Is this because formal training programs attracted diligent learners who remain eager to learn even decades later, or because these programs made learners appreciate the importance of learning new things? Does this path dependence at the firm or individual levels explain the great leaning performance of the industry as a whole? These questions are deferred to future research.

References

Akoten J, Otsuka K (2007) From tailors to mini-manufacturers: the role of traders in the performance of garment enterprises in Kenya. J Afr Econ 16(4):564–595

Easterly W (2002) The elusive quest for growth: economists' sdventures and misadventures in the tropics. The MIT Press, Cambridge, MA

Fleisher B, Hu D, McGuire W, Zhang X (2010) The evolution of an industrial cluster in China. China Econ Rev 21(3):456–469

Higuchi Y, Nam VH, Sonobe T (2015) Sustained impacts of Kaizen training. J Econ Behav Organ 120:189–206

Mlachila M, Yang Y (2004) The end of textiles quotas: a case study of the impact on Bangladesh, IMF Working Paper No. WP/04/108. International Monetary Fund, Washington, DC

Mottaleb KA, Sonobe T (2011) An inquiry into the rapid growth of the garment industry in Bangladesh. Econ Dev Cult Chang 60(1):67–89

Nam VH, Sonobe T, Otsuka K (2010) An inquiry into the development process of village industries: the case of a knitwear cluster in northern Vietnam. J Dev Stud 46(2):312–330

Rhee YW (1990) The catalyst model of development: lessons from Bangladesh's success with garment exports. World Dev 18(2):333–346

Siddiqi HGA (2005) The readymade garment industry of Bangladesh. The University Press Limited, Dhaka

Sonobe T, Otsuka K (2006) Cluster-based industrial development: an East Asian model. Palgrave Macmillan, Basingstoke

Sonobe T, Otsuka K (2011) Cluster-based industrial development: a comparative study of Asia and Africa. Palgrave Macmillan, Basingstoke

Sonobe T, Otsuka K (2014) Cluster-based industrial development: KAIZEN management for MSE growth in developing countries. Palgrave Macmillan, Basingstoke

Sonobe T, Hu D, Otsuka K (2002) Process of cluster formation in China: a case study of a garment town. J Dev Stud 39(1):118–139

Suzuki A, Nam VH, Sonobe T (2014) Willingness to pay for managerial training: a case from the knitwear industry in Northern Vietnam. J Comp Econ 42(3):693–703

Yamamura E, Sonobe T, Otsuka K (2003) Human capital, cluster formation, and international relocation: the case of the garment industry in Japan, 1968–98. J Econ Geogr 3(1):37–56

Yoshino Y (ed) (2011) Industrial clusters and micro and small enterprises in Africa: from survival to growth. World Bank, Washington DC

Part III
Central Role of Producer Cooperatives

Chapter 6
Trade Associations and Economic Regulation in the Lyons *Fabrique*: From the 1860s to the 1920s

Pierre Vernus

Abstract In the 1860s Lyons was the main European center for the production of silk fabrics and one of the major global silk trade centers. Its *fabrique* (silk industry) exhibited the characteristics of the Marshallian industrial district or those of a cluster. This chapter deals with the actions of the *chambres syndicales* (trade associations) founded by silk merchants and merchants-manufacturers in the 1860s onward. It will first map the institutional landscape that enabled the working of the *fabrique* before the end of the 1860s. Next, it will examine the emergence of formal trade associations and the challenges, arising from shortage of high-quality raw silk produced in Europe, among other things that these associations had to deal with. Lastly, it will identify the kinds of responses that they attempted to provide for maintaining credibility of the Lyons *fabrique* in specific fields such as commercial and economic information, product quality, and evolving commercial customs.

Keywords *Fabrique* (silk industry) • Lyon • Marshallian industrial district • *Chambres syndicales (trade association)* • Product quality

6.1 Introduction

Silk fabrics and garments were among the main French exports prior to the Great Depression in the 1930s. Commencing from the eigteenth century, Lyons rose to become the main European center for the production of silk fabrics and one of the major global silk trade centers. In the 1860s the Lyons silk industry, known as the *fabrique*, exhibited characteristics that matched those of the Marshallian industrial district or those of a cluster (Marshall 1932, p. 285–286; Porter 2000, p. 254–256).

P. Vernus (✉)
Rhône-Alpes Historical Research Unit (LARHRA), Lyon University, Lyon, France
e-mail: pierre.vernus@ish-lyon.cnrs.fr

T. Hashino, K. Otsuka (eds.), *Industrial Districts in History and the Developing World*, Studies in Economic History, DOI 10.1007/978-981-10-0182-6_6

The Lyons *fabrique* was an example of a *fabrique collective* (collective manufacture).[1] As noted by Cottereau (1997, p. 82), the *fabrique collective* constituted "the framework for capitalist industrialization more frequently than the allegedly 'classic' [that is to say the factory system] path of which 'universality' is purely mythical." Individual types of fabriques collectives could be distinguished from each other according to their production structures, the characteristics of the interconnecting networks or the division of labor that linked their actors, and the extent of the common sphere that was regulated. While Le Play may have favored rural *fabriques collectives*, he evoked examples of those in urban areas, above all, the one in Paris that he described as "the largest collective manufacture in the world." (Le Play 1874, p. 154)

The Lyons *fabrique* was also an example of an urban *fabrique collective*. It was centered in a large town, the second largest city in France, after Paris, in the 1860s. Lyons silk industry was a geographically located mesosystem of production based on a division of labor between small, medium, and some larger enterprises, each of which was specialized in relation to one or a small number of specific phases of the production process. Thus, the Lyons *fabrique* was an industrial mesosystem, the structure of which was based on the processing and production of silk, ranging from raw silk to a wide range of silk fabrics, and on upstream to downstream trade flows extending from suppliers to customers. It formed a coherent and dynamic network of firms, institutions, rules, practices, and customs. The individual or collective actors involved were heterogeneous in terms of their nature, activities, and status and could even participate simultaneously in several mesosystems. However, this was contingent on certain common factors such as available material, techniques, and markets, and on macroeconomic constraints relating to the regulation of the global production system in which they were embedded. From the first decades of the nineteenth century, increased production of silk fabrics was achieved as a result of weaving becoming more widespread in increasingly distant rural areas, especially in the nearby Isère *département* (for further elucidation of the concept of an industrial mesosystem, see De Bandt 1991, p. 232–238).

The Lyons *fabrique* was a well-established industrial district, as the production of silk fabrics was initiated during the first half of the sixteenth century. Silk fabric producers in Lyons became proficient in producing not only plain silk, but also patterned silk fabrics, and began to compete with the luxury-oriented Italian

[1]The name of the first merchants-manufacturers' union, created in 1868, was *Association de la fabrique lyonnaise*. Alain Cottereau, who revisited the *fabrique* at the beginning of the 1980s, noted that the concept of the *fabrique collective* was prevalent in the 18th century and was deployed as an analytical tool in the 1860s by Frederic Le Play, a French social scientist. The *fabrique collective* was one among the four categories of large industries (that is to say industries that shipped huge quantities of products to distant consumers) distinguished by Le Play. This author defined a *fabrique collective* as an ensemble of little workshops concentrated within the same area and completing domestic production. These workshops served *fabricants* (merchants-manufacturers), usually located in a town or port near this industrial area. The *fabricants* ordered products to be made by the workers, providing them with the requisite materials, and sold the outputs or exported them to distant markets (Cottereau 1986 and 1997; Le Play 1874, p. 150–158).

production from the seventeenth century onward, thanks to several innovations in reeling, throwing, weaving, and dyeing techniques. Moreover, because of its innovative technological capacity, supported by the authorities, as well as the implementation of a creative marketing strategy during the eighteenth century, Lyons surpassed all of its national and international rivals and was transformed into the leading European production center for silk fabrics (Léon 1967; Poni 1998; Ciriacono 1981). While the rise in production generated a growing demand for raw silk imported from Italy, it also favored the expansion of silk production, reeling, and throwing across a large area that encompassed sections of the Dauphiné and Forez regions and of the Rhône valley. The evolution of this industry connected these regions more closely with Lyons, so that the city's influence spread over an ever expanding area. However, the period of the French Revolution constituted a rupture in the history of the silk industry in Lyons. During this period, the city was besieged and threatened with destruction. Its prosperity was ruined, its administrative influence diminished, and major bodies within the institutional framework of the *fabrique* were dismissed. However, from the latter half of the 1790s, and especially after 1815, a new institutional framework was developed, foreign merchants returned, and silk fabric production rose once more. Consequently, during the first half of the nineteenth century, Lyons reasserted its predominance over other national or European silk fabric production centers, even though new competitors had emerged in the interim. By the time that the Second Empire (1852–1870) was established, between seven-tenths and eight-tenths of Lyons' silk fabric production was being exported and silk fabrics comprised one of the main French exports. By the end of the 1860s, the value of silk fabric production was about three times greater than that of the overall production of the other industries in Lyons. The *fabrique* constituted the pillar of Lyons' economic prosperity and dominated its economy throughout the century.

During the early stages of its development, the *fabrique* underwent the two phases identified in the Sonobe-Otsuka model: a quantity expansion phase followed by a quality improvement phase (Sonobe and Otsuka 2011; Hashino and Otsuka 2013). The latter was especially relevant as Lyons became the leading Western center for the production of silk fabrics during the eighteenth century. However, this model which focuses on the emergence and development of industrial districts does not consider the challenges faced by the Lyons *fabrique* from the middle of the nineteenth century. These entailed the adaptation of its production to meet a growing demand for less luxurious and expensive fabrics. Moreover, from the 1850s, Lyons was threatened with a shortage of raw silk because of the outbreak of silkworm disease.[2] These factors favored the use of cheaper Asian silk. In addition, the depression of the 1880s resulted in a dramatic decrease in the number of master weavers in the town, escalating the migration of weavers out of Lyons. Simultaneously, technical improvements and the growing scale of production fueled mechanization and the concentration of the silk industry within plants of varying sizes. The urban workshops and industries of the master weavers were steadily replaced by weaving mills located in the countryside or small towns around Lyons.

[2] See Chap. 2 of this volume for an extension and elaboration of the original Sonobe-Otsuka model.

Studies on localized industrial systems have emphasized the roles of different categories of institutions. For example, studies of Italian districts have contributed to the Marshallian concept of an industrial atmosphere. They have suggested that such districts share common values that are often based on the establishment of institutions aimed at increasing the economic efficiency of a district by favoring cooperation among firms in areas such as improvement of input or product quality, resource mobility, marketing, economic information, and innovation. Other institutions then work to develop the required social consensus in several districts (Becattini 1987). Studies on industrial districts have also emphasized the roles of different kinds of institutions in providing training, education, information, support, and setting quality standards (Porter 2000).

This chapter deals with the actions of a particular category of French voluntary business interest associations, namely the *chambres syndicales*. These assumed the functions of trade or employers' associations. A range of such organizations were founded in the Lyons silk industry, especially from the 1860s onward. This raises several questions. Why did these emerge at this point in time? How did they contribute, not to the genesis, development, and the consolidation of the district, but to adressing the challenges faced by the Lyons *fabrique* at that time? How did these trade associations favor agglomeration economies? More precisely, this study focuses on the trade associations founded by silk merchants and *fabricants*, because these groups were the most influential in the working of the *fabrique*, as were their associations To address these issues, this chapter will first map the institutional landscape that enabled the working of the *fabrique* before the end of the 1860s. Next, it will examine the emergence of formal trade associations and the challenges that these associations had to deal with. Lastly, it will identify the kinds of responses that they attempted to provide in specific fields such as commercial and economic information, product quality, and evolving commercial customs.

6.2 The Institutional System of the Silk Trade and Industry

In the mid-1860s, a set of institutions existed to ensure the collective management of the Lyons silk trade and industry, safeguarding of its interests, promotion of technical innovation, fraud prevention, arbitration of disputes, and the development of customs or practices. Some of these institutions were formed as a result of post-revolutionary reorganization, which in some cases recreated and adapted pre-revolutionary institutions. An example of this was the *Tribunal de commerce* (Commercial Court) that replaced the *Conservation des privilèges et des foires de Lyon* established in 1463 (Godart 1905), and the Chamber of Commerce. By 1869, of the 15 members of the Chamber of Commerce, four were silk merchants and four others were silk *fabricants*. In addition, there was one broker of silk fabrics and one silk dyer. The president and the secretary-treasurer of the Chamber were both silk merchants. Moreover, the Chamber controlled the *Condition publique des soies* (Public Silk Conditioning House), created in 1805 to check the weight and quality of bales of silk (Soria 1997; Pariset 1889; Perret 1878). Despite the fact that the silk trade and industry were of less importance and significance in the *Tribunal de commerce*, its presidents in the late 1860s belonged to these sectors.

The Lyons *Conseil des prud'hommes* (Labour Relation Board), established in 1806 for the silk industry at the behest of members of the *fabrique*, was the first of its kind in France. Its main purpose was to regulate individual labor disputes between *fabricants* and master weavers, or between the latter and their workers or apprentices (Cottereau 1997).

Some of the other institutions established during the first half of the nineteenth century were also specific to the *fabrique*. For instance, the *Caisse de prêt au chefs d'ateliers* (Fund for Loans to Masters Weavers) was established through a governmental ordinance in 1832 following an uprising of silk weavers that occurred in November 1831. It sanctioned loans to master weavers confronting difficulties resulting from a shortage of work or any other reason so that they were not compelled to sell their equipment. The repayment of debts was guaranteed by the community of *fabricants* who provided the weavers with work. This fund was aimed at preventing social unrest and the migration of skilled weavers to foreign silk fabric production centers. Some of the institutions were voluntary ones such as the *Société de lutte contre le piquage d'onces*, created by *fabricants* and authorized by the French government in 1843. This institution was established to prevent the embezzlement and traffic of silk. Initially, its purpose also included improving the industry's competitiveness by reducing overheads and re-establishing order and loyalty.[3] Occasionally, this society coordinated the activities of *fabricants* or preselected their candidates for the *Conseil de prud'hommes (L'Echo* 1844*)*.

Moreover, given the influence of silk manufacturing on the economic prosperity of Lyons, its interests were also supported by the city municipality within which silk merchants and *fabricants* were strongly represented. For instance, in 1869, a silk fabric broker headed the municipal commission. Of the 34 other members of the commission, 10 were silk manufacturers, two were silk merchants and one was a former silk broker.

Given that silk and the trade in silk fabrics required a large amount of capital, silk trading was often associated with banking, with some firms being involved in both activities. Of the eleven administrators of the local branch of the Bank of France, three were silk merchants and three were silk fabric manufacturers (Guide indicateur 1868). Moreover, to resolve new financial problems and needs resulting from the growth and escalation of business, the most dynamic silk merchants or *fabricants* took part in the establishment of new credit institutions. For instance, they participated actively in the creation of the *Crédit lyonnais* in 1863 (Bouvier 1961, pp. 108–127).

[3] Archives départementales du Rhône, 8 Mp 77.

6.3 The Emergence of the *Chambres Syndicales*

Recent studies have offered new insights on French business interest associations, particularly at the local and regional levels (Fraboulet et al. 2013; Vernus 2002). It has long been assumed that the major motivation underlying initial attempts to organize business was the defense of protectionism, with Lyons playing only a minor role in these attempts because the supply and export markets of its silk industry were foreign-oriented (Lefranc 1976). Contrary to these assumptions, it has been found that the structuration of the business community in and beyond Lyons was relatively advanced.

The formation of the *fabricants*' union, known as the *Association de la fabrique lyonnaise* (AFL), in 1867, was a turning point because it paved the way for the establishment of numerous other unions. By the middle of the 1880s, there was at least one union for each major activity representing the different stages of silk manufacturing. Following the formation of the *Cercle des teinturiers* (Dyers' Club created in the 1850s), and of the AFL, the *Union des marchands de soie* (UMS, Silk Merchants' Union) was founded in 1869. The reelers' and throwsters' unions in the Valence and Aubenas areas were created in 1874 and 1875, respectively.[4] The union of mechanical silk weaving employers, known as the *Association des patrons tisseurs de soieries*, was founded in 1884, and the following year, it was renamed the *Chambre syndicale des patrons tisseurs de soieries*.[5]

There were multiple areas of inequality between these trade associations. The nature of their membership constituted one of the key parameters. For example, some members of the AFL and of the UMS were among the richest people in the city. Some unions were only for artisans, whereas others were only for industrialists, contractors, or subcontractors. In fact, the AFL and the UMS occupied central positions in the network of unions, reflecting the prominence of silk merchants and *fabricants* within the silk industry mesosystem. Social and economic capital were concentrated within these unions, at least with respect to the most important firms that retained more economic power than their subcontractors, mainly comprising small and medium-sized firms. The leaders of these unions had strong institutional positions and power, primarily because they were often members of the Chamber of Commerce with which the UMS and AFL maintained strong links.

However, the question remains as to why these new business associations were created despite the existence of this dense network of institutions in the 1860s, and the strong influence of representatives of the silk trade and industry in the municipal and credit institutions. The first parameter that needs to be considered is the evolution of the legal framework. The Le Chapelier Law of March 1791, banning groups attempting to defend their interests, the law of April 10, 1834, and several articles of the French *Code pénal* had constrained the creation of associations, including those related to trade. However, from the 1860s, the government adopted a more liberal

[4] Both of these unions were local chapters of a common organization.

[5] AM Lyon, 1101 WP 100, Folder Syndicat du tissage mécanique des soieries (1884–1913).

stance. The Second Empire recognized the freedom of coalition in 1864, and the Third Republic established a legal status for unions, in 1884. These decisions were directed at workers' associations, but they also applied to trade associations. However, these latter associations were already accepted in practice by the authorities. Thus, even if their legal situation became less uncertain, it remains to be explained why the new legal opportunities were availed of by businessmen.

In reality, the new trade associations had to face problems that were either not dealt with, or were poorly handled by existing institutions.

Changes in the trade networks for the supply of silk and the marketing of silk garments seem to have provided a major impetus for the genesis of some of the *chambres syndicales*. First, pebrine and other diseases that devastated the silkworm populations in the Mediterranean basin, especially from the 1850s onward, reduced the predictability of outputs and prices. They led to deterioration as well as greater heterogeneity relating to the quality of silk. The expansion of Chinese or Japanese silk imports resulted in increased dependence of the silk trade and prices on Asian outputs and modified the trade networks (Federico 1994, p. 58–67; Klein 2002, 2013; Hamaide 1999). Moreover, the reorganization of trade networks and practices relating to silk fabrics heightened market uncertainty for *fabricants*. From the beginning of the nineteenth century, sales to Great Britain and the US had grown steadily, whereas the share of the European continental markets had receded. During the first stage of this evolution, specialization of economic agents was encouraged. Merchants and brokers from Lyons made business deals in foreign countries, whereas *fabricants* concentrated on production. This trade relied on a credit system based on interpersonal trust. Up to the end of the 1860s, the merchants and commissioners of Lyons retained numerous sales outlets worldwide. However, improvements in transport and communication encouraged buyers from foreign countries, especially those from Great Britain and the US, to deal directly in France with the *fabricants*, without the mediation of commission merchants (Cayez 1980 and 1993). Whereas commission merchants and their networks of correspondents provided a safeguard against unethical trade behaviors, this was evidently not always sufficient when dealing with new and unknown buyers. Consequently, the degree of uncertainty and associated transaction costs increased for *fabricants*. Thus, the AFL was founded after wrongdoings of a representative of a foreign firm had seriously damaged local companies (Syndicat des fabricants de soieries de Lyon 1927). In addition, the expanding scale of trade relationships gave rise to new commercial practices and, at the same time, disrupted old personal trade networks, or made their rebuilding necessary. This resulted in the need to adjust trade customs to adapt them to the new conditions.

Moreover, these transformations and the onset of the depression of the 1880s altered the balance between the main actors in the silk market. By extensively modifying the positions of reelers and throwsters, the pebrine outbreak and the geographical mutations of silk imports also provided the impetus for collective action. First, the collapse of French silkworm breeding weakened the foundation of French reeling, because imported silk were reeled, especially after reeling factories were established in China and Japan from the 1870s, based on the application of European methods. Second, most of the reelers and throwsters became increasingly dependent, economically, on Lyons silk merchants or *fabricants* who imported silk, consequently becoming subcontractors for them (Cayez 1993). From the mid-1870s, they began to request protection against the importation of silk. Subsequently, with the manifestation of the effects of the depression in the 1880s, protectionist ideas progressed and inspired the creation of unions such as the *Syndicat général du moulinage français* (General Union of French Throwing) in 1890[6] and the *Association de la soierie lyonnaise* (Lyons Silk Industry Association, ASL), which was formed as a result of secession from the AFL at the end of 1892.

While identification of challenges is one aspect to be considered, the passage to collective action within an organization is another matter. The spatial concentration of silk merchants and *fabricants* facilitated their collective mobilization. Indeed, most of the firms were located in a downtown quadrilateral of about 25 ha in area, and in some cases, three or four of these firms were located in the same building. Proximity facilitated daily contact and information exchange. It is not coincidental that the UMS and the AFL established their offices in this area.

Moreover, some individuals acted as catalysts, facilitating informal mobilization to establish a formal organization. For instance, Claude-Philippe Testenoire (1815–1878) appears to have played such a role.[7] As the son of a merchant in Saint-Etienne, he associated with a ribbon manufacturer before becoming the director of the branch in Lyons, assuming charge of marketing functions in 1867. Under Testenoire's leadership, the firm became one of the most important actors in the Lyons silk trade. As a member of the Chamber of Commerce, the administrator of the local branch of the Bank of France, one of the founders of the *Crédit Lyonnais*, and a member of the Lyons municipality, he belonged to the commercial elite of the city at the conclusion of the Second Empire. Ultimately, he was elected as the first president of the UMS.

6.4 The Activities of the *Chambres Syndicales*

How then did the new organizations respond to the challenges that confronted them? We will focus on three issues: economic information, production quality, and trade customs.

[6]This union was created to obtain a 3 francs tax on imported thrown silk, especially Italian ones. Its statutes disallowed silk merchants and *fabricants* from becoming members, because they would subsequently defend free admission of foreign silk into France.

[7]Archives of the UMS, AG, January 14, 1879.

6.4.1 Commercial Intelligence and Statistics

Two aims were prioritized and their achievement featured among the first accomplishments of the associations. These were: gathering information about the creditworthiness of trading partners and compiling and publishing data about silk production.

Both the AFL and the UMS developed commercial intelligence. They did not innovate, because in the aftermath of the credit crisis of 1848, the *Chambre syndicale des tissus de Paris* (Paris Fabrics Merchants' Association) had the same purpose (Lincoln 1981). The centralization of commercial information that was useful for the *fabrique* was one of the major aims of the AFL (Association de la fabrique lyonnaise 1869). Such a function took the form of a card filing system, synthesizing data on the main buyers in Lyons compiled from different sources. Members were asked to contribute their own data about their buyers, but the AFL set up its own network of information providers. Procuring access to this file seems to have been a strong incentive for acquiring membership of the AFL, because the *Association de la soierie lyonnaise* (ASL), which was created as a result of a scission of the AFL in 1892, declared commercial intelligence gathering to be one of its purposes and quickly implemented such a file system.[8] By 1900, it maintained 3436 cards (Association de la soierie lyonnaise 1901), while the AFL file comprised 57,600 cards. The growing number of cards reflected the increasing prevalence of direct trade relations between the *fabricants* and their foreign buyers. The compiled information contributed to the reduction of uncertainty regarding the trustworthiness of purchasers and, consequently, to a reduction in transaction costs. Establishing such a file system was also one of the top priorities of the UMS.

With the increasing volatility of silk production in the Mediterranean basin because of silkworm diseases, information about the quantity of cocoons, and the availability of reeled or thrown silk assumed vital importance. Indeed, in 1870, Testenoire acknowledged that none of the members of the UMS knew what the annual production of cocoons in France was. Furthermore, the official statistics were of poor quality. Consequently, predicting the trajectory of silk supplies and, thereby, of prices, had become very difficult.[9]

The limited resources of the UMS restricted its capacity to collect data. Consequently, the association began to set up a network of data providers; a task of long duration based on its members' connections. The inception period was difficult. Initially, letters were sent to a selected number of persons to ascertain the quantity of cocoons bought by the reelers in these individuals' localities, quantities reeled by the cocoons producers themselves, and quantities purchased by speculators. However, these only elicited a limited number of responses, resulting in doubts that the project would actually be realized. Notwithstanding this situation, new

[8] Archives départementale du Rhône (ADR), 10 Mp F 71, ASL file, Statutes adopted on December 29, 1892.

[9] UMS Archives, General Assembly, July 27, 1870.

attempts resulted in the expansion of the network of data providers. Thus, as early as 1872, a report on French silk production in 1871 was published with financial support provided by the Lyons Chamber of Commerce (Syndicat de l'union des marchands de soie de Lyon 1872). This effort was prolonged and intensified over the following years. However, data synthesis continued to be partially dependent on official statistics. In 1874, the annual report of the UMS criticized the apathy of French officials in relation to data collection on silk production despite ministerial instructions. This was contrasted with the "clever measures" taken by the Italian Chambers of Commerce regarding the collection of data on the quantity, quality, and prices of the cocoons sold in each market and the publication of the detailed results of their investigations. Data pertaining to the other silk producers were communicated by UMS members who had connections or owned plants in these countries. Initially the data collected on production capacities was very sketchy. However, this effort was extended and resulted in regular publications.

6.4.2 Defining and Controlling the Quality of Silk

If one considers quality not as an absolute standard but rather as a contingent notion, that is, as a social construction, the following question arises: How is a buyer able to judge whether a product corresponds to the expected quality? In other words, what is the common benchmark for evaluating whether an item is consistent with what was expected of it, and how is this benchmark determined (for an elaboration of this argument see Gomez (1994) especially part 3)?

Trade unions played a great part in establishing methods for checking the quality and weight of the silk sold in Lyons. This process entailed three parts: checking the quantity of water absorbed by the silk (*conditionnement*), checking the number of threads or yarns (*titrage* or sizing), and checking the proportion of gum or other substance (degumming or scouring) included in the silk (Perret 1878; Vignon and Isidore 1914). From 1805, the *Condition des soies* had acquired a monopoly over the *conditionnement* process. Moreover, the methods of measuring the degree of moisture of the silk had improved and stabilized, so that a "normal" level of moisture (10 % of the absolute weight determined by the *Condition*) had been defined, with the excess amount being removed for the benefit of the buyer, and a lack being adjusted to benefit of the seller.

The *titrage* and the degumming processes were more challenging. While improvements in the techniques and methods of reeling and throwing mills in Europe may have enabled greater consistency of European threads and yarns for the *titrage* process, this was not the case for Asian silk, which was imported in increasing quantities. Prior to 1858, when a public board controlled by the *Condition* was created for conducting tests, there was no standard. Only private testers existed. This issue generated keen debates between the UMS and the AFL and the throwsters' unions. Immediately upon being formed, the silk merchants' union denounced some of the prevailing practices as being dysfunctional for the following reasons.

First, the tradition of payments in kind made to private testers, who retained the silk sample used for testing, was said to favor embezzlement of silk. Second, they complained of the excessive number of tests required by buyers (above all, the *fabricants*), whereas the sellers had to pay for these. Silk merchants and *fabricants* agreed rather easily to favor monetary payments that had already been implemented by the public testing board. The instituting of a monopoly in favor of this public board had eventually been abandoned because it did not seem to fit with the ideological context of the time wherein liberty and free competition were considered laudable.[10] Moreover, the public testing board was criticized for the slowness of its operations and for its lack of organization. An exemplary testing board initiated by silk merchants and *fabricants* was launched in the middle of 1885 and was functional up to the post-First World War period. However, in practice, the tests conducted by the public board, whose equipment had been improved, became the *de facto* reference, essentially because their results were judged to be the most reliable (Union des marchands de soie de Lyon 1913). Moreover, negotiations between the UMS and the AFL led to an agreement regarding the number of tests that could be performed and their prices (Association de la Fabrique lyonnaise 1874).

Degumming is done to determine the proportion of gum in the silk, enabling the reduction in the weight of the silk after dyeing to be predicted. It also enables the elimination of extraneous substances. From 1856, the degumming process was systematized by the *Condition publique* for silk submitted to conditioning based on the procedures defined in 1855. In 1882, the UMS and the AFL reached an agreement regarding a list based on the results published by the *Condition* during previous years that indicated weight losses for each kind of thrown silk after undergoing degumming, according to its geographical provenance. This was established as a reference for transactions entailing an absence of particular specifications. However, as early as 1886, the UMS declared that it wanted to renounce this list. Its members complained that the increasing diversity of silkworm species that were the outcome of crossbreeding and the modification of reeling methods, had made the list unreliable. After several years of discussions and negotiations, UMS, the AFL, the ASL, and the reelers' and throwsters' unions were unable to reach a general agreement (Association de la fabrique lyonnaise 1888; 1892; 1893; 1894; *Bulletin des soies et soieries* 1893a, b, c, d, e).

6.4.3 Adjusting Trade and Industrial Usages

The *Usages des prud'hommes* (a code of customary practices established by the conseil des prud'hommes) essentially dealt with relations between *fabricants* and masters weavers. As previously noted, following the depression of the 1880s, the number of urban weavers receded dramatically, with weaving being relocated out of Lyons and becoming more mechanized and industrialized. Further, numerous

[10] Record of the minutes of the meetings of the *chambre syndicale* of the UMS, May 24, 1870.

reelers and throwsters lost their autonomy and increasingly shifted to being subcontractors for silk merchants or fabricants. Consequently, monitoring the quantity of silk, before and after reeling, throwing or weaving, became a major issue both for contractors and subcontractors.

The process of manufacturing crepe fabrics that were in high demand required a high degree of twisting and moistening with water or other substances, with respect to throwing. Thus, the question of tolerance for this moistening process arose. Usually, a tolerance of 0.5 % or 1 % between the degumming of the raw silk and that of the yarn was considered accepted. In 1892, the throwsters wanted this to be raised to 2 %. However, their demand did not receive a positive answer from the *fabricants*' unions.

Changes in the materials used during the manufacturing process constituted another area in which customary practices were questioned. In 1886, the lower quality of silk that was largely attributed to the increased use of Asian silk, the quality and consistency of which remained lower than those of European silk, prompted the union of subcontracted weavers to demand an alteration of the percentage of silk wastes traditionally admitted during the weaving process. Despite several meetings being held on this subject, no agreement was reached with the AFL, with the *fabricants* arguing that the qualities of silk were so diverse that no unique rate could be established.

Thus, in the 1880s and 1890s, a series of transformations relating to the geography of silk imports, the fabrics produced, technical improvements, and shifts in the relationships between the agents disrupted some of the old usages and generated a need for new rules. However, the time for stabilization had not yet arrived. This occurred during the 1900s when efforts to codify customs were apparent in different places. In 1908, within the AFL, a group of manufacturers of piece-dye fabrics was created to negotiate customs with subcontractors and clients. In 1909, the *Chambre syndicale des importeurs de tissus asiatiques* (Union of the Importers of Fabrics from Asia)[11] had codified its own customs (Chambre syndicale des importateurs de tissus asiatiques 1909).

For its part, the UMS codified silk trade usages in Lyons based on key decisions taken by its board when arbitrating disputes (Union des marchands de soie 1895; 1901 and 1904). Consequently, in accordance with French jurisprudence, it was for the party to prove the existence of trade customs to the judge. When asking a trade association to confirm the existence of particular usages, the judge was very often confronted with conflicting opinions. Thus, the codification set up by the UMS could be used as evidence in a trial (Stanziani 2012). Freedom of contract still remained and the associated usages were applied unless otherwise indicated. While the leaders of the UMS emphasized that imprecisely drafted special conventions were dangerous, the UMS did not elaborate a standard contract like the one developed by the Silk Association of America (Ishizaki 1928). Silk merchants individually produced their own printed forms. Some companies printed these forms or wrote the following text on them: "In case of dispute, the parties undertake to carry

[11] This union was founded in Lyon in June 1907.

their dispute to the arbitration of the board of the UMS." It is important to understand that this codification did not freeze older practices, because while the contractual framework was stabilized, it could also be modified, as illustrated in successive editions of the Code from 1895 onward. The codification was amended when new sources of dispute emerged, or when trade conditions required a change in usages.

After World War I, the silk trade and industry associations continued to monitor their customs. If these could be modified with the consent of all the interested parties, one of these parties could also try to steer the development of the customs in a direction that was more favorable to its own interests by demonstrating that the practices it wanted to enforce were standard. In others words, the objective was to create a precedent. Consequently, it was very important for the unions to quickly curb the practices of their members that contradicted the customs. For instance, in 1926, a *fabricant* wanted to dictate conditions of silk checking that were contrary to the usages to his suppliers. Immediately, the UMS committee warned members of the union. This problem was crucial during the post-war years when economics disturbances prompted some economic actors not to follow the customs. Genuine collaboration between unions was particularly useful for putting an end to bad practices. Thus, in 1929, when the UMS pointed out a departure from customs regarding payment for silk testing, it got the *Syndicat des fabricants de soieries* (Silk Fabrics Manufacturers' Union, henceforth SFS) to send out a circular reminding the *fabricants* that both of the unions wanted the customs to be respected. This was crucial for the UMS, because the credibility of the Lyons silk market was at stake. As it wrote to its members: "*In business as in games, competition must work sheltered by a common rule: it might have neither business nor games if the transgression of this rule was permitted.*"[12]

At the same time, endeavors to codify local customs were underway. Those that applied to throwing finally succeeded after several years. This was important because during the 1920s, crepes were in vogue and several conflicts occurred between throwsters and their principals. In 1921, a special committee proposed a draft codification of the customs in throwing that was rejected, because the different interested parties did not succeed in reaching a consensus. Negotiations resumed in 1923 and concluded with an agreement being reached between the UMS and the *Syndicat général du moulinage français* (Union des marchands de soie 1924, p. 38–40).

[12]"Dans les affaires comme dans les jeux, c'est à l'abri d'une règle commune que doit s'exercer la compétition; il n'y aurait plus d'affaires ni de jeux s'il était permis de la transgresser." (Union des marchands de soie 1927, p. 23–24).

6.4.4 Towards an International Codification

During the 1920s, the codification of silk trade usages extended to the international level. International meetings aiming at harmonizing norms in the textile industry had already taken place before the First World War. For instance, in 1874, a congress was held in Brussels to develop a common standard for the number of textiles threads and yarns. Another congress on the silk weight issue was held in Turin in 1905.

After the Congress of Milan that established the statutes of the International Silk Federation (ISF) in June 1927, a project of a code of the usages for the trade of crepes and highly twisted yarns was examined by the unions that dealt with silk, silk fabrics, and twisting. In December, a code formulated for the customs associated with twisted silk trade was adopted. This was essentially based on the proposals of the UMS. The unions were responsible for its enforcement, commencing from 1928 (Union des marchands de soie 1928, p. 23–24 and 1929, p. 31–32).

Shortly thereafter, the UMS elaborated a preliminary plan for codifying customs relating to raw and thrown silk in the yarns. This was examined by a special committee of the ISF and, subsequently, by a second-level committee gathering of French, German, Swiss, Italian, and Spanish silk merchants or *fabricants*. At the last step in this process, it was ratified by a congress held in Zurich in September 1929 and enforced in 1930 (Union des marchands de soie 1930, p. 25–28). A monitoring committee was established to follow the process of the enforcement of the codification and to study scientific methods that could improve the inspection of silk.

In 1929, in collaboration with the International Chamber of Commerce, the UMS studied another plan on international arbitration and it was examined to encourage the relevant parties to insert a special clause on this issue in their contracts. It must be emphasized that the codifications adopted in 1927 and 1929 anticipated this by encouraging recourse to this type of arbitration.

Commencing from 1930, the silk fabric trade also engaged with the process of codification. Harmonization was not limited to Europe; rather, it was expanded by relationships between European organizations and associations in Asia. For example, in 1932, the Silk Association of Shanghai sent the UMS its code relating to customs in Shanghai, requesting comments (Union des marchands de soie 1933, p. 35). However, the collapse of the silk and silk fabrics trade put an end to these endeavors.

6.5 Conclusion

Between the state and firms, there exists a whole range of mesolevel institutions. Some studies have underscored how important these institutions were in France during the first half of the nineteenth century (Hirsch 1991; Hirsch and Minard 1998; Lemercier 2003). However, their role during more recent periods must not be neglected.

In silk-related industries, trade associations, at least the more important and more lasting among these, have shaped a network of organizations. From their relations has emerged a whole gamut of rules that have played a considerable part in the regulating of this economic subsystem. Trade usages cover numerous fields such as quality standards; classification; production of goods; trade of raw materials, and finished goods; and industrial relations. This kind of autonomous regulation was not limited to local industries and trade. Thanks to the connections forged between organizations, it could extend beyond national borders and contribute to the standardizing of international trade practices.

This kind of regulation complemented State legislation and free contracting. In practice, these customs applied when no special clauses were specified in contracts between economic actors. They could be used by law courts as a basis for jurisprudence. Trade associations demanded State legislation as an ultimate solution when there was no agreement between them, or when an agreement had ceased to exist. However, additional research is required to assess how closely connected these three kinds of regulations were, and how their relationships evolved.

References

Association de la fabrique lyonnaise (1869) Rapport présenté à l'assemblée générale du 17 décembre 1868 (Report to the general assembly of December 17, 1868), Lyon

Association de la fabrique lyonnaise (1874) Rapport présenté à l'assemblée générale du 17 décembre 1873 (Report to the general assembly of December 30, 1873), Lyon

Association de la fabrique lyonnaise (1888) Rapport présenté à l'assemblée générale du 8 février 1887. Exercice 1886 (Report to the general assembly of February 8, 1887. Year 1886), Lyon

Association de la fabrique lyonnaise (1892) Rapport présenté à l'assemblée générale du 8 février 1892, Exercice 1891 (Report to the general assembly of February 8, 1892. Year 1891), Lyon

Association de la Fabrique lyonnaise (1893) Rapport présenté à l'assemblée générale du 1 février 1893, Exercice 1892 (Report to the general assembly of February 1, 1893. Year 1892), Lyon

Association de la Fabrique lyonnaise (1894) Rapport présenté à l'assemblée générale du 27 février 1894, Exercice 1893 (Report to the general assembly of February 27, 1894. Year 1893). A. Rey, Lyon

Becattini G (1987) Introduzione: il distretto industriale marshalliano: cronaca di un ritrovamento (Introduction: the marshallian industrial district, chronicle of a rediscovery). In: Becattini G (ed) Mercato e forze locali: il distretto industrial. Il Mulino, Bologna

Bouvier J (1961) Le crédit lyonnais de 1863 à 1882. Les années de formation d'une banque de dépôts (The *Crédit Lyonnais* from 1863 to 1882. The formatives years of a deposit bank), vol 1. SEVPEN, Paris

Bulletin des soies et soieries (Silk and Silk fabrics Bulletin) (1893a), June 24: 3–4

Bulletin des soies et soieries (Silk and Silk fabrics Bulletin) (1893b), July 1: 3–4

Bulletin des soies et soieries (Silk and Silk fabrics Bulletin) (1893c), July 8: 3–4

Bulletin des soies et soieries (Silk and Silk fabrics Bulletin) (1893d), July 22: 3–4

Bulletin des soies et soieries (Silk and Silk fabrics Bulletin) (1893e), June 29: 2–3

Cayez P (1980) Crises et croissance de l'industrie lyonnaise, 1850–1900 (Industrial crisis and growth in Lyon, 1850–1900). Éditions du CNRS, Paris

Cayez P (1993) Le commerce Français des soies et soieries (XVIIIe – XXe siècles) (The French Silk and Silk Fabrics Trade, 18th – 20th centuries). In: La seta in Europa secc. XIII-XX (Silk in Europe 13th – 20th centuries. Serie II – Atti delle « Settimani di Studi » e altri Convegni 24. Le Monnier, Prato

Chambre syndicale des importateurs de tissus asiatiques (1909) Codification des usages de la place de Lyon pour la vente des tissus asiatiques en vigueur au 1er janvier 1910 (Union of the importers of fabrics from Asia. Code of the common practices for the sales of fabrics from Asia in Lyon, in force since January 1, 1910), Lyon

Ciriacono S (1981) Silk manufacture in France and Italy in the XVIIth century: two models compared. J Eur Econ His 10(1):167–199

Cottereau A (1986) The distinctiveness of working-class cultures in France. In: Katznelson I, Zolberg AR (eds) Working-class formation: nineteenth-century patterns in Western Europe and the United States. Princeton University Press, Princeton, pp. 1848–1900

Cottereau A (1997) The fate of collective manufactures in the industrial world: the silk industry of Lyons and London. In: Sabel CF, Zeitlin J (eds) World of possibilities: flexibility and mass production in Western industrialization. Cambridge University Press, Cambridge, pp. 1800–1850

De Bandt J (1991) La filière comme méso-système (Industrial sector as a meso-system). In: Arena R., Benzoni L., De Bandt J., Romani P.-M. (eds) Traité d'économie industrielle. 2nd edn, Economica, Paris, pp. 232–238

Federico G (1994) Il filo d'oro: l'industria della seta dalla restaurazione alla grande crisi (The golden Thread: the World Silk Industry from the Restoration to the Great Depression), 1st edn, Storia e scienze sociali. Marsilio, Venezia

Fraboulet D, Locatelli AM, Tedeschi P (eds) (2013) Historical and international comparison of business interest associations: 19th–20th centuries. P.I.E. Peter Lang, Brussels

Godart J (1905) La Juridiction consulaire à Lyon: la conservation des privilèges royaux des foires, 1436–1791, le tribunal de commerce, 1791–1905 (The Commercial Court in Lyon). A. Rey, Lyon

Gomez P-Y (1994) Qualité et théorie des conventions (Quality and convention theory). Economica, Paris

Guide indicateur de la Ville de Lyon et du département du Rhône (1868). Année 1868 (Guide-directory to the city of Lyon and the Rhône département. Year 1868), E.-B. Labaume, Lyon

Hamaide E (1999) Les relations entre Lyon et la Chine au XIXe sièce: essai d'histoire commerciale (The relationship between Lyon and China during the 19th cenury). PhD thesis, University Lumière Lyon 2, Lyon

Hashino T, Otsuka K (2013) Cluster-based industrial development in contemporary developing countries and modern Japanese economic history. Journal of the Japanese and International Economies 30:19–32

Hirsch J-P (1991) Les deux rêves du commerce : entreprise et institution dans la région lilloise (1780–1860) (The two dreams of trade: entreprise and institutions in the Lille region (1780-1860)), Editions de l'EHESS, Paris

Hirsch J-P, Minard P (1998) "'Laissez-nous faire et protégez-nous beaucoup': pour une histoire des pratiques institutionnelles dans l'industrie française (XVIIIe-XIXe siècle)," in *La France n'est-elle pas douée pour l'industrie?*, ed. Louis Bergeron and Patrice Bourdelais, Belin, Paris, 1998 ("Let us do and protect us a lot": a history of institutional practices in French industry, 18th–19th centuries)

Ishizaki M (1928) Le droit corporatif international de la vente des soies. Les contrats-types américains et la codification lyonnaise dans leurs rapports avec les usages des autres places (International corporate law for the sales of silk. II The interacting of US standard contracts and the Lyon codification with the common practices in the other markets). M. Giard, Paris

Klein J-F (2002) Soyeux en mer de Chine: stratégies des réseaux lyonnais en Extrême-Orient (1843–1906) (Silk merchants in the China Sea: strategie of the Lyons networks in the Far-East (1843–1906)). PhD thesis, University Lumière Lyon 2, Lyon

Klein J-F (2013) Les maîtres du comptoir: Desgrand père et fils: réseaux du négoce et révolutions commerciales (1720–1878) (The masters of the sales counter, Desgrands father and son: trade networks and trade revolutions 1720–1878). PUPS, Paris

L'Echo de la Fabrique de 1841 (1844) December Issue, Lyon
Lefranc G (1976) Les organisations patronales en France du passé au présent (Business interests organizations in France from past to present). Payot, Paris
Lemercier C (2003), Un si discret pouvoir: Aux origines de la Chambre de commerce de Paris, 1803–1853 (The origin of the Paris Chamber of Commerce), La Découverte, Paris
Léon P (1967) La région lyonnaise dans l'histoire économique et sociale de la France. Une esquisse (XVIe-XXe siècle) (The Lyons region in the economic and social history of France, 16th–20th century). Revue historique 237(481):31–62
Le Play F (1874) La réforme sociale en Frane: déduite de l'observation comparée des peuples européens (Social reform in France infered from the comparative study of the peoples of Europe), vol 2, 5th edn. Mame fils, Tours
Lincoln A (1981) Le syndicalisme patronal à Paris de 1815 à 1848: une étape dans la formation de la classe patronale (Employers' and Trade union in Paris from 1815 to 1848: a stage of the making of the employers' class). Le Mouvement social 114:11–34
Marshall A (1932) Industry and trade: a study of industrial technique and business organization; and of their influences on the conditions of various classes and nations, 3rd edn. Macmillan and Co Limited, London
Pariset E (1889) La chambre de commerce de Lyon: étude faite sur les registres de ses délibérations: Vol. 2e partie, dix-neuvième siècle (The Lyons Chamber of Commerce: studies from its deliberation records). Association typographique, Lyon
Perret A (1878) Monographie de la condition des soies de Lyon (Monograph on the *Condition des soies* in Lyons). Imprimerie Pitrat aîné, Lyon
Poni C (1998) Mode et innovation: les stratégies des marchands en soie de Lyon au XVIIIe siècle (Mode and innovation: Lyons silk merchants' strategies in the 18th century). Revue d'histoire moderne et contemporaine 45(3):589–625
Porter M (2000) Locations, clusters, and company strategy. In: Clark GL, Feldman MP, Gertler MS (eds) Oxford handbook of economic geography. Oxford University Press, Oxford
Sonobe T, Otsuka K (2011) Cluster-based industrial development: a comparative study of Asia and Africa. Palgrave MacMillan, Hampshire
Soria A (1997) La chambre de commerce de Lyon au XIXe siècle: 1832–1908 (The Lyons Chamber of Commerce in the 19th century. 1832–1908). PhD thesis, Université Lumière Lyon 2, Lyon
Stanziani A (2012) Rules of exchange: French capitalism in comparative perspective, eighteenth to the early twentieth centuries. Cambridge University Press, Cambridge
Syndicat de l'Union des marchands de soie de Lyon Union des marchands de soie de Lyon (1872) Statistique de la production de la soie en France. Récolte de 1871 (Statistics for Production in France. Harvest in 1871). Imprimerie du Salut public, Lyon
Syndicat des fabricants de soieries de Lyon (1927) Le syndicat des fabricants de soieries de Lyon. La Soierie de Lyon 1:306–323
Union des marchands de soie de Lyon (1895) Codification des usages de la place de Lyon pour la vente des soies asiatiques (Code of the common practices in Lyon for the sales of silk from Asia). Imprimerie Alexandre Rey, Lyon
Union des marchands de soie de Lyon (1901) Codification des usages de la place de Lyon pour la vente des soies asiatiques en mer et sur les marchés d'origine (Code of the common practices in Lyon for the sales of silk from Asia at sea and on the home markets). Imprimerie Alexandre Rey, Lyon
Union des marchands de soie de Lyon (1904) Codification des usages de la place de Lyon pour la vente des soies asiatiques en mer et sur les marchés d'origine, approuvée par l'assemblée générale du 29 janvier 1895, modifiée et complétée par les assemblées générales du 28 janvier 1896 (art. VII) et du 12 avril 1904 (art. I) (Code of the common practices in Lyon for the sales of silk from Asia at sea and on the home markets, approved by the general assembly on January 29, 1895, amended and supplemented by the general assemblies on January 28, 1896 and April 12, 1904). impr. de A. Rey, Lyon

Union des marchands de soie de Lyon (1913) Codification des usages de la place de Lyon (Code of the common practices in the Lyon market). imp. de A. Rey, Lyon

Union des marchands de soie de Lyon (1924) Rapport sur les travaux du syndicat pendant l'année 1923 (Report on the work carried out during the 1923), Lyon

Union des marchands de soie de Lyon (1927) Rapport sur les travaux du syndicat pendant l'année 1926 (Report on the work carried out during the 1926), Lyon

Union des marchands de soie de Lyon (1928) Rapport sur les travaux du syndicat pendant l'année 1927 (Report on the work carried out during the 1927), Lyon

Union des marchands de soie de Lyon (1929) Rapport sur les travaux du syndicat pendant l'année 1928 (Report on the work carried out during the 1928), Lyon

Union des marchands de soie de Lyon (1930) Rapport sur les travaux du syndicat pendant l'année 1929 (Report on the work carried out during the 1929), Lyon

Union des marchands de soie de Lyon (1933) Rapport sur les travaux du syndicat pendant l'année 1932 (Report on the work carried out during the 1932), Lyon

Vernus P (ed) (2002) Les organisations patronales: une approche locale (XIXe–XXe siècles) (Trade and employers' organisations. A local approach 19th – 20th centuries). Cahiers du Centre Pierre Léon d'histoire économique 1, Centre Pierre Léon d'histoire économique et sociale, Lyon

Vignon L, Isidore B (1914) La soie au point de vue scientifique et industriel (Silk from a scientific and industrial perspective), Paris

Chapter 7
Development of High-Value Agricultural Districts: The Role of Producer Cooperatives in Japan and Developing Countries

Keijiro Otsuka

Abstract Like manufactured products, quality variations are large in high-value agricultural products (HVPs) such as vegetables, fruits, and livestock products. Yet, it is difficult for retailers and consumers to identify immediately the quality as well as safety of HVPs. Like manufacturing industrial districts, innovation holds the key to the development of agricultural districts. Thus, producer cooperatives ought to play a key role in introducing new technologies, obtaining marketing information, and ensuring the quality of HVPs. This chapter attempts to demonstrate not only similarities in development patterns between industrial and agricultural districts but also in the role played by producer cooperatives. With a view to drawing lessons from historical experience for the development of agricultural districts in developing countries, this chapter reviews the development experience of apple-producing district in prewar Japan and compares it with the contemporary development of a large number of agricultural districts in Asia and sub-Saharan Africa.

Keywords High-value agricultural products • Agricultural districts • Quality and safety • Innovations • Producer cooperatives • Contract farming

7.1 Introduction

Broadly speaking, agriculture consists of staple crop sectors and high-value product (HVP) sectors.[1] The former produce rice, wheat, maize and other grains, whereas the latter produce fresh fruits, vegetables, and livestock products such as milk, pork, and poultry. While grains are generally characterized by small variations in quality,

[1] Omitted from this categorization is the sector that traditionally produces such commercial products as coffee, cocoa, rubber, and sugarcane. Analytically this sector is not too different from the crop sector if producers are smallholders. If production is by plantations, we argue that it should be replaced by contract farming.

K. Otsuka (✉)
Graduate School of Economics, Kobe University, Kobe, Japan
e-mail: otsuka@econ.kobe-u.ac.jp

T. Hashino, K. Otsuka (eds.), *Industrial Districts in History and the Developing World*, Studies in Economic History, DOI 10.1007/978-981-10-0182-6_7

with rice being one major exception,[2] HVPs are characterized by high variations in quality and safety. Since wholesalers, retailers, and consumers cannot immediately identify the quality and safety of HVPs, spot markets seldom function as described by Akerlof (1970). Moreover, since many HPVs are newly introduced in developing countries, farmers may not know how to grow them, and also lack access to new improved seeds, appropriate inorganic fertilizer, safe pesticides, and credit. Therefore, the development of HVP sectors is likely to be constrained by imperfect or absent markets.

Unlike for grains, income elasticity for demand for HVPs is high, meaning that HVP sectors are potentially growing sectors. Furthermore, HVPs can be exported from developing countries to supermarkets in high-income countries (Reardon and Berdegué 2002; Reardon and Timmer 2012). Therefore, HPV sectors are potentially profitable and their development can contribute to poverty reduction (World Bank 2007). The critical question is how HVP sectors have developed in high-income countries, such as Japan, and how they can be developed in low-income economies in Asia and Africa.

One solution is contract farming,[3] in which the contractor is often an agent of supermarkets, whether in developed countries or domestically, and provides improved seeds and appropriate chemical inputs on credit to farmers, together with technical services. In return, farmers deliver the contractor a specified quantity and quality of product at a scheduled time. The contractor offers either a fixed price in advance or a pricing formula that depends partly on market prices, and engages in marketing of HVPs. This pricing system reduces price risk for farmers. To assure the quality and safety of HVPs, the contractor exerts considerable effort on the supervision of production processes and the use of inputs. In this way, contract farming mitigates or overcomes the problems of imperfect or absent markets. Interestingly, contract farming resembles putting-out contracts in manufacturing. As in the case of putting-out contracts, the transaction costs of contract farming are substantial, because the contractor must prevent the diversion of provided inputs for other purposes and side-selling of products to other buyers and agents, in addition to supervising production activities. To reduce transaction costs, the contractor may prefer to make a small number of contracts with large farmers, rather than a large number of contracts with small farmers. It is therefore argued that although contract farming is conducive to modernization and efficiency improvement of agriculture as it introduces new improved farming systems, it may be detrimental to equity as it tends to favor large-scale farmers.

To reduce the transaction costs borne by contractors in securing HVPs from small farmers, the formation of agricultural districts and the establishment of producer cooperatives play key roles. Transaction costs can be reduced if agricultural producers are clustered, as in the case of manufacturing entrepreneurs in industrial

---

[2] The quality of grain seeds also varies considerably, and consequently contract farming is often applied to seed production as well as HVPs.

[3] See Otsuka et al. (2016) for the latest review of the literature on contract farming.

districts.[4] Producer cooperatives can reduce transaction costs for contractors, as it may be possible to effectively monitor member production based on social capital, and to directly make contracts with the contractor. Alternatively the cooperative can guarantee the quality and safety of HVPs to the contractor, where each small farmer is engaged in contract farming. Even in the absence of contract farming, producer cooperatives can play a critical role by introducing new products and production methods, providing credit, guaranteeing product quality and safety, and undertaking product marketing. Such activities generate positive externalities and collective actions thus are indispensable for the development of high-value agricultural districts.

This chapter explores the role of producer cooperatives in the development of HVP sectors in both Japan and developing countries. Section 7.2 discusses why small-scale family faming is dominant in agriculture worldwide, including the production of HVPs, and why producer cooperatives must play a key role in the development of high-value agricultural districts where small-scale family farms dominate. Section 7.3 reviews the role of producer cooperatives in the successful development of Japan's apple-producing districts, whereas Section 7.4 examines the role of producer cooperatives in developing countries in Asia and sub-Saharan Africa.[5] Section 7.5 concludes this chapter by providing policy implications for the development of high-value agricultural districts in developing countries.

7.2 Dominance of Family Farms and the Emergence of Contract Farming

Farm production is generally subject to scale diseconomies beyond the farm size manageable by family labor because of the high cost of monitoring hired labor in spatially dispersed and ecologically diverse agricultural production environments (Deininger and Byerlee 2012; Feder 1985; Hayami and Otsuka 1993).[6] This is particularly the case in low-income economies, where the intensive use of labor is less costly than a mechanized production system. Hired labor is employed for simple tasks such as weeding, transplanting, and harvesting, but not for care-intensive activities such as water and pest management, or the application of fertilizer and other purchased inputs (Hayami and Otsuka 1993). Restated, labor markets fail to function in care-intensive activities in agriculture. This is why family farming is dominant worldwide.[7] In fact, large plantations in Asia, haciendas in Latin America,

[4] This point is discussed in Chaps. 1 and 2.

[5] Some literature on Latin America is also included.

[6] To my knowledge, a major exception is large-scale flower production in greenhouses, a production system similar to the factory system in terms of a fine division of labor. See, for example, Mano et al. (2011).

[7] In practice, more important than the labor market in adjustment of different factor endowments across farming households is the land rental market (Otsuka et al. 1992; Otsuka 2007). Although the majority of family farms are owner-cultivated, they include tenant-cultivated farms.

and estates in sub-Saharan Africa were created primarily by colonial governments rather than market forces (Otsuka 2007).[8] This also explains why plantation-based production of pineapples, sugarcane, and bananas in the Philippines is outcompeted by peasant-based production of the same tropical products in Thailand (Hayami 2001). However, peasants or small-scale farmers may not know how to grow and sell HVPs and also lack access to improved seeds and other inputs as well as credit. Thus, successful peasant-based production of HVPs in Thailand presumably was possible because of the use of contract farming.

Rather than operating their own large farms, non-agricultural firms, often supermarkets, prefer to enter contracts with farmers, who rely primarily on family labor. Labor market failures thus can be avoided. To overcome the failure of input and credit markets and the absence of technology provision services,[9] private firms or their agents provide seeds and other inputs on credit, together with technical services, and closely supervise production.[10] According to tradition in Asia, landlords, rice millers, and fertilizer dealers provide inputs on credit (Bardhan 1980; Hayami et al. 1999; Otsuka et al. 1992), but they do not provide new inputs and improved technical knowledge.

To reduce information asymmetry regarding the quality and safety of HVPs between producers, retailers, and consumers, supermarkets guarantee the products they sell. Thus, the reputation of a particular supermarket as a reliable seller of high-quality products is very important. As Grosh (1994) argues, because HVPs are perishable, coordination of delivery from producers to retailors at the proper time is also critically important, and so modern market chains use cold storage facilities and other indivisible equipment. The importance of reputation and the use of indivisible equipment confer scale economies in marketing. In fact, supermarkets are usually gigantic.

Clearly, although contract farming is generally more efficient than plantation-type, integrated, large-scale production systems, it is undoubtedly costly. The empirical literature suggests that contractors choose large farmers as partners, particularly in the early stage of the development of contract farming, to economize on transaction costs (e.g., Reardon et al. 2003). Gradually, however, small farmers also form producer cooperatives to facilitate contract farming (Otsuka et al. 2016). In fact, cooperatives procure improved seeds and chemical inputs on behalf of small farmers, supervise production processes, and examine product quality and safety. Thus, the cooperative may be able to reduce transaction costs for contractors, although it must incur extra transaction costs itself. Therefore, it seems reasonable

[8] Once large production units are established, it is difficult to resolve them even if they are inefficient partly because of the credit constraints of small-scale farmers, who are potentially more efficient producers, and partly because of the inability of employed workers of large production unit, who may be eligible to be land reform beneficiaries, to manage production of such products.

[9] This assumes malfunctioning of public-sector extension systems in developing countries in general and in Africa in particular.

[10] Strictly speaking, this is called the production contract. Another type of contract farming involves a marketing contract, in which the contractor designates the use of particular inputs. See Otsuka et al. (2016) for further details.

to hypothesize that producer cooperatives contribute to the rise of contract farming between large marketing agents and small-scale farmers.

Although the empirical literature on contract farming seldom states explicitly, producers of HVPs are clustered. This is evident from the fact that case studies of contract farming typically cover small areas. An exception is Briones (2015), who finds that clustering helps small-scale tobacco producers in the Philippines promote contract farming. Needless to say, clustering reduces the transaction costs of contract farming. Also clustering is obviously necessary for the establishment of effective producer cooperatives.

Contract farming has long been practiced in developed countries, including the case of sugar production in nineteenth century Taiwan (Little and Watts 1994). However, contract farming has become increasingly common in developing countries, driven by increased consumer interest since the 1990s in the quality and safety of HVPs and the development of supermarkets. Even in the absence of contract farming, in the history of HVP production in developed countries, small-scale farmers interested in the production of HVPs must have faced the same problems as those facing contract farmers now. They include the introduction of new products and production methods, the improvement of access to input and output markets, and the assurance of product quality and establishment of a good reputation. To solve these problems, collective action is needed because all these actions entail production externalities. Restated, how to internalize externalities lies at the heart of the development issues of industrial districts discussed in Chaps. 1 and 2.

In the next section we will take up the case of the historical development of Japan's apple-growing districts before World War II. It will be shown that common issues exist in this historical case and contemporary cases involving developing countries, to be discussed in Sect. 7.4.

As mentioned earlier, contract farming resembles a putting-out contract in manufacturing, in which the contractor provides materials as well as technical and marketing services. Such contracts have been historically practiced in Europe and Japan (Abe and Saito 1988; Hashino and Otsuka 2013; Landes 1969; Marglin 1974). Gereffi (1999) recently turned attention to the growing role of global buyers, often supermarkets in developed countries as in the case of contract farming. Observing that global buyers provide putting-out contracts to small-scale producers in developing countries, he argues that producers in Asia learn not only production methods from global buyers but also marketing methods, which enable those producers to upgrade their status from subcontractors receiving putting-out contracts to independent exporters. While Schmitz and Knorringa (2000) agree that learning from global buyers is important,[11] producers in developing countries learn primarily production technologies and generally fail to learn marketing methodologies, since marketing is a core competence of global buyers. A recent review of the literature on contract framing by Otsuka et al. (2016) suggests that small-scale farmers in developing

[11] Schmitz and Knorringa (2000) argue that willingness to learn from outsiders is one of the main reasons for China's success and India's failure.

countries learn production technologies from contract farming but not marketing methods.

Historically, the putting-out contract was replaced by the factory system, with important reasons for this being scale economies in production arising from the use of large machines, the fine division of labor, and the ease of supervising factory workers (Landes 1969; Marglin 1974). Landes emphasizes that embezzlement is a major source of transaction costs in the putting-out system, which is conceptually identical to the conversion of provided inputs for other purposes under contract farming. Conceptually, the factory system resembles an integrated large-scale production system, such as a plantation in which not only production but also processing and marketing are carried out by a single production unit. The question then arises of whether contract farming will be replaced by the integrated production system, as occurred in the history of manufacturing sectors. Our answer is negative. Family farms dominate in the U.S. despite the huge farm size there. In Latin America, private companies manage large mechanized farms but do not adopt an integrated production system.[12] Little sign exists in developing countries that farm size expands under contract farming, large-scale farms dominate in contract farming, or contracting companies undertake their own large-scale production. To my knowledge, one exception is Senegal, where contracting companies operate large-scale farms to produce high-quality vegetables for export (Maertens and Swinnen 2009). However, the case of Senegal is likely to be a temporary exception because the advantage of an integrated production system increased with the sudden increase in quality and safety standards in the EU.

The rise of a large-scale factory system replacing small-scale production units in manufacturing and the continued dominance of family farms in developing countries reflect the fundamental difference between manufacturing and farming. While the former is increasingly characterized by scale economies in production, the latter is constrained by the high monitoring cost for hired workers, which leads to scale diseconomies (Otsuka et al. 2016). Thus, we expect that contract farming will continue to prevail in the production of HVPs in developing countries and that whether truly small-scale farmers are excluded from or included in the production of HVPs through contract faming depends on the strength of their collective action to establish and maintain effective producer cooperatives.

7.3 Historical Development of Apple-Growing Districts in Prewar Japan[13]

As will become clear, the role and functions of producer cooperatives are surprisingly similar between the historical case of Japan, discussed in this section, and contemporary cases in Asia and sub-Saharan Africa, discussed in the next section.

[12] It appears that, according to interviews with managers of agricultural firms in Brazil, the monitoring cost for hired workers is lower under a highly computerized system.

[13] This section draws on Shirai (2012, 2013).

Aomori Prefecture is one of the most famous apple growing prefectures in Japan. Yet, commercial apple production there began only in 1875, when several farmers tried to grow apples. Apple production gradually increased and the total area planted with apples in Aomori Prefecture increased from 1200 ha in 1900 to 12,500 ha in 1935 (Shirai 2012). Apple production accounted for 21 % of agricultural production value in Aomori Prefecture by 1935, increased from a mere 4 % in 1900. The momentum behind this success came from the establishment of the Takedate Apple Producers' Cooperative in 1907 in Takedate village, located at the center of the apple producing districts in Aomori Prefecture.

The number of cooperative members increased from 50 in 1907 to 279 in 1917, and increased further to 314 in 1927. Following the rise of the Takedate Cooperative, as many as 29 other producer cooperatives, which dealt with apples, were established from 1908 to 1911 in Aomori Prefecture. As far as the Takedate Cooperative is concerned, 80 % of apple growing farmers in its neighborhood were members of this cooperative around 1910. Compared with non-members, members were mostly relatively prosperous owner farmers.

The first major function of the Takedate Cooperative was collective marketing, i.e., joint purchase of materials and joint sale of products. While non-members sold apples to local agents and wholesalers, members regularly sold their products through the cooperative to designated wholesalers in urban markets, with whom a strong trust-based relationship was developed. The cooperative also operated its own retail shops in large cities. This was reminiscent of township-village enterprises in industrial clusters in China, which sold their high-quality products directly to urban wholesalers as well as selling to consumers through their own retail shops, rather than relying on local traders and wholesale markets (Sonobe and Otsuka 2006). The second major function was to control production, by providing guidelines on pruning, weeding, and pest and disease controls. This can be considered a technical service to produce high-quality products. Product quality and production value were assessed by experts and farmers with unsatisfactory performance were given recommendations for improvement. In this way, the Takedate Cooperative successfully produced standardized high-quality products. The third function was to provide cheap credit to cooperative members. To do this, the Takedate Cooperative borrowed from major banks, local banks, and credit associations.

Clearly, the role of the cooperative was essentially the same as that of the contractor offering contract farming, namely providing inputs, credit, technical services, and marketing services. The major difference is that the decisions of the producer cooperative were made by farmers, whether individually or through a selected group, whereas contract farming was designed by contractors, supermarkets, and their agents.

The Takedate Cooperative earnestly attempted to standardize its apples and improve their quality. Thus, the cooperative promoted apple grading and branding. Depending on taste, color, and size, apples were classified into five categories and the highest quality category were marked with the trademark of the Nakadate Cooperative. Apples produced by members of the cooperative received awards at agricultural exhibitions and trade fairs. As a result, apples produced by members of the Takedate Cooperative often fetched prices 100 % higher than the average for apples from Aomori Prefecture in the early twentieth century.

Similar activities were carried out by other producer cooperatives in agricultural districts in Japan. One notable example is the Mitsukabi Mandarin-Orange Producer Cooperative from the late 1960s to the late 1990s (Matsubara 2014). The Mitsukabi Cooperative upgraded the quality of oranges by introducing high-quality specie, and providing technical training, standardizing and grading the products, adopting branding, and selling the products to supermarkets and other large outlets. In short, similar to the Takedate Cooperative, the Mitsukabi Cooperative carried out product, process, and marketing innovations, which led to considerable growth of high-quality mandarin-orange production in the Mitsukabi area.

Ironically the success of the Takedate Cooperative in the 1910s and 1920s led to its failure in the 1930s. The reputation the cooperative gained for its high-quality apple producers attracted traders from urban areas throughout Japan. Competition among traders in turn led to cooperative members being approached directly and offered high prices, which resulted in rampant side-selling. Since the prices offered to cooperative members were often lower than market prices because of deductions made to cover the costs of member services, members were tempted to sell to outside traders, even though this violated their agreements with the cooperative. This is consistent with the argument of Poulton et al. (2004) that competition among buyers expands the opportunity for side-selling in developing countries, so that competition and "contract farming" are incompatible. In fact, Waldron et al. (2010) report that side selling caused the break-down of contract farming among beef farmers in China. Punishment of side-selling was weak because forfeiture of the cooperative membership was the main threat used to enforcement the cooperative agreement. In fact, the proportion of apple growing farmers who were members of the Takedate Cooperative declined from 80 % in the 1910s to roughly 20 % by around 1935.

It is fair to conclude that for small farmers to produce and market HVPs, a producer cooperative should be formed to undertake procurement of inputs, provide technical services, and guarantee product quality. The advantage of this system over contract farming is that rewards for such services would accrue to the cooperative and eventually to its members. However, producer cooperatives alone may be unable to sustain production of high-quality products due to a weak punishment mechanism for violations of the collective agreement.

7.4 Contract Farming and Producer Cooperatives in Developing Countries

Globally, large farmers participate more actively in contract farming than small farmers (Otsuka et al. 2016). In developing countries, statistical analyses consistently show that the coefficient of farm size in the contract farming participation function is almost always positive and significant. This appears to imply that smaller farmers tend to be excluded from contract farming. However, many sample farmers in case studies are small-scale farmers and the difference in farm size between participants and non-participants is relatively small, e.g., 0.76 vs. 0.55 ha in Indonesia (Winters et al. 2005). Thus, we can hardly conclude that small-scale farmers are generally excluded from contract farming in developing countries.

One reason for the participation of smallholders in contract farming is likely to be the establishment of smallholder cooperatives. Unanimous agreement exists among researchers of contract farming that to overcome the handicap arising from the small quantity of transactions by smallholders, smallholders must form producer cooperatives to reduce contractor's transaction costs and enhance their capacities to provide a consistent and timely supply of high-quality and safe products (Barrett et al. 2012; Boselie et al. 2003; Glover and Kusterer 1990; Kirsten and Sartorius 2002; Neven and Reardon 2004; Poulton et al. 2010; Reardon and Barrett 2000; Reardon et al. 2009; World Bank 2007). Many of these researchers are pessimistic about the prospects for the emergence and development of smallholder producer cooperatives. However, smallholder cooperatives, which supply HVPs to domestic supermarkets, have been emerging in China (Ito et al. 2012; Jia and Huang 2011), India (Trebbin 2014; Narrod et al. 2009), Kenya (Neven et al. 2009; Rao et al. 2012; Okello and Swinton 2006), Tanzania (Barham and Chitemi 2009), and Vietnam (Wang et al. 2014). Okello and Swinton (2006) and Rao et al. (2012) report that smallholders established producer cooperatives to ensure compliance with increased safety standards for the export of HVPs to European markets or to supply to domestic supermarkets.

There are two types of smallholder cooperatives. One is the intermediary type: this is a producer cooperative that makes contracts with buyers on behalf of its members, who procure inputs and sell outputs only through the cooperative. Examples include tobacco faming in the Philippines (Briones 2015) and hybrid maize seed production in Java (Winters et al. 2005). Such cooperatives resemble the collective marketing function of the Takedate Cooperative. The second type is the facilitator-type: this type of cooperative is designed to facilitate contracts between the contractor and smallholders by providing group members with technical assistance, modern inputs, and marketing information. This type of cooperative exists in watermelon production in China (Ito et al. 2012) and elsewhere (Boselie et al. 2003). This cooperative model resembles the second function of the Takedate Cooperative, which provided technical services for production control. Finally, some producer cooperatives provide credit to their members that resembles the third function of the Takedate Cooperative (Bellemare 2012; Briones 2015; Winters et al. 2005).

Notably, although producer cooperatives help smallholders participate in contract farming, their members are relatively large-scale farmers (Fischer and Qaim 2012; Francesconi and Heerink 2010; Ito et al. 2012; Winters et al. 2005). For example, in China the average farm size of cooperative members is 0.48 ha, versus 0.43 ha for non-members (Ito et al. 2012). The corresponding numbers for East Java are 0.59 ha and 0.36 ha (Winters et al. 2005). It may well be that producer cooperatives prefer to assist relatively large-scale farmers to save on the transaction costs associated with providing inputs and technical services and monitoring the behaviors of small-scale farmers. Thus, it must be understood that the establishment of producer cooperatives alone may not be able to solve the problem of small farmer exclusion from contract farming. However, considering the relatively small gap in farm size between the two groups, it is unlikely that farm size is the decisive factor affecting participation in contract farming among smallholders.

Many producer cooperatives lack advanced production technology. Thus, there are many cases in which NGOs provide technical services (Escobal and Cavero 2012: Michelson et al. 2012; Rao et al. 2012; Rao and Qaim 2011). This is partly because contract farming has evolved from production contracts, in which the contractor controls production, to marketing contracts, in which the contractor designates the use of particular inputs and production methods. In the latter case, producer cooperatives cannot rely entirely on the contractor in acquiring new technological knowledge, even though the acquisition of such knowledge is socially desirable. Thus, the provision of new technological knowledge by NGOs makes sense. Unfortunately, however, rigorous assessment of the impact of NGO training has not been attempted in the literature.

While many case studies find significant and positive income effects of contract farming assisted by producer cooperatives, it is puzzling that in many countries the prevalence of producer cooperatives is reported to be limited (Dries and Swinnen 2004; Hellin et al. 2009; Maertens and Swinnen 2009; Minten et al. 2009; Roy and Thorat 2008; Singh 2002; Trebbin 2014). There are several possible interpretations. First, researchers focused on successful cases of producer cooperatives in their case studies, meaning the research results may not show the general picture of contract farming in the country as a whole. Second, and consistent with the first interpretation, the operation of producers cooperatives is not profitable and so many are supported by the government, as in China (Jia and Huang 2011; Ito et al. 2012), Ethiopia (Bernard et al. 2008), and Tanzania (Barham and Chitemi 2009). Third, and consistent with the experience of the Takedate Cooperative, although the functions of producer cooperatives are socially beneficial, they do not function effectively due to the high cost of coordinating cooperative members so as to internalize externalities. If the third interpretation is valid, room exists for effective government interventions.

To summarize, while many case studies suggest critical roles are played by producer cooperatives in contract farming, none have successfully inquired into the conditions under which producer cooperatives are viable and profitable. Considering the utmost importance of trade unions in realizing innovations in industrial districts reported in this book, it is worthwhile to explore the role of producer cooperatives in realizing innovations in high-value agricultural districts in developing countries.

7.5 Concluding Remarks

Surprisingly large similarities exist not only between producer cooperatives in prewar Japan and contemporary developing countries but also between producer cooperatives or associations in manufacturing and high-value agriculture. Product markets commonly fail because of information asymmetry related to product quality. To produce high-quality products requires the application of improved inputs and appropriate technological knowledge. However, input markets and markets of improved technological information are either absent or imperfect. Furthermore, standardization, quality-upgrading, and quality assurance must be facilitated. Producer cooperatives or associations must play a central role in solving all these problems.

In other words, in the absence of significant scale economies in production, cooperatives, whose members are small-scale producers, must undertake activities that produce positive externalities. One example is the introduction of new technologies, production methods, and products, which are likely to spillover from initiators or innovators to neighbors. Another example is the establishment of reputations as high-quality producers and as a high-quality production area, a reputation that benefits all producers in associated industrial or agricultural districts. Needless to say, appropriate inputs must be used, proper production methods must be adopted, and strict quality inspections must be carried out, to establish a high reputation.

While similarities exist among producer associations in manufacturing, producer cooperatives in prewar Japanese agriculture, and producer cooperatives in developing countries, there is one essential difference, which relates to who plays the role of entrepreneur. In the case of contract farming, it is contractors and supermarkets that play the role of entrepreneurs, even though producer cooperatives play certain roles in technological, managerial, and marketing innovations. As Joseph Schumpeter (1912) emphasized, entrepreneurs introduce innovations in technology, management, and marketing and receive sizable entrepreneurial profits. Similarly, Theodore Schultz (1975) argues that high income is the return realized from the ability to deal with disequilibria arising from the adoption of new technologies and responses to dynamic market changes. Viewed from this perspective, we cannot simply assume that the benefits of contract farming, which involves innovation, accrue to small-scale farmers as they are not entrepreneurs in this context. Particularly, farmers' production autonomy is highly restricted under production contracts, so that little room exists for farmers' entrepreneurship.

Thus, while establishing producer cooperatives will contribute to the participation of small-scale farmers in modern supply chains, nurturing their human capital or entrepreneurship is also needed to achieve the truly inclusive development of contract farming. As Gereffi (1999) assumes, some small-scale farmers may have learned technology and marketing from participation in contract farming. Masakure and Henson (2005), Minten et al. (2007, 2009), and Glover and Kusterer (1990) note that production methods learned from contract farming for the production of high-quality products for export and domestic supermarkets are applied to other crops. However, to the best of my knowledge there is no empirical study that reports the case of farmers who have acquired not only new technology but also new marketing methods from contract farming and, hence, become more independent commercial producers.

To improve the welfare of small farmers interested in contract farming requires investment in the human capital of smallholders by means of management and marketing training, as in the case of management training of micro, small, and medium-scale entrepreneurs in industrial clusters in Asia and Africa (Sonobe and Otsuka 2011, 2014). If such training is designed by the producer cooperatives and is financially and technically supported by the public sectors and international donors, small-scale farmers will be able to significantly enhance their entrepreneurship and so obtain a new source of higher income. Also if training is offered only to cooperative members, side-selling, which troubled the Takedate Apple Producers' Cooperative, may be prevented or at least significantly mitigated.

References

Abe T, Saito O (1988) From putting-out to the factory: a cotton-weaving district in late-Meiji Japan. Text Hist 19(2):143–157

Akerlof GA (1970) The market for "lemons": quality uncertainty and the market mechanism. Q J Econ 84(3):488–500

Bardhan PK (1980) Interlocking factor markets and agrarian development. Oxf Econ Pap 32(1):82–98

Barham J, Chitemi C (2009) Collective action initiatives to improve marketing performance: lessons from farmer groups in Tanzania. Food Policy 34(1):53–59

Barrett CB, Bachke ME, Bellemare MF, Michelson HC, Narayanan S, Walker TF (2012) Smallholder participation in contract farming: comparative evidence from five countries. World Dev 40(4):715–730

Bellemare MF (2012) As you sow, so shall you reap: the welfare impacts of contract farming. World Dev 40(7):1418–1434

Bernard T, Taffesse AS, Gabre-Madhin E (2008) Impact of cooperatives on smallholders' commercialization behavior: evidence from Ethiopia. Agric Econ 39(2):147–161

Boselie D, Henson S, Weatherspoon D (2003) Supermarket procurement practices in developing countries: redefining the roles of the public and private sectors. Am J Agric Econ 85(5):1155–1161

Briones RM (2015) Small farmers in high-value chains: binding or relaxing constraints to inclusive growth? World Dev 72(1):43–52

Deininger K, Byerlee D (2012) The rise of large farms in land abundant countries: do they have a future? World Dev 40(4):701–714

Dries L, Swinnen JFM (2004) Foreign direct investment, vertical integration, and local suppliers: evidence from the Polish dairy sector. World Dev 32(9):1525–1544

Escobal J, Cavero D (2012) Transaction costs, institutional arrangements and inequality outcomes: potato marketing by small producers in rural Peru. World Dev 40(2):329–341

Feder G (1985) The relation between farm size and productivity: the role of family labor, supervision and credit constraints. J Dev Econ 18(2/3):297–313

Fischer E, Qaim M (2012) Linking smallholders to markets: determinants and impacts of farmer collective action in Kenya. World Dev 40(6):1255–1268

Francesconi GN, Heerink N (2010) Ethiopian agricultural cooperatives in an era of global commodity exchange: does organizational form matter? J African Econ 20(1):153–177
Gereffi G (1999) International trade and industrial upgrading in the apparel commodity chain. J Int Econ 48(1):37–70
Glover D, Kusterer K (1990) Small farmers, big business: contract farming and rural development. Palgrave Macmillan, Hampshire
Grosh B (1994) Contract farming in Africa: an application of the new institutional economics. J Afr Econ 3(2):231–261
Hashino T, Otsuka K (2013) Hand looms, power looms, and changing production organizations: the case of the Kiryu weaving district in early twentieth-century Japan. Econ Hist Rev 66(3):785–804
Hayami Y (2001) Ecology, history, and development: a perspective from rural Southeast Asia. World Bank Res Obs 16(2):169–198
Hayami Y, Otsuka K (1993) The economics of contract choice. Clarendon, Oxford
Hayami Y, Kikuchi M, Marciano EB (1999) Middlemen and peasants in rice marketing in the Philippines. Agric Econ 20(1):79–93
Hellin J, Lundy M, Meijer M (2009) Farmer organization, collective action and market access in Meso-America. Food Policy 34(1):16–22
Ito J, Bao Z, Su Q (2012) Distribution effects of agricultural cooperatives in China: exclusion of smallholders and potential gains in participation. Food Policy 37(6):700–709
Jia X, Huang J (2011) Contractual agreements between farmer cooperatives and buyers in China. Food Policy 36(5):656–666
Kirsten J, Sartorius K (2002) Linking agribusiness and small-scale farmers in developing countries : is there a new role for contract farming ? Dev Southern Afr 19(4):503–529
Landes DS (1969) The unbound prometheus: technological change and industrial development in Western Europe from 1750 to the present. Cambridge University Press, Cambridge
Little P, Watts M (1994) Living under contract: contract farming and agrarian transformation in sub-Saharan Africa. University of Wisconsin Press, Madison
Maertens M, Swinnen JFM (2009) Trade, standards, and poverty: evidence from Senegal. World Dev 37(1):161–178
Mano Y, Yamano T, Suzuki A, Matsumoto T (2011) Local and personal networks in employment and the development of labor markets: evidence from the cut flower industry in Ethiopia. World Dev 39(10):1760–1770
Marglin SA (1974) What do bosses do? the origins and functions of hierarchy in capitalist production. Rev Radical Polit Econ 6(1):33–60
Masakure O, Henson S (2005) Why do small-scale producers choose to produce under contract? lessons from nontraditional vegetable exports from Zimbabwe. World Dev 33(10):1721–1733
Matsubara H (2014) Chiiki Kakushin to Shugoteki Kigyouka Kodo (Innovation for agricultural district and collective action of entrepreneurs). Soshiki Kagaku Org Sci 47(3):52–63
Michelson H, Reardon T, Perez F (2012) Small farmers and big retail: trade-offs of supplying supermarkets in Nicaragua. World Dev 40(2):342–354
Minten B, Randrianarison L, Swinnen JFM (2007) Spillovers from high-value agriculture for exports on land use in developing countries: evidence from Madagascar. Agric Econ 37(2/3):265–275
Minten B, Randrianarison L, Swinnen JFM (2009) Global retail chains and poor farmers: evidence from Madagascar. World Dev 37(11):1728–1741
Narrod C, Roy D, Okello J, Avendanõ B, Rich K, Thorat A (2009) Public-private partnerships and collective action in high-value fruit and vegetable supply chains. Food Policy 34(1):8–15
Neven D, Reardon T (2004) The rise of Kenyan supermarkets and the evolution of their horticulture product procurement systems. Dev Policy Rev 22(6):669–699
Neven D, Odera MM, Reardon T, Wang H (2009) Kenyan supermarkets, emerging middle-class horticultural farmers, and employment impacts on the rural poor. World Dev 37(11):1802–1811

Okello JJ, Swinton SM (2006) Compliance with international food safety standards in Kenya's green bean industry: comparison of a small- and a large-scale farm producing for export. Rev Agric Econ 29(2):269–285
Otsuka K (2007) Efficiency and equity effects of land markets. In: Evenson RE, Pingali PL (eds) Handbook of agricultural economics, vol 3. Elsevier, Amsterdam
Otsuka K, Chuma H, Hayami Y (1992) Land and labor contracts in agrarian economies: theories and facts. J Econ Lit 30(4):1965–2018
Otsuka K, Nakano Y, Takahashi K (2016) Contract farming in developed and developing countries. Annual Rev. Res. Econ. forthcoming
Poulton C, Gibbon P, Hanyani-Mlambo B, Kydd J, Maro W, Larson MN, Osorio A, Tschirley D, Zulu B (2004) Competition and coordination in liberalized African cotton market system. World Dev 32(3):519–536
Poulton C, Dorward A, Kydd J (2010) The future of small farms: new directions for services, institutions, and intermediation. World Dev 38(10):1413–1428
Rao EJO, Qaim M (2011) Supermarkets, farm household income, and poverty: insights from Kenya. World Dev 39(5):784–796
Rao EJO, Brümmer B, Qaim M (2012) Farmer participation in supermarket channels, production technology, and efficiency: the case of vegetables in Kenya. Am J Agric Econ 94(4):891–912
Reardon T, Barrett CB (2000) Agroindustrialization, globalization, and international development: an overview of issues, patterns, and determinants. Agric Econ 23(3):195–205
Reardon T, Berdegué JA (2002) The rapid rise of supermarkets in Latin America: challenges and opportunities for development. Dev Policy Rev 20(4):371–388
Reardon T, Timmer CP (2012) The economics of the food system revolution. Ann Rev Res Econ 4:225–264
Reardon T, Timmer CP, Barrett CB, Berdegué J (2003) The rise of supermarkets in Africa, Asia, and Latin America. Am J Agric Econ 85(5):1140–1146
Reardon T, Barrett CB, Berdegué JA, Swinnen JFM (2009) Agrifood industry transformation and small farmers in developing countries. World Dev 37(11):1717–1727
Roy D, Thorat A (2008) Success in high value horticultural export markets for the small farmers: the case of Mahagrapes in India. World Dev 36(10):1874–1890
Schmitz H, Knorringa P (2000) Learning from global buyers. J Devel Stud 37(2):177–205
Schultz TW (1975) Ability to deal with disequilibria. J Econ Lit 13(3):827–846
Schumpeter JA (1912) The theory of economic development. Oxford University Press, New York
Shirai I (2012) Sangyo kumiai niyoru seisan-ryutsu katei no tosei (Control of production and marketing processes by industrial cooperative). Shakai Keizai Shigaku Soc Econ His 78(2):3–26
Shirai I (2013) Kindai Nihon niokeru nosakumotsu sanchi no keisei to sangyoukumiai (Formation of agricultural districts and industrial cooperative in the modern Japan). Ph.D. dissertation, Graduate School of Economics, Osaka University
Singh S (2002) Contracting out solutions: political economy of contract farming in the Indian Punjab. World Dev 30(9):1621–1638
Sonobe T, Otsuka K (2006) Cluster-based industrial development: an East Asian model. Palgrave Macmillan, Hampshire
Sonobe T, Otsuka K (2011) Cluster-based industrial development: a comparative study of Asia and Africa. Palgrave Macmillan, Hampshire
Sonobe T, Otsuka K (2014) Cluster-based industrial development: KAIZEN management for MSE growth in developing countries. Palgrave Macmillan, Hampshire
Trebbin A (2014) Linking small farmers to modern retail through producer organizations: experiences with producer companies in India. Food Policy 45:35–44
Waldron S, Brown C, Longworth J (2010) A critique of high-value supply chains as a means of modernizing agriculture in China: the case of the beef industry. Food Policy 35(5):479–487
Wang H, Moustier P, Loc NTT (2014) Economic impact of direct marketing and contracts: the case of safe vegetable chains in northern Vietnam. Food Policy 47(1):13–23
Winters P, Simmons P, Patrick I (2005) Evaluation of a hybrid seed contract between smallholders and a multinational company in East Java, Indonesia. J Dev Stud 41(1):62–89
World Bank (2007) World development report, 2008: agriculture for development. World Bank, Washington, DC

Part IV
Supporting Role of Local Government

Chapter 8
Industrial Districts in Europe: Policy Lessons for Developing Countries?

Hubert Schmitz and Bernard Musyck

Abstract In the 1970s and 1980s, industrial districts in Europe achieved international competitiveness and attained high employment standards, even though they were based on local small- and medium-sized firms and concentrated on traditional sectors. This makes them of special interest to less-developed countries in the South and East. This paper examines what policy lessons can be drawn from this European experience. It does so by focusing on the role of public and private institutions in four fields: (a) the provision of credit, (b) the training of workers and entrepreneurs, (c) the provision of real services, and (d) wage negotiations. The paper suggests that institutions played more of a role in later than earlier phases of growth. It points toward a new model of industrial policy based on local institutions but emphasizes that there is as yet little systematic assessment of the role of such institutions.

Keywords Small-firm industrial districts • International competitiveness • Europe • Public and private institutions • Small enterprise development • Industrial policy

8.1 Introduction

This paper is addressed to the researchers and practitioners in the field of small enterprise development, particularly those working on developing countries. Our central question is what policy lessons can we learn from the recent European experience with small-scale industry? This question is of particular interest because in advanced countries, particularly in Europe, there has been a reemergence of small enterprises in the course of the 1980s (see, for example, Sengenberger et al. 1990). There are various forces behind this reemergence. The one that has probably

---

This chapter is a reproduction of Hubert Schmitz and Bernard Musyck (1994), "Industrial Districts in Europe: Policy Lessons for Developing Countries?" *World Development* 22(6):889–910.

H. Schmitz (✉)
Institute of Development Studies, University of Sussex, Brighton, UK
e-mail: h.schmitz@emeritus.ids.ac.uk

B. Musyck
School of Economic Sciences and Administration, Frederick University, Nicosia, Cyprus

T. Hashino, K. Otsuka (eds.), *Industrial Districts in History and the Developing World*, Studies in Economic History, DOI 10.1007/978-981-10-0182-6_8

received most attention is the success of European small-firm industrial districts in achieving international competitiveness and attaining high employment standards (Pyke and Sengenberger 1992). A key question for researchers and practitioners alike is whether such success was the result of intervention by public or private institutions. If so, some of the measures adopted could perhaps be replicated elsewhere.

Investigating this issue is a daunting task. First, there are conceptual problems which hinder the analysis. Second, our empirical understanding of why and how the European industrial districts grew is far from complete. Third, the research material which does exist suggests that there are considerable variations in industrial districts. Nevertheless, some policy lessons can be drawn and the purpose of this paper is to bring them out. This is done by examining the role of formal institutions in four European regions: the Third Italy, Baden-Württemberg in Southern Germany, West Jutland in Denmark and South-West Flanders in Belgium. In carrying out this task we benefited from other studies which focus on formal institutions in industrial districts, most notably Murray (1991) and Pyke (1992a). Our objective was, however, not to list examples of what institutions can do, but to assess – as far as possible – what they have actually done in the selected regions. The paper is based primarily on secondary sources, but for the cases of Baden-Württemberg and South-West Flanders we have also drawn on our own previous research (Musyck 1992, 1993, 1995; Schmitz 1992).

Section 8.2 explains briefly what we mean by “industrial districts” and introduces the four European regions mentioned above. Sections 8.3, 8.4, 8.5 and 8.6 constitute the core of the paper – the role of public and private institutions is examined in four areas: the provision of credit, training, and real services, as well as the negotiation of wages and working conditions. This is followed by a discussion of whether the importance of local and regional institutions has changed over time. Section 8.7 suggests that such institutions have played more of a role in later rather than earlier phases of growth. In Section 8.8 the analysis switches to the macro level but concludes that little can be learned from the industrial district experiences about the macro policy environment. The more interesting conclusions emerge at the meso (sectoral/regional) and micro (enterprise/local) level. Section 8.9 asks whether a new model of industrial policy emerges from the reviewed experiences. Finally, Section 8.10 discusses whether there are any lessons for what donor agencies can do in promoting local industry in less-developed countries (LDCs).

8.2 Key Features of Industrial Districts

This paper is not concerned with small-scale industry in general, but with a particular form of industrial organization, the so-called industrial district in which small firms are particularly prominent. The term industrial district goes back to Alfred Marshall who used it for the “concentration of specialized industries in particular localities” (Marshall 1920). The Italian economist Becattini (1989, 1990) used the concept to capture the success of agglomerations of small firms in some areas of his country and the Italian experience has given impetus to research on industrial districts in a number of advanced country regions during the last decade (Pyke and Sengenberger 1992).

From this international debate the following have emerged as the main attributes of industrial districts: geographical proximity, sectoral specialization, predominance of small- and medium-sized firms, close interfirm collaboration, interfirm competition based on innovation rather than lowering wages, a socio-cultural identity which facilitates trust relations between firms and between employers and skilled workers, active self-help organizations, and active regional and municipal government which strengthens the innovative capacity of local industry. It should, however, be emphasized that there are many variations among industrial districts and that the weight of the above attributes varies a great deal.

It is also worth mentioning that a number of concepts other than the industrial district have been used. For example, Garofoli (1983) introduced a typology of "local productive systems." Similarly Courlet and Pecqueur (1991) talk in terms of a "socio-territorial industrial system." Piore and Sabel (1984) refer to it as flexible specialization but this term is also used for other forms of industrial organization (see Rasmussen et al. 1992). The result is confusing because different concepts are used to describe the same reality or sometimes the same concept is used to describe different realities. Perhaps the key point that comes out of this debate is that industrial success cannot be grasped by analyzing individual firms. Their strength lies in clustering and cooperative competition which open up efficiency and flexibility gains which individual producers can rarely attain. Elsewhere (Schmitz 1990) we have used the concept of "collective efficiency" to capture these gains.

The renewed interest in the industrial districts was fuelled particularly by the experience of, what has come to be called, the "Third Italy". The concept of the Third Italy started to be used in the late 1970s. At that time it became apparent that while little economic progress was in sight in the poor South (Second Italy), the traditionally rich First Italy (North West), based on large industrial concentrations, was facing a deep crisis. In contrast, the small firms districts of the North East and Center[1] of Italy showed fast growth which attracted the attention of social scientists.

The most common sectors represented in the Third Italy are textiles, shoes, furniture, tiles and mechanical engineering. The Danish experience reviewed in this paper refers to the region of West Jutland which has industrial districts specializing in garments and furniture. In German case of Baden-Württemberg, the main sectors are metal working and mechanical engineering. Finally, the strength of South-West Flanders rests on the carpet weaving and upholstery, chipboard, and frozen vegetables sectors among others.[2] Overall, these regions are specialized mainly in

[1] The concept of the "NEC model" (North East and Central Italy) was also introduced (Fuà 1983).

[2] The inclusion of South-West Flanders along with the other three well-known cases of European industrial districts may surprise some readers. This region in Belgium is a particularly clear case of autonomous industrialization, as documented in detail by Musyck (1992, 1993, 1995). While

traditional industries which are technologically compatible with the small-scale family structure of most local firms.

This takes us to the question of why these cases are of particular interest to LDCs. There is a combination of answers:

- they have clusters of indigenous firms
- operate mainly in traditional sectors (in which LDCs are thought to have a comparative advantage)
- compete successfully in international markets.

They have also had a favorable growth and employment performance.[3] There are variations among the regions considered but so as to give a comparative measure, it is worth mentioning that all regions considered performed over the last two decades better than most – if not all – other regions in their respective countries. They had among the highest GDP growth rates and lowest rates of unemployment in the 1970s and 1980s. But it is not clear whether they are coping better than other regions with the current recession in Europe.[4]

One of the main points made in the industrial district literature is that this performance was achieved by taking the "high road" to competitiveness (Sengenberger and Pyke 1992). This means seeking to compete by innovating, that is, adopting new technologies, developing new or better products and reacting more speedily to market changes. Investing in the labor force is seen as the key to achieving this. In contrast, the "low road" means trying to compete on the basis of low wages and flouting labor standards.

Institutions are seen as essential in steering enterprises toward the high road. This is explicit in Piore and Sabel (1984) who suggest that local institutions in the Third Italy have a double role: they ensure that standards in remuneration and use of labor are obeyed and that they provide assistance through vocational training, technology centers and the like.

The strongest statement on the role of institutions in helping industry to take the high road can probably be found in Herrigel's analysis of the case of Baden-Württemberg:

> My argument is that the success of Baden-Württemberg firms is based on a system that socialises risk across a broad array of public and private institutions. Small firms do not have to bear the entire burden of: (a) developing new technologies; (b) finding new markets; (c) training skilled engineers and workers; or (d) raising capital. Many of the costs of specialization are shared by or embedded in a thick network of institutions… (Herrigel 1988, p. 2).

---

sharing many features with the other regions, its inter-firm division of labor is less deep and in this respect its inclusion as an industrial district can be questioned.

[3]The evidence is scattered over many references used in the remainder of this paper.

[4]For example there seems to be a relative slowdown of economic performance in the Third Italy (Bianchi 1992) and in Baden-Württemberg (*Wirtschaftswoche*, January 15, 1993). Cooke and Morgan (1993) call them "growth regions under duress."

This is a particularly useful quote because it recognizes explicitly that taking the high road requires investments and involves risks. As will be seen in the course of this paper, however, there is little empirical evidence on how institutions have influenced investment decisions or the perceptions of risk by the entrepreneur.

Before investigating the institutions in detail, it is worth recalling that the purpose of this paper is to draw lessons for LDCs from the four above mentioned regions. This calls for a brief reflection on the limits of transferability. One of the key features of industrialization in all four regions is that it has deep social roots, in particular a common history of small-scale agriculture, a strong tradition of self-employment, and a socio-cultural identity which facilitates trust and reciprocity between local firms (Illeris 1986; Canullo 1990; Colletis et al. 1990). Such constellations can also be found in some LDCs. Each of the regions considered, however, also has its own very specific historical features. For example, in the case of the Third Italy, Trigilia (1989, 1990) stresses that the local Communist and Catholic subcultures were essential to the emergence and growth of the industrial districts and of the local institutions. Do such historical specificities render the question of replicability absurd? Our answer is a simple one: history matters, but it is equally important not to become (mentally) imprisoned by history. If one is not concerned with replications based on blueprints but with applications of selective lessons, then some of the experiences reviewed in this paper are at least worth considering.[5]

8.3 The Provision of Credit

As stated above, our main objective is to explore what policy lessons can be derived for developing countries from the European experience of industrial districts. A later section shows that there is very little that this literature provides at the macro level (Sect. 8.8), but at the meso and micro level there is more to learn; reviewing the experiences at this level is what constitutes the core of the paper. This section focuses on the role of financial institutions in the four regions; followed by a review of experiences in training (Sect. 8.4), real services (Sect. 8.5) and wage negotiation (Sect. 8.6).

As regards finance for small-scale industry in LDCs, the two main results that can be found in the literature are:

- small enterprises rely overwhelmingly on savings of the owner or his/her family and
- access to credit is of key importance.

At first sight this seems a contradiction but closer inspection tends to show that credit is indeed a problem; not for all small enterprises but for those who seek to expand or innovate. Since our interest in the small-firm industrial districts of Europe

[5] For a useful discussion on the replicability of industrial districts see Zeitlin (1992).

is fuelled precisely by their apparent ability to grow and innovate it is important to know more about access to credit in these cases.

The main finding that emerges from our review is that credit tended to be available and local banks played a major role in providing that credit. By local banks we mean institutions which have grown primarily from collecting savings of local people and lending to local entrepreneurs. While such banks cannot isolate themselves from national or international capital markets their expansion is not geared by national or international strategies but by local and regional considerations. Such local banks, however, were not the only providers of credit and we also seek to draw lessons from the experience of other financial institutions. In what follows we deal with the four regions one by one.

(a) *Third Italy*

In his conceptualization of the industrial district, Becattini (1990, p. 47) stresses the relevance of local credit provision or what he calls the "theory of the local bank."

> The local bank is an organism, born and bred in the district, that is very closely linked with local entrepreneurs (and often with other local social and political lobbies) and deeply involved in local life, which it knows in detail, and to which it gives direction to a considerable extent.

A local bank has the advantage that it can pay more attention to the personal qualities of the applicant and the prospects of his/her investment project. According to Signorini (1992), however, there are also drawbacks associated to it. The author mentions the case of the *Cassa di Risparmi e Depositi di Prato*, a typical example of a local bank, which experienced a serious bad-loan crisis in 1987. According to Signorini, the bank's local roots can sometimes result in overlending: "In districts, it appears, banks are 'generous' in the sense that they regard as normal a higher degree of leverage than elsewhere" (Signorini 1992, p.24). In regard to the cost of credit, Signorini indicates that interest rates charged by local banks to district firms are not significantly different than elsewhere. He therefore concludes, "that the 'local bank' effect may have more to do with the quantity of credit than with its price" (p. 21). In this sense, the role of local banks in facilitating access to credit is confirmed.

Another local credit initiative worth mentioning are the Loan Guarantee Consortia of Modena in the Emilia-Romagna region (Brusco and Righi 1989; Murray et al. 1989; Murray 1991; Best 1990). One of the local consortia includes 3500 small and medium-sized firms who provide mutual credit guarantees. Each firm pays a membership fee which makes up a loan guarantee fund which is supplemented with contributions from the municipal, regional and national governments. Applications are vetted by specialized subcommittees and the consortium's board, which is composed of local entrepreneurs and a small staff. If accepted, the application is sent to a commercial bank with a partial guarantee (from 50 % upward) for the loan.

This particularly helped small firms to gain access to loans for investment and working capital, and it did so on the basis of the strength of their projects and community standing and not just on traditional collateral. Failure rates were minimal with repayment records far superior to similar loans in the Italian banking sector as a whole.[6] There are other such loan consortia in Modena and – according to G. Garofoli (personal communication, November 1992) – they are common in many parts of Italy, not only in industrial districts. Unfortunately no studies seem to be available which investigate why and how local loan consortia became particularly important in industrial districts and how they affected the perceptions of risk by banks and borrowers. More generally, given the paradigmatic standing of the Third Italy in the industrial district debate, the role of financial institutions is explored very little.[7]

(b) *Baden-Württemberg*

The German case lends further importance to the role of the local bank in lending to small- and medium-scale industry. In addition, there are self-help and government institutions providing credit specifically for innovation projects.

Baden-Württemberg has a strong local and often cooperative banking system. Of particular importance are the municipal banks (the Sparkassen) and the cooperative banks (the Kreditgenossenschaften, or Volks- or Raiffeisenbanken). They account for most lending to the so-called Mittelstand – the small- and medium-sized firms. The strength of both types of bank appears to owe much to local knowledge and reciprocal obligations.

> The boards of directors of the cooperative banks are typically comprised of the owners or directors of the leading firms in the district; and since the firms are thus, in effect, indebted to each other, they form a kind of consortium. Aside from permitting close reciprocal social control… the system guarantees that judgements regarding the granting of credit or the need to fuse distressed firms will be made by persons long familiar with the companies and personalities concerned, and, moreover, who are dedicated to advancing the interests of the local community (Sabel et al. 1989, p. 395).

Even if this quote overrates the prevalence of the communal interest there is little doubt about the important role of the municipal and cooperative banks in lending to local small- and medium-scale industry. In contrast, the Frankfurt-based national and international banks have sometimes found it difficult to penetrate this local banking market. There are indications that their share of local bank business decreased over recent decades (Sabel et al. 1989). We should, however, add that there does not seem to be a thorough study focusing on the role of the local banks in the otherwise well-researched Baden-Württemberg economy.

While commercial banks are the main source of credit in Baden-Württemberg, mention must be made of other credit institutions which seek to foster innovation

---

[6] According to Brusco, "… the person who receives a loan from the cooperative will stay up at night thinking of ways of repaying his loan; whereas the person who receives a bank loan will stay up at night thinking of ways of not repaying his loan" (1985, p. 25).

[7] Zacchia (1984) suggests that low-cost credit made available to small- and medium-scale industry through regional banks, was relatively easy to obtain in Italy in the 1960s and first half of the 1970s, but the data are not sufficiently disaggregated to analyze the uptake in the industrial districts of the Third Italy.

in local industry. Self-help institutions facilitate access to finance for innovative ventures. Where commercial banks find that loans for technical innovations are too risky, producers can lean on the Bürgschaftsbank Baden-Württemberg. This bank was set up by the chambers of industry and commerce and other self-help institutions to provide credit guarantees. Such guarantees are available for up to 80 % of a loan, at an annual 1 % commission and for up to 23 years. Since the upper limit is DM 1 million it is of relevance mainly to small or medium enterprises. The same applies to another financial self-help institution, the Mittelständische Beteiligungsgesellscheft. It makes available venture capital of up to DM 300,000 provided that at least 25 % of the total investment is the entrepreneur's own capital.[8]

Finally, there is the Landeskreditbank (LKB), a public institution which is in charge of the regional government's low-cost credit programmes for innovating firms. The LKB provides financial support for entrepreneurs who:

- develop new products or processes;
- put new techniques into practice;
- set up new technology intensive enterprises.

The support consists primarily of subsidised credit.[9] During 1984–1988 over 2600 enterprises benefited from these programs, mostly for the second purpose, resulting in public expenditure amounting to DM 214 million (Becher and Weibert 1990). This is the only case of institutional support for which we found an effectiveness study. According to Becher et al. (1989–1990), over half of the enterprises benefiting from such support would have innovated anyway, but they intensified or speeded up the process because of the support; one-quarter of beneficiaries made no changes to what had been planned. Only one-sixth of the benefiting enterprises started innovation projects which would not have seen the light of day without support.

The main conclusion which can be derived from this German case is that small- and medium-scale industry in Baden-Württemberg is able to obtain credit from a variety of sources, local commercial banks, self-help credit institutions and the regional government. It is hard to judge from available accounts whether such choice also existed in the other three regions considered in this paper.

(c) *West Jutland*

Kristensen (1992, p.149) describes the importance of small local savings banks during the setting up of business in the district of Salling (West Jutland):

> … many furniture makers have traditionally used skills as carpenters and cabinet-makers to start up in the building and construction industry during boom periods… In such initial

---

[8] In addition, this organization acts as a conduit for venture capital of up to DM 1 million from federal sources.

[9] The Steinbeis Foundation, which can draw on extensive sector-specific expertise, participates in the assessment of applications. The loans are channeled to the firms through their local commercial banks whose role is thus further heightened.

periods the small local savings banks have been able to use their detailed local knowledge as a basis for providing loans for the creation of new building and construction businesses.

In this case, "the theory of the local bank" is again at work. More so perhaps in Jutland because local savings banks go far back into history: "...farmers had set up their own local savings banks in the mid-19th century to gain independence from the merchants of larger towns..." (Kristensen 1992, p. 137). For the other districts he analyzes (Herning and Ikast), he reports that a new regional bank was created from the fusion of small local banks. The new bank would be in a better position to provide long-term finance for local small- and medium-sized enterprises. Following Kristensen's account, the local anchorage of the regional bank was so strong that "the population of the area proved itself ready to defend the regional bank from incorporation into one of the dominant Copenhagen banking groups" (p.149).

(d) *South-West Flanders*

Apart from the Bank van Roeselare, there has been no indigenous bank that has survived until today in the region. Although the Bank van Roeselare has been growing steadily in recent years, it probably did not play a more important role than the national banks in the development of the region during the last two decades.

As the local economy grew, however, so did the Bank van Roeselare. It remains a local bank with about 75 agencies and has been playing a growing role in South-West Flanders in recent years. The reasons seem to be encapsulated in the "theory of the local bank" mentioned above.[10] Like almost all firms in the region, the bank has sought to grow without compromising its independence: the bank has not involved itself in risky operations abroad, for example; and it has kept a fairly local profile in its operations. In conclusion, while the Bank van Roeselare cannot be credited with a major role in laying the foundations of the regional growth, it is a direct product of the local development and, in turn, has become an important lender to local industry.

(e) *Conclusion*

On the basis of the evidence available to us it is hard to draw firm conclusions on the provision of credit. It is true that in the industrial districts reviewed self-finance, especially through the family, plays an important role[11] but this can hardly explain the absence of more detailed studies on credit provision.

---

[10] Like the case of the cooperative banks in Baden-Württemberg, South-West Flemish industrialists are members of the board of the Bank van Roeselare (Martens 1990). It is interesting to note that the bank is also involved in an important informal activity. It holds two file-card boxes, one with details of entrepreneurs who wish to sell their business, the other with details of those entrepreneurs interested in acquiring a new business. By doing so, the bank has created a network where information circulates by word of mouth.

[11] In the South-West Flemish case, survey results indicate that 76 % of entrepreneurs financed the growth of their business mainly by their own means. A comparable figure for the rest of Belgium was 65 %. Other survey results in South-West Flanders indicate that over 90 % relied entirely on family capital when they started their business (Musyck 1993).

For those seeking to draw lessons from the limited information available two aspects deserve most attention: the importance of the local bank and of self-help in credit provision and guarantees. So as to fully appreciate their significance it is worth recalling two principles which affect the provision of loans and their repayment: trust and reciprocity. The very word credit is derived from the Latin verb *credere* – to believe or to trust. Local banks have a particular advantage in assessing where to put their trust through their knowledge of the entrepreneurs, the locality and sometimes also the sector. The pressure to repay is influenced by reciprocity. Mechanisms for grouping lenders and borrowers – through financial guarantee consortia or credit cooperatives – increase the sense of mutual obligation and reduce the risk of default (Murray 1991).

What are the implications for lending to small-scale industry in LDCs? Although, the above conclusions do not break new ground, there is in fact a large body of literature on credit to small- and medium-sized enterprises in LDCs (see for example Levitsky 1986 and Germidis et al. 1991). The experience of European industrial districts tends to reinforce the conclusions derived from this body of literature. The emphasis on local credit institutions and self-help initiatives does, however, create a dilemma for international development and finance agencies which seek to support small-scale industry in LDCs (and more recently also in Eastern Europe). They need local intermediaries to disburse their funds. State development banks do not have the branch network to reach local industry (outside main cities). Large commercial banks may have the network but their local branches often take the concerns of national headquarters more seriously than those of the local economy; as a result they are often passive banks, *vis-à-vis* local small industry, relying merely on standardized assessment and loan procedures and on the existence of collateral. Identifying and helping to build up local credit institutions is a slow and difficult process.[12] Still, they are likely to be the most effective intermediaries; effective in lending to small enterprises at a low default rate, but not effective in solving the immediate "disbursement problem" of foreign donors.

8.4 Training

Of all support measures for small industry in LDCs, managerial and technical training has been the most widely used. The reason is straightforward: providing training is easier than most other measures. It is certainly easier than changing the context in which small enterprises operate. Indeed, training can have an ideological function in that the obstacles are seen in the people who run the enterprises rather than in the (often hostile) environment in which they operate. This is not to argue against

[12] The difficulty of using or creating local financial institutions for the purpose of distributing funds on behalf of donor agencies is underlined by Canullo (1990) who suggests that in Southern Italy it has reinforced the existing clientèle system.

training but against making it the all-out focus and divorcing it from other measures. This is, however, not the place to review the LDC experience.[13]

The purpose of this section is to ask what lessons (if any) the small-firm industrial districts of Europe provide on the importance, form and organization of training. The general finding is that proactive measures in investing in human resources are a general feature of the successful industrial districts. Key features of the training programs are that they are very practically orientated and codetermined by the private sector. In other words, private local firms and their associations play a major role in designing the content, in carrying out, and in monitoring the training.

(a) *Third Italy*

In the Italian case, the problem of training has probably been best analyzed by Capecchi (1987) in a paper especially dedicated to this issue. He declares that the existence of technical schools is the most important point in explaining the development of flexible specialization in the mechanical engineering industry of Emilia-Romagna. The author indicates that the region is able to coordinate the activities of the organizations which administer professional training; these organizations can be part of the public sector (municipality) or the private sector (unions, artisans associations, professional organizations, etc.). The author also underlines the different types of training available in the Emilia-Romagna region. They include training for employees with low or higher levels of formal education, but also include schemes aimed at entrepreneurs or would-be entrepreneurs. The main advantage of this regional structure of educational and training services lies in the fact that coordinated solutions can be found for local problems. Capecchi insists on this flexible character of the provision of education and training which draws on the resources of various public and private institutions but is geared to the needs of local industry.

It is hard to tell from the available literature if education and training played an equally important role in other sectors and regions in Italy. Roberta Rabellotti (personal communication, September 1992) provided us with further examples of training institutions in industrial districts. Similarly G. Garofoli (1992) confirmed that there are many useful training schemes and that *they are run in conjunction with the private sector*. Garofoli (1992) emphasizes, however, that this came about in a rather twisted way. In the 1970s, the authority for training was shifted from the national to the regional government. Apparently this provoked the disappearance of many municipal-sector specific technical schools, while professional training schemes at the regional level became overly standardized resulting in a mismatch between what was offered and what was needed. During the 1980s, local agents tried to overcome the gap between training needs at municipal level and the inadequate public training supply of regional institutions. New local schemes based on the resources of public institutions, employers' associations and private firms were introduced in several Italian industrial districts. Garofoli (1992) concludes that the emergence of these training schemes confirms the local level as the most appropriate

---

[13] On the discussion of training for small-scale industry in LDCs see, for example, Boehm and Kappel (1990); Fluitman (1989).

level for the provision of training, and the important role of the private sector in coregulating and cofinancing these schemes (personal communication, November 1992).

(b) *West Jutland*

In his work on West Jutland, Kristensen (1992) examined the role of regional training schools in two industrial districts, one specializing in knitwear, the other in furniture. By drawing on the examples of the Herning Textile School and Skive School for Cabinet Making, Kristensen stresses that the presence of such schools has played an important role in the development of local industry. In both Herning and Skive the localities had the ability "to transform central institutions into locally oriented systems" (1992, p. 165). The point the author makes is that the centrally funded education institution is controlled in such a way that it serves the needs of the local economy.

> Herning was able to have the school relocated (even though Herning had yet to become the main centre of the garment industry), thus providing a new institutional framework for their own educational needs. Since then, every educational reform and every new programme to advance knowledge on the new technologies has been skillfully exploited to develop the school to serve the needs of local enterprises (Kristensen 1992, p. 165).

Kristensesn stresses that the orientation of the schools toward the needs of local industry was orchestrated by local powers, notably the employers association and unions. For example, in Herning, which has been successful in establishing a number of different education and training institutions, the director of the chamber of commerce and industry has moved away from a strategy of simply making occasional use of new opportunities toward a more purposeful approach to increase educational choice. School leaders meet under his chairmanship to "discuss plans or possibilities for new initiatives, courses or subjects, so that they can work together instead of competing for students, thereby maximising the region's ability to acquire support from government grants" (Kristensen 1992, p. 166). The local provision of education and training adapted to the needs of the industry helps to maintain the social and family network on which the industrial district is based. The fostering of a regional concentration of specialized skills and the growth of local industry seem to reinforce each other.

(c) *South-West Flanders*

In South-West Flanders there is also a great emphasis on vocational training. As shown by aggregate statistical data in Musyck (1993), the proportion of students following technical and vocational education is higher in South-West Flanders than in the rest of the country. At the same time, the number of university students in South-West Flanders remains relatively low compared with Belgium. Practical rather than academic know-how is preferred in the region. In addition to the traditional vocational and technical schools, the Vormingsinstituut voor KMO (training institute for small- and medium-size enterprises) plays a key role. This institute was first created in the region (in 1960) and later copied elsewhere in the country. The advantage of the institute over traditional vocational schools is that it promotes permanent education by providing training for new and existing entrepreneurs. Permanent education means that young people can start learning a job under an apprenticeship scheme; later they can take up training courses to become entrepreneurs; and finally they have the opportunity to update their know-how regularly by following proficiency courses on technical and managerial issues. These three components of the institute's training program are worth explaining in more detail.

The apprenticeship program is open to students from the age of 15. Students work four days a week in a firm and attend the institute on the fifth day. The entrepreneurs' training is the most important program on offer by the Vormingsinstituut voor KMO. The scheme is designed for people with professional experience who wish to acquire the necessary qualifications to start their own business. The course is spread over two to three years with between four and eight hours tuition per week, normally during evenings and Saturdays. The third program is aimed at established entrepreneurs or managers. The aim is to update know-how on managerial and technical issues through seminars and evening classes. Teaching is based on lecturing by specialists and exchange of know-how between participants. Overall, over 37,000 participants were enrolled in the program of the Vormingsinstituut of West Flanders in 1990–1991. The fastest growing courses were those for new and existing entrepreneurs. Comparisons between various regions in Belgium suggest that South-West Flanders has the highest teaching intensity in such vocational courses (Musyck 1993).

An essential characteristic of the Vormingsinstituut is that it is close to the local industrial community. This is partly ensured by the financing, 50 % of which comes from the private sector. Local industry is also represented on the board of directors of the institute. The program content is usually determined in close cooperation with local entrepreneurs, some of whom participate in the teaching itself. While a definite assessment of the relative importance of the Vormingsinstituut is hard to undertake, it is revealing that the number of courses and students has increased steadily over the last three decades in South-West Flanders (Musyck 1993).

(d) *Baden-Württemberg*

The case of Baden-Württemberg is similar to that of South-West Flanders in that the local education and training system is geared toward the needs of local industry and that the private sector plays an important role in financing and organizing the training. There are, however, two differences. One is that Baden-Württemberg has probably a longer tradition than South-West Flanders in providing such education and training, and second, that the emphasis on the applied and the practical has not occurred at the expense of academic institutions and basic research. The region boasts a high number of universities and research institutes (Kohler 1987).

For the purpose of this paper other institutions are of more importance. At the level of higher education mention must be made of the Fachhochschulen (polytechnics) since their curricula are closely linked to the needs of local industry. These schools are of particular relevance for those aiming for careers as engineers or managers in the specialized local enterprises. For the majority of workers the vocational training colleges (Berufsschulen) are of greater importance. They cater for apprentices who work three days a week in a local firm and spend two days at college. This is the well-known German dual system of vocational training. The chambers of industry and commerce play a key role in this dual training system particularly in the design and supervision of courses and in the examination of apprentices.

There is, however, a recognition that this dual system is insufficient to prepare workers for the rapidly changing skill requirements which come with the adoption of new technologies and organizational methods. Professional and industrial associations as well as chambers of industry and crafts have therefore created, since the mid-1970s, a number of training and technology centers. Their function is to organize seminars and courses for retraining or updating of know-how. Some of these courses are combined with examinations and the award of certificates which give formal recognition to the mastering of technical and managerial skills. The above institutions and courses both cater to the needs of local industry but they are not specifically geared to the needs of small industry. As regards small-scale industry, the most important institutions are the craft chambers (Handwerkskammern) and their branch specific divisions (Innungen). They preside over training for all skill levels, from the apprentice to the Meister (Master Craftsman who employs apprentices) (Boelcke 1987).

This system of education and training has a long tradition in Baden-Württemberg and is well developed. It has to be said, however, that the same intermediary institutions are also in charge of industrial training in other parts of Germany, including those regions which are economically less successful. If there is a difference it does not lie in the institutional structure but more likely in the especially close collaboration between education and training institutes and local enterprises in Baden-Württemberg (Schmitz 1992).

(e) *Conclusion*

This section has shown some of the distinctive characteristics of the training facilities offered in the four studied regions. To sum up, in all four regions an active policy of training is pursued for both workers and entrepreneurs. The private sector plays a major role in regulating the training schemes, influencing their content and monitoring them. It seems that in this way a close match is achieved between what is taught and what local enterprise needs.

Given that local industry in the four regions had above average growth rates in the 1970s and 1980s and is internationally competitive, it is tempting to conclude that the training systems discussed above were an essential causal factor in this success. The reader needs to be reminded, however, that this section had to be based primarily on descriptions of the training systems and that there is little or no material on their effectiveness.

Keeping in mind these words of caution, what lessons can be derived for LDCs? This is not to ask for blueprints which can be exported; such attempts rarely work. German aid agencies, for example, have found that introducing the German dual apprenticeship training with all its regulations in LDCs does not make for a cost-effective and sustainable training system (Boehm and Kappel 1990). There is, however, a principle which comes out of the reviewed experiences and which seems worth adhering to in other countries. The principle is that of involving the private sector itself in regulating and cofinancing the training. This helps to ensure that the formal training is relevant, up-to-date and cost effective. Adopting the above principle may not always be possible. Where industry is dispersed it is much more difficult to achieve than where industry clusters, that is, where it is geographically and sectorally concentrated. Clustering facilitates the emergence of private sector institutions (e.g., associations or chambers) and their involvement in formal training programs.

8.5 The Provision of Real Services

Among the support measures for small-scale industry the two most traditional and widely practiced ones are credit and training, both of which have been discussed above. In the European industrial district debate there is, however, another group of measures which has attracted much more attention: the provision of real services. What is meant by this? According to Brusco (1992),

> …the provision of real services involves supplying companies, in return for payment, with those goods or services that they require instead of giving them the money that they need to go out and buy these goods or services on the market (p.187).

Real services can be wide ranging. To take some of the author's examples, they can include the translation of tenders advertised in foreign countries, the provision of information regarding the technical standards enforced by law in various foreign countries for a set of products, or the provision of testing facilities for raw material used in the production (testing the quality of steel or silk for example). Selling real services does not only mean providing information or services at a cost:

> The need for information is there but the awareness of this need is not. To sell information really means getting involved in the process of making that awareness grow, which is similar in many ways to a process of technology transfer (Brusco 1992, p. 189).

In this respect, real services can also be considered as a kind of innovation policy. The purpose of this section is to explore how important the provision of real services was in our four European regions and who should provide such services.

(a) *Third Italy*

Real services in the Third Italy can be best illustrated with the example of CITER (Centro Informazione Tessile Emilia- Romagna) described by Brusco and Righi (1989). CITER is located in Modena, and operates in the knitwear field. The center provides four major services. First, it edits a half-yearly periodic report on market trends. This report is a compilation of all available information on import and export flows, on production, on the evolution of the industry in other countries, and various other issues dealing with the activity of the sector at home and abroad. The second task of CITER is to inform the artisans about the prices and nature of yarns which are available on the market. Third, CITER informs its members on the availability of equipment, by preparing technical notes on the machines used in the sector and by collecting and making all relevant literature available to its members.[14] Finally, a major role of CITER is to inform the local business community about the fashion trends. Because of its close relationship with the large department stores, CITER can obtain privileged information on the purchasing trend of various fashion lines offered on the market. It also collects data on the evolution of tastes, values and motivations of the consumer, and purchases the expensive catalogues of fashion institutes around the globe. To summarize, the most important task of CITER is the collection, analysis and distribution of all information that is relevant for the local business community. It is important to note that CITER was initially financed with public funds when it was created in 1980, but that a decade later, only 30 % of the total budget is supported by government funds. CITER now depends directly on member companies, either in the form of subscriptions or as payment for specific services (Pyke 1992a). The experience of CITER is interesting because the organization also sold its services to other textile areas. In a sense this opens new opportunities for interregional cooperation among local productive systems. For developing countries, this could also mean that a transfer of knowledge is possible via this path.

The regional development agency of Emilia-Romagna, ERVET in Bologna, "lies at the heart of a 'service system' which involves dedicated sectoral service centres" such as the CITER centre described above, but also CERCAL (shoes), QUASCO (building industry) and CESMA (farm machinery). In addition, EVRET is involved in four service centers which operate "transversally" or "laterally," i.e. providing services to different sectors: SVEX (export promotion), RESFOR (promotion of subcontracting in metal industry), CERMET (quality upgrading) and ASTER (technology development). Other examples of real services include: Centro Servizi (Pisa) which serves the footwear and leather industry by offering a data bank on machinery, markets, clients and other information relevant to the sector; TECNOTEX in the town of Biella which offers professional training, research and technological experimentation for the textile industry; and the Comitato Servizio Tondenze Moda in Empoli which provides professional training and information on fashion trends (Murray 1991; Pyke 1992a). The experience of the Emilia-Romagna region for real services is probably the most widely publicized one. Interesting cases also exist, however, in other Italian industrial districts (see Garofoli 1991, chapter 6).

The mere existence of such services does not mean that they function well or are effective, although this is often implied in the literature (for instance Pyke 1992a;

[14]An experiment is currently being conducted with the collaboration of Enea (a public agency operating in the technology diffusion area). The aim of the project is the creation of an image data bank for the textile clothing industry. The system is based on a personal computer, a video disk unit and a CAD system. According to Camagni and Rabellotti (1992), this user-friendly "off-the-shelf" technology is offered at a competitive price, and can therefore also be used by small-and medium-sized enterprises.

Murray et al. 1989; Best 1990). The only assessment of real services that could be found was that of the above described CITER by Brusco and Righi (1989); they conclude

> ...everything seems to indicate that its role has been a determining element in moving the sector towards the more sophisticated segments of the market, where quality is as important as price, or even more important, and where the danger of NIC competition is less worrisome (p.419).

The authors underline the success by referring to the increase in the number of members, the drop in the annual contribution from local authorities (i.e. CITER becomes self-sufficient), and finally, the fact that other producer associations have asked CITER to repeat for their members the reports on market and fashion trends.[15]

(b) *Baden-Württemberg*

In Baden-Württemberg the provision of real services is most pronounced in technology transfer. Support for the provision of technology services was particularly strong during the 1980s. This is significant because internationally the agenda of economic policy making in the 1980s was set by the neoliberals. In a neoliberal world, market forces can be relied upon to maximize innovations and solve issues of technology transfer. The startling success stories of rapid innovation and industrial growth in Japan, the Republic of Korea and Taiwan contradicted this view (White 1988), yet the neoliberal agenda remained very influential throughout the 1980s. In Germany, regional governments took the lead in shaking off the simplistic neoliberal prescription for innovation. The government of Lothar Späth, Prime Minister of Baden-Württemberg, was in the vanguard of making innovation policy a central concern for regional government. There was a clear recognition at the regional government level that innovation is costly and risky (Späth 1985, 1987).

Indeed, there are several institutions which provide or arrange advice at various stages of searching for or introducing new processes and products. The key actor is the Steinbeis Foundation which has the multiple task of working on technology policies strategically, acting as a center which advises entrepreneurs who can help them, and providing specialized assistance itself through its technology transfer centers located throughout the region. It is the latter which fall most squarely under the heading of provision of real services. Such services are provided by over 100 Steinbeis Transfer Centers. The operating costs for these services are almost totally covered by the fees charged by the centers.

There is a powerful ethos that the Foundation and its individual Transfer Centers should be self-financing: 95 % of the Foundation's overall budget is earned by selling services (Pyke 1992b). A limited subsidy is received from the state government for opening new Transfer Centers and buying initial equipment. Once functioning, 7 % of fees received by each Transfer Center is paid to the Steinbeis Foundation to cover central administration costs (Cooke and Morgan 1990).

[15] In another paper, Brusco (1989) asks how an assessment can be made of the effectiveness of public money involved in the provision of real services. Although the possible costs and benefits are identified, it is not an empirical evaluation of the actual effectiveness of real service centres.

Some of these centers are attached to Fachhochschulen (polytechnics) which themselves are expected to work closely with local enterprises and to assist with technical and related managerial problems. Thus, there exists a decentralized net of specialized technology support services. Industry contributes in varying degrees to the financing and organization of these services. This also applies to the 10 technology parks established in the region.

An assessment of these centers which specialize in the transfer of technology to local small- and medium-size industry is difficult and probably premature. Most of them only started operating in the course of the 1980s. All we can do at this stage is to offer some reflections on the provision of such real services and their potential (in)significance.

Because of the seeming success of industry in Baden-Württemberg to cope with the challenge of rapid technical change, a number of other Länders copied measures adopted by the regional government of Baden-Württemberg. But the fact that Baden-Württemberg was a pace-setter in such technology policy neither proves that it is better at executing it nor that such provision of real services matters.[16] An assessment of the Steinbeis centers would need to investigate how they have affected the entrepreneur's perception of risk and, as a result, how effective have they been in bridging the gap between available and applied technology. Such assessments could not be found. One could, however, plausibly argue that the existence of such centers reduces the cost of searching for advice and makes it more likely that possibilities of product and process innovation are explored. The fact that the centers specialize in specific types of technology and that they have been able to self-finance themselves lends support to this argument.

While the question of the effectiveness of real services for technology transfer remains open, there are some principles that deserve attention and are highlighted by the Baden-Württemberg experience:

(i) There was a recognition that the government required staff that could work on technology strategically, develop new practical approaches and coordinate the work of relevant institutions. It is interesting that this strategic role was not entrusted to an existing government department, let alone a new department created for this purpose, but to an institution which is not part of the civil service: the Steinbeis Foundation.[17] While working directly for the government, and financed partially by government, constitutionally it is a non-government organization which reports to a *Kuratorium* consisting of representatives of craft, trade and industry, the scientific community, political parties and regional administration. The point to be made is that the fostering of innovation requires an approach to policy making which combines the capacity to think and act

[16] For a more detailed examination of regional technology policy in Baden-Württemberg, see Schmitz (1992).

[17] The Landesgewerbeamt used to play an important role in Baden-Württemberg's regional innovation policy (Reuss 1986) but its functions in this respect are now largely carried out by the Steinbeis Foundation.

strategically but works at the same time through a decentralized institution close to the enterprise.

(ii) In Baden-Württemberg, government support has traditionally been linked to self-help. It was a principle of the pioneer Ferdinand Steinbeis last century and remains the principle in current technology support services (Kohler 1987; Maier 1987), and also in the provision of credit and training (see previous section). The form and extent to which industry, trade and craft contribute varies, but their active participation is in most cases a precondition for government support.

(iii) Governmental, semi-governmental and independent institutions frequently offer similar services. This could be interpreted as undesirable overlap and duplication. This is not our view – to start with there is complementarity and collaboration between these institutions as stressed in official publications (MWMT 1990). There is, however, also rivalry and competition, both between institutions and with private sector. For technology support services, for example, Cooke and Morgan (1990) have pointed to the tensions between the chambers of industry and commerce, the private consultancy industry and the Steinbeis transfer centres. Not surprisingly, the competing agents see this as a problem. Such competition could, however, be seen as a strength of Baden-Württemberg's institutional infrastructure. It gives the user a choice and makes the supplying institutions and enterprises more prone to cater for the needs of local industry and to do so effectively.

In this section on Baden-Württemberg we concentrated on the provision of real services in the area of technology transfer. This is easily the most widely provided and therefore the most interesting real service provided in this region. It is not, however, the only one. It is worth mentioning that the provision of real services extends to overseas marketing. The Foreign Trade Foundation (Stiftung Aussenwirtschaft) is an institution created jointly by the chambers of industry and commerce, industrial associations and regional government. The Foundation's main task is to facilitate exports of small- and medium-sized enterprises. In view of the high export intensity of the region's industry (for example, in 1988 46 % of machine tools were exported) the Foreign Trade Foundation seems an important initiative but studies of its effectiveness are not available.

Another interesting example of the provision of a real service is the establishment of a quality control center in the Heuberg region which specializes in the production of metal tools and parts for various local industries. Semlinger (1991) studied in detail how this quality center emerged as a result of joint action between local small metal-working firms and local government. Again, however, it is too soon to assess the relative importance and effectiveness of this center.

(c) *South-West Flanders*

In South-West Flanders the provision of real services is more limited. To our knowledge there are no technology transfer centers of the kind prominent in Baden-Württemberg. There is, however, a Center for Quality Control (Centrum voor

Kwaliteitszorg) which is an offshoot of the Vormingsinstituut voor KMO discussed earlier. The center is a self-help institution created in 1971 by local entrepreneurs. It is financed by membership fees and income from services supplied to industry.

(d) *West Jutland*

In accounts of the industrial districts of West Jutland the provision of real services does not figure prominently. Kristensen (1992) merely mentions the existence of the Clothing Technological Institute in the Herning district. This institute is involved in consultancy for local firms, the experimentation of new products and processes and advice for the local textile schools on courses and training programs. We learned from Sven Illeris (personal communication, September 1992) that the institute was set up by the textile sector's industrial organization, which is dominated by Herning-Ikast firms. The institute has recently become a branch of the Danish Technological Institute, which is a non-profit-making organization for technical development and advice.[18] Central Government grants account for an insignificant share of the budget of the institute.

Another real service is the establishment of exhibition and congress facilities in Herning. These facilities are used for various different occasions, the main being textile fairs, which are among the largest in Northern Europe (Illeris 1992). Forty-nine percent of the fair and congress facilities are owned by the municipality, which quite often subsidizes activities that take place on the premises. According to a recent survey carried out by the Herning municipality, private sector firms rank the venue amongst the most appreciated public facilities (S. Illeris, personal communication, September 1992). Pedersen (1986) and Hansen (1991) warn us, however, not to overrate the importance of institutions in providing producer services in West Jutland. Their research shows that real services supplied by private firms are more significant.

(e) *Conclusion*

As in previous sections, only a very patchy picture emerges on the provision of public real services in the European regions considered. It is hard to tell whether this patchiness arises because such services play a minor role or because they were not studied. Nevertheless, some tentative conclusions can be drawn. In doing so we keep in mind our guide question of what policy lessons can be derived from the European experience for institutional support to small-scale industry elsewhere, especially in developing countries.

The crucial lesson is that real services, to the extent that their relevance could be ascertained, were rarely provided by the public sector itself. It seems that the successful interventions were carried out by private sector institutions or were joint private/public sector initiatives. Public bodies in themselves can become the catalyst in support programs for small-scale industry or can make important financial and infrastructural contributions, but on their own can rarely carry or operate such

[18] For details on the activities of this institute, particularly its network program in various parts of Denmark, see Pyke (1992c).

schemes. Among the main reasons are expertise and finance. A great deal of sector and sometimes even product-specific expertise is required for an effective delivery of real services. In addition, the financial sustainability of such programs requires that the private sector itself makes a major and generally growing contribution to their existence.

While the effectiveness of real service centers remains underexplored, they have attracted a great deal of attention internationally. Is this attention premature? Probably not. As said above, these centers rely increasingly on self-finance. If they continue to do so, this is probably their best relevance test.

The question then arises as to how LDC institutions can learn from these experiences. Transferring institutional know-how is not easy. It is also costly. This is perhaps an area where donor agencies can help by supporting "learning-by-visiting". This includes financing the preparation of documents and videos and paying the centers and related enterprises for receiving visiting delegations. Such learning by visiting,[19] however, would only be useful if a realistic (i.e. not a rosy) picture is provided of how the centers emerged and how they function.

8.6 The Role of Trade Unions

In a paper which examines institutional support for small-scale industry it may seem unusual to deal with the role of trade unions. One of the main competitive advantages of small firms is often seen in their easy access to cheap labor, especially non-unionized labor. The European industrial district experience does not support this. On the contrary, it seems that the success of these industrial districts was not based on low wages but on innovation and flexibility. Sengenberger and Pyke (1992) present them as examples of the "high road" to competitiveness. The main purpose of this section is to explore the role which trade unions play in making firms embark on the innovation rather than low-wage route.

(a) *Third Italy*

According to Trigilia (1989), unionization has been relatively high in the Third Italy. He attributes this to the political subculture which provided "institutional and identity resources which favored the organization of workers in small-firm districts" (p. 184). This situation was most pronounced in areas in which the Communist Party was strong or traditions of association existed. Trigilia also points out that wage negotiations were held in a peaceful social climate:

> …the existence, in many areas, of deeply rooted, territorial political subcultures favored the growth of unionization, but at the same time it contributed to directing union activity so that

[19]This was practiced, for example, by Robin Murray of IDS. He led an Industrial Strategy Mission to Cyprus (funded by UNIDO/UNDP) which was greatly influenced by the experience of the Third Italy (Murray et al. 1988). As a follow-up of this mission he took a Cypriot delegation (consisting of private and public representatives) to Italy for visits to real service centres and firms.

> it neither hindered the process of economic development nor weakened the local subculture itself (Trigilia 1989, p. 186).

Moreover, the particular social structure of the studied area (low proletarianization, "deep-rooted ties with the traditional institutional and cultural context" (Trigilia 1989, p. 186)) did not favor the development of militant unionism found in the large industrial centers. To conclude,

> ...structural constraints and the characteristics of the working class directed the unions towards a negotiative and localist type of representation ... In general, however, union agreements and activity did not impose rigid constraints on the mobility and flexibility of the work force. In exchange, the unions obtained benefits of a prevalently economic type and a high level of recognition on the part of the entrepreneurs (Trigilia 1989, p. 187).

Best (1990) stresses further the causal connection between unionization and innovation in industry:

> In Modena unions have benefited from strong artisan associations with which they could bargain.
>
> The existence of national associations of artisans and national unions exerts pressure on artisan firms to compete on the basis of innovation and quality as opposed to wages ... Equally important is the pressure that high wages put on artisan companies to adjust productivity upwards rather than the pressure in a competitive wage environment to adjust wages downwards to match low productivity levels.
>
> The pressure for innovation ... is crucial to the long term viability of small firms. In Modena, where wages are about the same in both small and large firms, small firms have to seek means of increasing productivity gains in large firms. In the south where wage discrepancies between small and large firms are substantial, small firms are generally fragmented, slow to innovate, and fit the traditional image of backward enterprise (Best 1990, pp. 221-223).

This strong emphasis on unionization and innovation does not mean all is well for labor in the Third Italy. For instance, Lazerson (1990) shows that the knitwear industry continues to use low-paid, non-registered home workers. F. Murray (1987) suggests that there are considerable differentials in stability of work, wage levels and working conditions, particularly between men and women. The unions themselves draw attention to "intolerable conditions of underpaid labour, breaches of labour contracts, and abnormal forms of labour relations" (Brutti and Calistri 1990, p. 138). All this indicates that there remain gaps in union protection of labor and that sweat shop methods have not entirely disappeared from the Third Italy.

(b) *Baden-Württemberg*

If high wages and labor standards are essential components of the industrial district model, Baden-Württemberg fulfills these criteria probably more so than the Third Italy. Industrial workers enjoy high wages and a short working week. A shortage of skilled workers and low rates of unemployment for unskilled work has enabled trade unions to negotiate high wages and a step-by-step introduction of the 35-hour week.[20] We do not know to what extent the degree of unionization varies

[20] Unlike in the Third Italy, other institutions such as the church, local government and political parties have little influence over wages and labor standards, but it should be mentioned that Lothar

between large and small firms, but the settlements reached apply to workers throughout industry in the region.

Pressure for innovation does not only come from high wages. The most powerful union in the region, IG Metall, has sought to accelerate innovation by arguing for increased investment in training, particularly for new skills. In stressing this forward looking attitude of IG Metall, it is not implied that employer-labor relations have been entirely harmonious. Far from it, in a number of respects these relations have been highly antagonistic, particularly in Baden-Württemberg. Effective strike action and negotiation have made the Baden-Württemberg unions pace-setters in Germany. IG Metall has been in the vanguard of the fight for a shorter working week and higher wages. Thus, "destructive competition" (Sengenberger 1990) by gaining advantages through squeezing wages and lowering labor standards had no chance. This pressure from the unions – made possible by the relative shortage of labor – contributed to the creation of a climate in which enterprises sought to become more competitive through innovation. This is of particular importance in a region which is both a producer and user of new technology.

(c) *West Jutland*

In Denmark, wages and labor conditions are regulated by collective agreements. This situation has evolved gradually throughout this century, but negotiations have become more decentralized in recent years (S. Illeris, personal communication, September 1992). Large and small firms do not receive differential treatment and the rate of unionization in West Jutland is high. This has resulted in a "strong inhibition against organizing production on the basis of cheap labour" (Kristensen 1992, p. 156). The author also claims that,

> Such wage regulation and standard setting could then be at least partly responsible for the prevalence in the industrial districts of competitive strategies aimed at dynamic innovation, quality, and design consciousness, rather than those aimed simply at all-out price and cost minimization (p. 157).

Kristensen also insists on the link between social cohesion of the small communities in West Jutland and the industrial strategies followed, which avoid cutting wage costs. Moreover, the flexible cooperation between workers and managers is also favored by such strategies. He illustrates this with two examples. The first one shows that the local community has counteracted a national policy favoring a widening of the wage gap between blue-collar and white-collar workers. The second example shows how the sense of community and trust among workers and employers was preserved by the new initiative of local entrepreneurs, who managed to increase wages beyond the national limit, while respecting the strict guidelines of the national employer's associations.

(d) *South-West Flanders*

As in Denmark, Belgian unions do not negotiate different pay deals for small and large firms; workers in small firms are entitled to the same wages as their colleagues

---

Späth, conservative Prime Minister of Baden-Württemberg until 1991, consistently argued against low wages (Schmid 1988, p. 31).

in large firms. Negotiations between employers and workers take place at the national level for each sector. Agreements lay out minimum wage conditions, but individual employers are free to offer higher salaries. This is exactly what is currently happening in South-West Flanders where wages tend to be above the minimum wage levels for the sector.

Because in most sectors wages and working conditions have always been negotiated at the national level, South-West Flanders has been affected by the various union policies, in the same way as other regions. For example, the policy on reduction of working hours has been implemented in the same way in South-West Flanders as in the rest of the country.[21] Competing on the basis of low wages has not been on the agenda in South-West Flanders, nor the rest of Belgium. On the contrary, since the early 1970s, Belgium has been renowned for having one of the highest labor costs in the world, with the unions continuing to press for a further reduction in working hours (Eyskens 1980). Overall, it is reasonable to accept that a tradition of strict social policies and labor regulations at the national level has contributed to pushing South-West Flemish entrepreneurs to increase levels of productivity by upgrading the labor force, rather than engaging on a downward spiral of low wages and poor productivity performances.

(e) *Conclusion*

The main message coming out of this section is that strong labor unions have contributed to competitive behavior which favors innovation. This is clearest in the cases of Baden-Württemberg and Italy where wages and working conditions are negotiated at the regional or local level. In Belgium and – until recently – Denmark negotiations have taken place at the national level but, in spite of this difference, these cases also confirm the general conclusion that the performance of local industry is not enhanced by low wages and weak labor unions. In a sense, one could say that the union blocked the "low road" to competitiveness.

Could this have any relevance for LDCs? In order to answer this question one needs to ask the prior question of what made the unions strong. A key factor in "our" European regions is the relative shortage of labor. In contrast, the typical situation in LDCs is one of large labor surplus. The likelihood of workers to unionize and exert effective pressure is small under conditions of excess labor supply. In this sense, the applicability of the European experience is rather limited.

The situation in LDCs, however, is neither uniform nor static. Where unions press for higher wages and better working conditions such claims are often seen as a threat to competitiveness. In such cases, it can be useful to refer to the European industrial districts as examples where the existence of strong unions has induced the search for product and process innovations (often in product lines in which LDCs

[21] Ironically enough, unions in the textile sector in South-West Flanders are now confronted with the fact that many of their members prefer not to follow strictly the national guidelines on shorter working times. Instead of 38 h per week, they prefer to work 40 h for an increased hourly salary. There has been a serious shortage of labor in the region for a few years. For a comprehensive review of labor relations in South-West Flanders, see Musyck (1993).

are thought to have a comparative advantage). Of course, the dynamic does not necessarily work that way. By the same token, product and process innovations are not precluded by weak unions. But the latter make the low route more likely.

8.7 Spontaneous and Institutionally Induced Growth

By examining the role of institutions in the four fields of credit, training, real services and wages one loses sight of how institutions and their measures sometimes reinforce each other. A review of the case material, region by region, however, would arrive at the following conclusion: none of the industrial districts are the result of planned action, of a local or regional industrial strategy. They all developed spontaneously. Public and private sector institutions did play a role in their growth process but they were not created by these institutions. In other words, in dealing with the need and potential of institutional intervention one has to distinguish between different stages. Let us explain.

None of the industrial districts studied in this paper relied entirely on the market. They all had regional or local institutions which supported industry, particularly small- and medium-sized firms. It seems that their relative importance increased over time. This comes most clearly out of Brusco's (1990) analysis of the Italian experience. He distinguishes between an industrial district model Mark I and Mark II. Mark I refers to the early growth which was largely spontaneous. In Mark II, industry requires support from local and regional institutions in order to speed up innovation, expand into new markets and thus consolidate growth.

Such a distinction between two phases also seems useful in the case of Baden-Württemberg where the regional government pursued a very active innovation policy in the course of the 1980s. The industrial structure on which the success was based, however, was largely in place beforehand (Schmitz 1992). In the Belgian case, the recent developments show an evolution similar to the German and Italian cases. In 1990, 190 South-West Flemish investors created an association to implement a comprehensive and strategic policy package to support the industrial development of South-West Flanders.[22] As far as the Danish case is concerned, discussion with Sven Illeris and Poul Ove Pedersen confirm that the relative importance of institutions has been increasing over time.

There is a policy implication which emerges from the similarity between these experiences. It is a conclusion which is almost obvious but which needs emphasizing in view of the desperation with which poor regions observe those which are prosperous. Governments or government-sponsored institutions cannot create an industrial organization which competes on the basis of collective efficiency. Once private initiative has led to a minimum concentration of industrial activity and

[22] The association, called Charter 99, set out its priorities to intervene in the fields of telecommunication, product development and design, export to Euro-region Northern France, training, environment and infrastructure, regional marketing and representation in Brussels (Musyck 1993).

know-how, however, they can play an important part in helping industry to innovate and expand.

The difficulty for the researcher as well as for the practitioner is that it is almost impossible to determine a threshold at which this critical mass exists. Nevertheless, there is a warning that the transferability of the industrial district experience is very limited where local small industry has to be built up from scratch.

This is not to say that nothing can be done to initiate small enterprises. Take, for example, the Republics of the former Soviet Union where small-scale industry was not allowed to develop under the previous central planning regime. Local authorities and foreign donors are now trying to foster the growth of small enterprises in order to demonopolize the economy, improve the availability of goods and services, and create employment. One way of going about this is to establish technoparks and business incubators. A key feature of this approach is that it provides start-up firms with access to two resources which are either not available at all small firms or only at prohibitive cost, namely space (site, building, workshops) and producer services (advice on preparation of business plans, production management, marketing, finance). This approach, while modeled on experiences in the West, seems particularly promising for the current conditions in these Republics of the former Soviet Union (EBRD 1992).

Even though groups of firms are supported in technoparks and business incubators, tenant firms are likely to work in parallel and engage in activities which are not related to each other. Collective efficiency may arise at a later stage but cannot be expected to result immediately from this approach. The general point to be made here is that the industrial district experience is of greater relevance to those institutions which seek to foster industrialization in areas which already have a minimal density and critical duration of local small industry.[23]

8.8 The Macro Policy Environment

This paper has so far concentrated on the role of regional and local institutions. In the recent experience with fostering small firms in LDCs, there has been an increasing emphasis on the role of the macro policy environment. This section recalls briefly why this occurred and then asks what lessons, if any, can be drawn from the European industrial district experience on the macro policy environment.

In the past, most initiatives in support of small-scale industry in LDCs were of the direct kind and occurred at the micro level. Assistance was provided in the form of managerial and technical training, special credit lines, the provision of sites and services, etc. Such measures have sometimes been useful but it is now widely acknowledged that their effectiveness remains limited for two reasons. First, the institutions providing support have to deal with a multitude of enterprises.

[23]These notions of minimal density and critical duration are used by Pecqueur and Silva (1992) in their work on diffuse industrialization.

Administrative costs are inevitably high and the managerial and executive capacity of such institutions is rarely sufficient for dealing with more than a small percentage of the clientele. Second, macroeconomic policies often favor large rather than small enterprises. Where general incentives discourage small enterprise growth direct support to such enterprises tends to have little if any effect. For example, the fostering of indigenous intermediate technology appropriate for small industry will have little if any effect if fiscal incentives facilitate the importation of foreign technology.

Indeed, there is now a consensus among researchers and practitioners that the priority must lie in improving the general policy environment for small-scale industry, that is, eliminating the bias toward large-scale industry (see, for example, Liedholm and Mead 1987; UNDP et al. 1988; Späth 1992; Stewart 1989). In practice this is difficult because existing policy regimes are not the result of misguided technocrats but of vested interests. The change is further hampered by institutional problems. Government personnel, in support of small-scale industry, tends to be concentrated in special agencies concerned with small firms and excluded from the decisions on general economic policy.

Contrary to the developing country experiences discussed above, the effect of macro policy environment on the development of small- and medium-sized enterprises is not dealt with in the industrial district literature. The reason probably lies in the fact that industrial districts are often studied in reference to, and in comparison with, the rest of the national economy. This automatically disregards the explanatory power of the national macroeconomic environment for the relative economic performance of industrial districts. Moreover, this literature also ignores the effects of a changing macroeconomic environment over time. Finally, even in comparisons between industrial districts located in different countries there is no assessment of the impact of macroeconomic policies.[24]

We are not saying that the macro policy environment did not matter, but that it was not dealt with. We can only speculate as to why this was so. One reason could be that with European integration national differences in economic policy are diminishing. The question is whether lessons can be drawn from the resulting common macro policy framework. The answer probably varies with the field of policy. Take, for instance, monetary policy. The stress on monetary stability in the four European countries considered seems desirable for all countries, even if monetary stability is more difficult to attain in LDCs. In the case of trade policy, emulating the European experience would be more controversial. Italy, Germany, Denmark and Belgium are relatively open economies. It would be wrong to conclude from this that a policy of protection is generally bad for small-scale industry. In the context of LDCs, the infant industry argument remains important even though the protection of LDC industry has a history of problems (Schmitz 1984). Indeed, on trade policy reform, the LDCs' own recent history offers more insights than the recent European experience (see, for example, Evans 1992).

[24] Macro economic regulation is discussed by Piore and Sabel (1984) but is only considered essential for mass production.

Another issue that needs to be raised in the discussion of the general policy framework is whether small firms were exempt from certain tax and social security regulations. On this issue the literature contains some references to the Italian case (Parisotto 1991). In Italy the "artisan statute" of 1956 grants small firms concessions on the number of legal requirements in matters of account keeping, taxation, social security contributions, etc. The importance of this national statute is hard to judge. If the thriving of small-scale industry of the Third Italy is seen as evidence for its importance one would need to set against this the poor performance of small-scale industry in the South where the same regulations apply. Apart from the Italian artisan statute there is little if any discussion of national policies or regulations in the industrial district literature. As seen in the previous sections, the emphasis is almost entirely on regional and local institutions. Our main findings on their role are drawn together in the following section.

8.9 Toward a New Model of Industrial Policy?

The European industrial districts have become a major reference point in the recent debate on industrial policy. In this paper we have tried to assess the role of formal institutions, both public and private, in these successful regions, primarily by reviewing the recent literature. This proved to be a difficult undertaking. There is little systematic assessment of the role of governmental or non-governmental institutions in the European industrial districts. In some cases it is hard to tell whether this is so because such institutions were unimportant or because they remained under researched.

The lacuna was most glaring at the macro level, that is the incentive structure set by central government. This is not to say that nothing can be learned at this level, but what we can derive are merely conclusions about what the growth of industrial districts does not represent. It is not the result of centrally administered incentives for particular regions. Nor are they the result of liberalization and deregulation.

More positive lessons emerge at the meso and micro level. The recent industrial district experience in Europe points toward a new model of local and regional industrial policy which:

- emphasizes delegation of functions to a diverse range of governmental and non-governmental institutions;
- operates through institutions close to the enterprises;
- extends the concern with entrepreneurship from the private to the public sector; and
- stresses self-help through business associations and producer consortia.

These were some of the main features which emerged from reviewing the experiences in the provision of credit, training and real services. For each of these areas a number of specific policy conclusions were derived.

One general conclusion, however, which needs reiterating is that the emergence of the industrial districts does not result from consciously pursued local or regional industrial strategy. It seems that the reviewed cases went through two stages: spontaneous growth, and institutionally enhanced growth. There was no clear-cut dividing line, but there was a common pattern of institutions playing more of a role in the later than in the earlier growth phase. In other words, to the extent that policy implications can be drawn from this experience they are not concerned with the emergence of industrial districts but with the path they took once they existed.

Even this cautious assessment of the role of institutions carries some question marks. In the industrial policy debate, the international attention given to the European industrial districts remains based on two observations: expanding and innovative local industry, and active local institutions. A causal connection is plausible, indeed we started this paper expecting to find rich case material. What we found, however, was largely descriptive material on what these institutions do, but little assessment of how they influenced the perceptions of risk and entrepreneurial decisions. On the other hand, it is worth recalling that many of the institutions and their services result from local initiative and are – at least partially – self-financed. This suggests that they probably matter to local industry.

Whether these cases justify using the term "industrial policy from below" is a matter of temperament rather than science.[25] But there can be little doubt that the industrial district experience contributed to a general shift in the recent European industrial policy debate. There has been an increasing concern with the role of regional and local institutions in enhancing industrial competitiveness (Best 1990; Hucke and Wollmann 1989; Murray 1991; Illeris and Jakobsen 1990; Zeitlin 1989). The remainder of this section contains some reflection on why such a decentralized approach is desirable. They are not conclusions that can be derived from the previous sections but observations which were triggered by our case studies and which can serve as propositions for further research.

We would suggest that regional and local institutions offer two advantages over central institutions: less ideology and more accountability. Let us explain. The break with ideology is clearest in the German and Italian cases. In Germany it was the regional government of Baden-Württemberg led by the Christian Democrats that took the lead in shaking off simplistic neo-liberal prescriptions about industrial policy. In the Third Italy, Communist-controlled municipal authorities broke with the doctrine of the Communist Party, which was anti small-scale industry, ignoring the fact that in some regions small industry was the backbone of the economy.

As regards the accountability of local and regional institutions, this issue was not investigated in the material reviewed. If information were available it would probably show that generalizations, across institutions and regions, are hard to make. But it seems plausible to suggest that in regional and local institutions there is more likely to be a sense of accountability and reciprocity benefiting the regional and local economy than in centralized institutions.

---

[25] An in-depth study of local institutions in Germany carries the title "Economic Policy from Below" (Nassmacher 1987).

This is not to argue for localness *per se* nor does it amount to local romanticism. We merely recognize that innovating industry, especially small industry, requires a supportive infrastructure and producer services, which the market does not necessarily deliver. In principle, these could be provided by central institutions, but they tend to be less transparent to the local user and more remote from local needs.

While such broad statements are inevitably controversial, it seems clear that in the cases reviewed new initiatives did in fact come from local and regional institutions. In the Danish case local authorities even trespassed central authority so as to be able to support local industry. More than that, in all four regions, one can trace the emergence of local government agencies, industry associations/chambers and sometimes unions. It seems that in the cases studied here such coalitions – while not free from internal conflict – played a positive role. But one cannot discount the possibility that in other circumstances they could block rather than enhance innovation.

8.10 Any Lessons for Donor Agencies?

This final section contains some reflections on the relevance of our findings for donor agencies. It is written with agencies operating in LDCs in mind, but some of it may also apply to those engaged in Eastern Europe and the former Soviet Union. Great hopes are pinned on the contribution of small-scale industry to economic reconstruction and income generation. Many national and international agencies have devoted an increasing share of their resources to small enterprise development, but are searching for ways of spending them. Donor agencies in particular have been looking for "models" of how institutions can foster such development and how this process can be supported from the outside with financial and technical assistance.

This paper does not provide simple recipes for providing such "injections." If anything, the four cases reviewed point toward the difficulties of fostering local industry from the outside.

Foreign donors need a funnel through which to channel their support. One of the main lessons of this paper is that there is no easy funnel. The European experience of supporting small-scale industry is a very decentralized one. If donors seek to draw a conclusion from this experience it would be: do not work through a central intermediary. The problem is that this makes the provision of aid more cumbersome, since it means not only a multitude of local intermediaries but also small projects. Most aid agencies prefer large projects, but in this field large injections of aid are more likely to generate clusters of rent-seekers than clusters of manufactures.

The message that aid would need to be channeled in small amounts through a diffuse net of local institutions is not an entirely new one in the aid business. Some donor agencies have come to this conclusion through their own experience in small enterprise development. They will see the findings of this paper merely as a confirmation for a strategy which they are pursuing anyway.

The emphasis we have given to regional, local and sectoral institutions does not mean that central government could or should be ignored. As mentioned before, in LDCs the general policy environment is often biased against small firms. Progress in improving the policy environment remains hampered because: (a) those forces in central government most concerned with small enterprise development are rarely in the "engine room" of economic policy making; (b) small-scale industry lacks both political clout and professional capacity to make its views felt; (c) clear arguments and information on the precise kind of required policy changes are rarely available. The European experiences reviewed in this paper do not offer a way forward, but since this issue is important mention should be made of how donor agencies can contribute to improve the policy environment.

Donor agencies can help to bring about both pressure and information by financing action research. To this end it can be useful to set up task forces which can draw on international and national expertise, in which government and private sector are represented, and which focus on a few selected industrial sectors and localities. The advantage of this sectoral approach are that the crucial constraints on small enterprises emerge most clearly in sector-specific studies, it is at the sectoral and local level that the private sector can engage most meaningfully in policy dialogue (through associations), and on some issues of economic policy (for example, tariffs) differentiation by sector is crucial. The argument is not to carry out separate policy studies but to include issues of central government policy on the agenda of sectoral task forces.

A reason for mentioning such task forces here is that sometimes international donor agencies can become the catalyst for bringing together government and industry as well as researchers and practitioners. Donors are also more likely than national institutions to have funds for a substantial investigation into "problems and opportunities."

The key points made above (albeit very briefly) concern the way such investigations should be carried out. The first stress is on the sectoral (or subsectoral) approach. It is at the sectoral level that the problems become "alive," that research findings are not just "data" but become "ammunition" for change. (This is particularly relevant for clustering firms since sectoral and geographical concentration facilitates collective action.) The second stress is on the participatory approach; that is, to involve practitioners in carrying out the research. It is certainly true that professional researchers will find it easier to work on their own and use the practitioners merely as informants rather than collaborators. Indeed, if the value of the research is judged by the delivery of a written report conforming to international standards, then the job is best left to the "professionals." The problem is that even a good report can only transmit a fraction of what is learned in the course of the investigation. If the purpose of the research is to generate information and insights which can be internalized by local actors, then it is useful to incorporate such actors into the process of unravelling the constraints on local industry.

As stated above, these are not conclusions that can be derived from the European industrial districts. They are based on operational experiences in small enterprise promotion in LDCs. These experiences suggest that – whatever the rhetoric –

central governments are unlikely to become the champions of small local enterprises. Regional and local institutions, both public and private, are more promising in this respect, whether as pressure groups for changes in economic policy or providers of producer services. When we started this paper, we expected that the institutional involvement in the growth of successful European industrial districts could provide a role model for institutions in poorer regions of the world. We found that the evidence was shaky. There seems to be a mismatch between the international attention given to these European cases and what is actually known about them.

References

Becattini G (1989) Sectors and/or districts: some remarks on the conceptual foundations of industrial economics. In: Goodman E, Bamford J (eds) Small firms and industrial districts in Italy. Routledge, London

Becattini G (1990) The Marshallian industrial district as a socioeconomic notion. In: Pyke F, Becattini O, Sengenberger W (eds) Industrial districts and inter-firm cooperation in Italy. International Institute for Labour Studies, Geneva

Becher G, Weibert W (1990) Technologiepolitik in Baden-Württemberg. Mimeo, Fraunhofer Institut für Systemtechnik and Innovationasforschung, Karlsruhe

Becher G et al (1989–1990) "Zwischenbilanz der einzelbetrieblichen Technologieförderung für kleine und mittlere Unternehmen in Baden-Württemberg," Mimeo, Part 1 (1989) and Part 2 (1990) (Karlsruhe: Fraunhofer Institut für Systemtechnik and Innovationasforschung, 1989–90)

Best M (1990) The new competition. Polity Press, Cambridge

Bianchi G (1992) Requiem per la Terza Italia? prime considerazioni sui risultati provvisori dei censimenti 1991. Instituto Universitario Europeo, Firenze, Mimeo

Boehm U, Kappel R (1990) Thesen zur Berufsbildungshilfe für Eutwicklungsländer. In: Boehm U, Kappel R (eds) Kleinbetriebe des Informellen Sektors und Ausbildung im Sub-Saharischen Afrika. Insitut für Afrikakunde, Hamburg

Boelcke W-A (1987) Organisation und Politik von Industrie, Handwerk und Handel. In: Schneider H (ed) Verbände in Baden-Württemberg. Kohlhammer Verlag, Stuttgart

Brusco S (1985) Local government, industrial policy and social consensus in the experience of Modena (Italy). Mimeo, New York

Brusco S (1989) The idea of the industrial districts. In: Goodman E, Bamford J (eds) Small firms and industrial districts in Italy. Routledge, London

Brusco S (1990) The idea of the industrial district: its genesis. In: Pyke F, Becattini G, Sengenberger W (eds) Industrial districts and inter-firm cooperation in Italy. International Institute for Labour Studies, Geneva

Brusco S (1992) Small firms and the provision of real services. In: Pyke F, Sengenberger W (eds) Industrial districts and local economic regeneration. International Institute for Labour Studies, Geneva

Brusco S, Righi E (1989) Local government, industrial policy and social consensus: the case of Modena (Italy). Econ Soc 18(4):405–424

Brutti P, Calistri F (1990) Industrial districts and the unions. In: Pyke F, Becattini G, Sengenberger W (eds) Industrial districts and inter-firm cooperation in Italy. International Institute for Labour Studies, Geneva

Camagni R, Rabellotti R (1992) Technology and organization in the Italian textile-clothing industry. Entrepreneurship Reg Dev 4(3):271–285

Canullo G (1990) Industrialisation of rural areas: the Italian NEC model. Paper presented at the OECD Conference on Enterprise and Employment Creation in Rural Areas (Paris, January)
Capecchi V (1987) Formation professionelle et petite entreprise: le développement industriel à specialization flexible en Emilie-Romagne. Form Empl 19(1):3–18
Colletis G, Courlet C, Pecqueur B (1990) Les systèmes industriels localisés en Europe. Institut de Recherche Economique sur la Production et le Développement Université des Sciences Sociales, Grenoble
Cooke P, Morgan K (1990) Industry, training and technology transfer: the Baden-Württemberg system in perspective, Regional Industrial Research Report. Department of City and Regional Planning, University of Wales, Cardiff
Cooke P, Morgan K (1993) Growth regions under duress – renewal strategies in Baden-Württemberg and Emilia-Romagna. Mimeo/Department of City and Regional Planning, University of Wales, Cardiff
Courlet C, Pecqueur B (1991) Local industrial systems and externalities: an essay in typology. Entrepreneurship Reg Dev 3(4):305–315
EBRD (1992) Approaches to conversion and industrial restructuring, Unpublished Mission Report by E. Wallace and H. Schmitz, European Bank for Reconstruction and Development, London
Evans D (1992) Institutions, sequencing and trade policy reforms. Report prepared for the Money. Finance and Development Division, UNCTAD, Geneva
Eyskens G (1980) Vijftig jaar welvaartsontwikkeling in Vlaanderen. Tijdschrift voor Economie en Management 15(2):289–300
Fluitman F (1989) Training for work in the informal sector. International Labour Office, Geneva
Fuà G (1983) Rural industrialization in later developed countries: the case of Northeast and Central Italy. Banca Nazionale Del Lavoro Quarterly Review 36(147):351–377
Garofoli G (1983) Industrializzatione diffusa in Lombardia. Franco Angeli, Milano
Garofoli G (1991) Modelli locali di sviluppo. Franco Angeli, Milano
Garofoli G (1992) The Italian model of spatial development in the 1970s and 1980s. In: Benko G, Dunford M (eds) Industrial change and regional development: the transformation of new industrial spaces. Belhaven Press, London
Germidis D, Kessler D, Meghir R (1991) Financial systems and development: what role for the formal and informal financial sectors? Development Centre, OECD, Paris
Hansen N (1991) Factories in Danish fields: how high-wage, flexible production has succeeded in peripheral Jutland. Int Reg Sci Rev 14(2):109–132
Herrigel G (1988) The political embeddedness of small and medium-sized firm networks in Baden-Württemberg. Paper delivered at the Workshop on Interfirm Innovation Dynamics, sponsored by the Six Countries Programme on Aspects of Government Policies towards Technological Innovation in Industry, Stuttgart
Hucke J, Wollmann H (eds) (1989) Dezentrale technologiepolitik? Birkhäuser Verlag, Basel
Illeris S (1986) New firm creation in Denmark: the importance of the cultural background. In: Keeble D, Wever E (eds) New firms and regional development in Europe. Croom Helm, London
Illeris S (1992) The Herning-Ikast textile industry: an industrial district in West Jutland. Entrepreneurship Reg Dev 4(1):73–84
Illeris S, Jakobsen L (eds) (1990) Networks and regional development. Nordisk Institut for Regionalpolitisk Forskning (Nordrefo), Copenhagen
Kohler H (1987) Konservative und sozialdemokratische Modernisierungskonzeptionen am Beispiel der Forschungs – und Technologiepolitik der Bundesländer Baden-Württemberg und Nordrhein-Westfalen – eine vergleichende Analyse. Diplomarbeit, Sozial-wissenschaftliche Fakultät, Universität Konstanz
Kristensen PH (1992) Industrial districts in West Jutland, Denmark. In: Pyke F, Sengenberger W (eds) Industrial districts and local economic regeneration. International Institute for Labour Studies, Geneva
Lazerson M (1990) Subcontracting in the Modena knitwear industry. In: Pyke F, Becattini G, Sengenberger W (eds) Industrial districts and inter-firm cooperation in Italy. International Institute for Labour Studies, Geneva

Levitsky J (1986) World Bank lending to small enterprises: a review, Industry and finance series 16. World Bank, Washington, DC
Liedholm C, Mead D (1987) Small scale industries in developing countries: empirical evidence and policy implications, International development paper no. 9. Michigan State University, East Lansing
Maier HE (1987) Das modell Baden-Württemberg: Über institutionelle voraussetzungen differenzierter qualitätsproduktion – Eine Skizze. Discussion Paper IIM/LMP 87-10a. Wissenschaftszentrum Berlin für Sozialforschung, Berlin
Marshall A (1920) Principles of economics, 8th edn. Macmillan, London
Martens J-P (1990) La région de courtrai: entreprises et groups d'entreprises. Courrier Hebdomadaire du CRISP, No. 1289
Murray F (1987) Flexible specialisation in the 'Third Italy.'. Capital Class 33:84–95
Murray R (1991) Local space, Europe and the new regionalism. The Centre for Local Economic Strategies and South East Economic Development Strategy, Brighton
Murray R et al (1988) Cyprus Industrial Strategy: report of UNDP/UNIDO mission. IDS, Brighton
Murray R, Best M, Pezzini M (1989) Consortia and the Third Italy. Unpublished dossiers, IDS, Brighton
Musyck B (1992) The characteristics of autonomous industrialization in South-West Flanders (Belgium). Paper presented at the Colloque international industrie et territoire: les systèms productifs lodalisés (Grenoble, 21–22 October, 1992). French version published in Courlet C, Soulage B (eds) Systèmes Productifs Localisés et Politiques Publiques (Paris: l'Harmattan, 1994)
Musyck B (1993) Autonomous industrialization in South-West Flanders (Belgium). Ph.D. dissertation, University of Sussex, Brighton
Musyck B (1995) Autonomous industrialization in South-West Flanders (Belgium): continuity and transformation. Reg Stud 29(7):619–633
MWMT (1990) Mittelstandsbericht 1990. Ministerium für Wirtschaft, Mittelstand und Technologie, Stuttgart
Nassmacher H (1987) Wirtschaftspolitik "von unten": ansätze und Praxis der kommunalen Gewerbestandspflege und Wirtschaftsförderung. Birkhäuser Verlag, Basel
Parisotto A (1991) The distinctive pattern of non-agricultural self-employment in Italy. Working Paper No. 48, World Employment Programme Research, ILO, Geneva
Pecqueur B, Silva M (1992) Territory and economic development: the example of diffuse industrialization. In: Garofoli G (ed) Endogenous development and Southern Europe. Avebury, Aldershot
Pedersen PO (1986) Business service strategies: the case of the provincial centre of Esbjerg, Report EUR 10611, FAST Series No. 19. EEC, Brussels
Piore M, Sabel C (1984) The second industrial divide: possibilities for prosperity. Basic Books, New York
Pyke F (1992a) Industrial development through small-firm cooperation: theory and practice. ILO, Geneva.
Pyke F (1992b) Strengthening small firms through co-operation and technical services: the roles of the Steinbeis Foundation and the Landesgewerbeamt in Baden-Württemberg. Paper presented at the International Conference on Endogenous Regional Development in a Global Economy: The roles of Technical Service Institutes and Co-operation Networks in Small Firm Economies, Valencia
Pyke F (1992c) A focus on the Danish technological institute and the Danish network co-operation programme. Paper presented at the International Conference on Endogenous Regional Development in a Global Economy: The roles of Technical Service Institutes and Co-operation Networks in Small Firm Economies, Valencia
Pyke F, Sengenberger W (eds) (1992) Industrial districts and local economic regeneration. International Institute for Labour Studies, Geneva

Rasmussen J, Schmitz H, van Dijk M-P (1992) Introduction: exploring a new approach to small industry. IDS Bull 23(3):2–6
Reuss K (1986) Die klassische Gewerbeförderung in Baden-Württemberg und ihre locale Verankerung. In: Maier HE, Wollmann H (eds) Lokale Beschäftigungspolitik. Birkhäuser Verlag, Basel
Sabel C, Herrigel G, Deeg R, Kazis R (1989) Regional prosperities compared: Massachusetts and Baden-Württemberg in the 1980s. Econ Soc 18(4):374–404
Schmid H (1988) Regionale Wirtschaftsförderung -- Schranke des 'Modells Baden-Württemberg'? Eine Untersuchung über Gründe und Effekte des Festhaltens an einem umstrittenen Politikbereich. (Doktorbeit Sozialwissen- schafliche Fakultät, Universität Konstanz)
Schmitz H (1984) Industrialisation strategies in less developed countries: some lessons of historical experience. J Dev Stud 21(1):1–21
Schmitz H (1990) Small firms and flexible specialization in developing countries. Labour Soc 15(3):257–285
Schmitz H (1992) Industrial districts: model and reality in Baden-Württemberg, Germany. In: Pyke F, Sengenberger W (eds) Industrial districts and local economic regeneration. International Institute for Labour Studies, Geneva
Semlinger K (1991) Das Steinbeis-Zentrum für Qualitätswesen – Eine Kleinbetriebliche Kooperationsinitiative auf dem Weg zum Erfolg. Mimeo, Institut für Sozialwissenschaftliche Forschung, München
Sengenberger W (1990) The role of labour standards in industrial restructuring: participation, protection and promotion, Discussion Paper No. 19. International Institute for Labour Studies, Geneva
Sengenberger W, Pyke F (1992) Industrial districts and local economic regeneration: Research and policy issues. In: Pyke F, Sengenberger W (eds) Industrial districts and local Economic Regeneration. International Institute for Labour Studies, Geneva
Sengenberger WG, Loveman G, Piore MJ (eds) (1990) The re-emergence of small enterprises: industrial restructuring in industrialised countries. International Institute for Labour Studies, Geneva
Signorini LF (1992) The price of Prato, or measuring the industrial district effect. Paper presented at the European Regional Science Association Conference, Brussels
Späth L (1985) Wende in die Zukunft. Spiegel/Rowohlt, Hamburg
Späth L (1987) Wirtschaftspolitische Umbrüche: Der Weg zur Innovationspolitik in Baden-Württemberg. In: Buddenburg H (ed) Umbrüche – Neve Strukturen in Wirtschaft und Gesellschaft. Busse Sewald, Herford
Späth B (1992) The institutional environment and communities of small firms. IDS Bull 23(3):8–14
Stewart F (1989) Macro policy mechanisms: new trends. In: Gosser A, Molenaar K, Teszler R (eds) Small enterprises, new approaches. Ministry of Foreign Affairs, Netherlands Development Cooperation, The Hague
Trigilia C (1989) Small-firm development and political subcultures in Italy. In: Goodman E, Bamford J (eds) Small firms and industrial districts in Italy. Routledge, London
Trigilia C (1990) Work and politics in the Third Italy's industrial districts. In: Pyke F et al (eds) Industrial districts and inter-firm cooperation in Italy. International Institute for Labour Studies, Geneva
UNDP, Government of the Netherlands, ILO, UNIDO (1988) Development of rural small industrial enterprise – lessons from experience. United Nations, Vienna
White G (ed) (1988) Developmental states in East Asia. Macmillan, London
Zacchia C (1984) Rural industrialization in Italy. J World Trade 18(2):110–124
Zeitlin J (1989) Local industrial strategies: introduction. Econ Soc 18(4):367–373
Zeitlin J (1992) Industrial districts and local economic regeneration: overview and comment. In: Pyke F, Sengenberger W (eds) Industrial districts and local economic regeneration. International Institute for Labour Studies, Geneva

Chapter 9
Promotion of the Weaving Districts in Modern Japan

Tomoko Hashino

Abstract In the case of the silk-weaving industry in modern Japan, local producers attempted to improve the quality of their products and to achieve a good reputation for their district brand for survival and sustainable growth. Such attempts often failed, however, due to the existence of free riders who did not care about the quality of products or did not possess proper knowledge of advanced technologies. Export of inferior-quality product from Japan led to heavy criticisms against Japanese products. Facing such a critical situation, not only producer cooperatives but also central and local governments introduced the quality inspection system and supported the quality-improvement activities of local producers to sustain the development of industrial districts. Policies of both local and central governments enabled the shift from the quantitative expansion phase of the industrial districts to the qualitative improvement phase, in which a limited number of innovative firms produced high-quality products with their established district brands.

Keywords Silk-weaving industry • Quality improvement • District brand • Inferior quality products • Producer cooperatives • Central and local governments

9.1 Introduction

The shift from the quantitative expansion phase, in which an increasing number of small firms produce low-quality products, to the qualitative improvement phase, in which a limited number of innovative firms produce high-quality products, is critical for both the survival and the sustainable development of industrial districts in contemporary developing economies (Sonobe and Otsuka 2006, 2011, 2014). The process of trial and error by which industrial districts struggle to improve the quality of their products may appear to be a 'crisis,' because profitability is very low at the beginning of the new phase. If there is no innovation, the district would not be able to grow, and would eventually decline. What kind of innovation is needed to promote the improvement of product quality? Who initiate this innovation? Sonobe and

T. Hashino (✉)
Graduate School of Economics, Kobe University, Kobe, Japan
e-mail: hashino@econ.kobe-u.ac.jp

T. Hashino, K. Otsuka (eds.), *Industrial Districts in History and the Developing World*, Studies in Economic History, DOI 10.1007/978-981-10-0182-6_9

Otsuka (2006) point out that it is entrepreneurs who drive the shift from the quantity expansion phase to the following prosperous phase. However, the question remains: who are these entrepreneurs?

As will be shown in Chap. 10 in this volume, it appears that not only technological innovation but also institutional and organizational innovations are critically important for the sustainable development of industrial districts in China. While such innovations are important in the development process of contemporary industrial districts, improvement in quality and earning a good reputation in the market are also critical issues in history and the developing world. For example, in their early periods of industrialization, both Germany and Japan developed a reputation for inferior-quality products. Needless to say, such reputations in international markets resulted in a decline in exports. Therefore, gathering information about international markets, especially about the reputation of exported goods in detail, and transmitting it to local producers via non-market institutions became a critical issue for industrial development. Building such a system, which Sugihara (1994) called 'informational infrastructure,' can be considered one of the most important institutional and organizational innovations the Meiji government carried out in the process of industrialization.

To use important information from international and domestic markets effectively, both competition and cooperation within industrial districts, consisting of small-scale local producers, were essential in Japan (Hashino 2007a). In fact, industrial districts in modern Japan were much more organized for cooperation than the Marshallian type of Anglo-Saxon regional economy characterized by competition (Hashino and Saito 2004; Abe 2012; Hashino and Kurosawa 2013). As is shown in Chap. 6 in this volume, the trade association in Lyon also played a leading role in solving problems arising from inferior raw materials supplied by new markets through cooperation. In addition, Chap. 7 points out that producer cooperatives in agricultural districts carried out quality improvement, standardization of products and processes, and marketing innovations cooperatively, which led to the sustainable growth of the districts.

It is worth noting that prefectural or local governments not only supported training institutes and trade associations in weaving districts but also established technical schools and public research institutes to promote sustainable growth by facilitating the quality improvement phase of industrial districts in Japan (Sawai 1999; Hashino 2012; Yamazaki and Abe 2012). Of course, the central government attempted to promote the transplantation of modern industries from the West, as well as the modernization of traditional industries. The establishment in 1873 of the large-scale state-owned Tomioka factory in the silk-reeling industry, which produced one of Japan's major export products, is a good example of 'industrialization from above,' as well as efforts to solve the quality problem.[1] However, as far as the promotion of improvement in the quality of products by industrial districts is concerned, local governments played a more important role than the central government by directly supporting industrial districts. They could more easily respond to

[1] Saito (2014) questions whether or not modern Japan was in a developmental state.

proactive local producers who were keen to learn how to use Western technology. Local governments also helped to establish rules to exclude free riders and protect the 'district brand.'

To explore the role of local governments in promoting the shift from the quantitative expansion phase to the quality improvement phase in industrial districts, the experience of weaving districts in Japan provides a good example. After the Meiji Restoration in 1868, *kabunakama* or traditional guilds were ordered to dissolve under the principle of freedom of trade. Rules and regulations under the traditional guilds were abolished. This resulted in business confusion, partly due to a large number of unscrupulous new entrants into the industry. This was the phase of quantitative expansion described by Sonobe and Otsuka (2006, 2011). In addition, immature technology and insufficient knowledge led to problems of inferior quality.

Not only in the domestic market, but also in the export market, the inferior quality of Japanese products was often a serious problem. As discussed in Chap. 4, plain silk fabric, which was called *habutae*, became a prominent export good shortly after production was launched in the mid-1880s. The export of *habutae* grew rapidly, but the inferior product quality gradually became a serious trade issue between the West and Japan. Consular Reports conveyed complaints about the inferior quality of Japanese *habutae* in both European and American markets and explained in detail how defective Japanese *habutae* was (Hashino 2010). Because the quantity of exported *habutae* as a share of all exported goods in terms of value had increased to as much as 10% by the turn of the century (Hashino and Otsuka 2013), both the central and local governments took this problem seriously and had to take action to improve the quality of *habutae* in cooperation with local producers in weaving districts. Having developed a poor reputation, what kinds of actions did the weaving districts and local governments take for recovery? This issue is addressed in this chapter.

The purpose of this chapter is to explore a role of trade associations, local governments, and the central government in the development of weaving districts in Meiji Japan. Section 9.2 explains how inferior product quality occurred in the traditional weaving industry in the early Meiji period (1870s–1880s). Section 9.3 examines how local producers or trade associations attempted to solve the problems in the domestic market by establishing training institutes and technical schools. Section 9.4 explores how quality problems with export *habutae* around the turn of the century were solved based on the Consular Reports, which were one of the fundamental pillars of informational infrastructure. It will be shown that not only trade associations and local governments, but more importantly the central government, played a positive and significant role in protecting and improving district brands to improve and maintain their reputation in international markets. Section 9.5 concludes the study and draws policy implications for contemporary developing economies.

9.2 Inferior Product Quality in the Early Meiji Period

After the Meiji Restoration in 1868, the Japanese people and the central government attempted to transplant modern industries such as cotton spinning, shipbuilding, railroads, papermaking,[2] and iron and steel manufacturing in search of complete import substitution and rapid modernization. In general, such industries were large scale and steam powered. The central government invested in these industries by establishing state-owned factories, which were later sold to the private sector. As mentioned before, the central government also established a model silk-reeling factory, even though silk reeling was indigenous and had developed to a significant level before the opening of the ports in the mid-nineteenth century. The aim of the establishment of this model factory was to introduce Western technology and factory production systems to improve the quality of the raw silk that was produced. In those days, Japanese raw silk had a poor reputation in the international market, even though it had become one of Japan's most promising export goods shortly after international trade started. However, the deterioration in the quality of Japanese silk was widely known (Sugiyama 1988, p. 96). Therefore, the central government took the matter seriously and decided to introduce and diffuse new technology by establishing a model factory.

It is interesting to note that indigenous or traditional industries also suffered from a poor reputation in the domestic market. The weaving industry was one of the most developed traditional sectors, and was a large contributor to the economy at the time. Abe (1983) surveyed the development history of eighteen traditional cotton-weaving districts in the early Meiji period and pointed out that fifteen districts faced the serious problem of inferior fabric quality (Abe 1983, p. 309). Generally speaking, there were two reasons for this inferior quality (Hashino 2007a, pp. 103–105; Hashino 2012, pp. 32, 34). One originated from the moral hazard in business transactions after the demise of traditional guilds, such as cheating by producers or distributors. In other words, the demise of the traditional guilds enabled inexperienced entrepreneurs to enter the industry, and dishonest producers and merchants who did not obey the traditional business rules caused problems. It is said that they often sold shorter lengths of fabrics than stated or dyed the fabrics with coarse dyestuffs. Dishonest producers sometimes added filler to increase the weight of fabrics. Surprisingly, it appears that the large number of new entrants in prewar Japan is quite similar to the large number of new firms that entered the market during the quantitative expansion phase in China described by Sonobe and Otsuka (2006, 2011) (see also Chaps. 2 and 10).

The second reason was an insufficient understanding of technology, e.g., new dyestuffs were used without proper knowledge amidst the introduction of Western synthetic dyes. Many of the inferior-quality problems were the result of misuse of

---

[2]The papermaking industry already had a long tradition in Japan, having originally come from China. However, a large-scale, mechanized Western-style paper industry was transplanted in the early Meiji period to satisfy new demand such as newspapers. See Kurosawa and Hashino (2012).

imported dyestuffs, as the producers did not understand the differences between the imported products and the familiar traditional dyestuffs (Uchida 1988, p. 165). According to Tamura (2004), who investigated the causes of defective dyed products, the problem was the use of synthetic dyestuffs without accompanying technological improvements in the scouring and bleaching processes (Tamura 2004, p. 156). In addition, many kinds of dyestuffs were imported without distinguishing between organic, mineral, and synthetic varieties. Because importers lacked information on dyestuffs, the textile manufacturers had to select them through a process of trial and error, which caused problems.

Realizing that the matter was serious, the central government (Ministry of Agriculture and Commerce; 1881–1925) changed their conventional laissez-faire policy and started supervision and training programs to improve the quality of products (Yui 1964, pp. 25–27). The Ministry of Agriculture and Commerce provided instruction and subsidies for improvement in major industrial districts from 1885, when the department of industry was established. The following year, a section was also established to promote industry by supporting and subsidizing competitive exhibitions in major local areas. In response to requests for training and subsidies from local governments, the central government also supported the improvement of production technologies in indigenous industries. By the mid-1880s, the dumping of inferior-quality products that had started in the early Meiji period troubled weaving districts. As a result, these districts became keen to regulate the sale of inferior-quality products and to explore new markets. This led local governments to ask the central government to promote a policy for improvement in the quality of products.

One of the industrial policies promoted by the Ministry of Agriculture and Commerce was the staging of expositions and competitive exhibitions, which were held frequently between 1880 and 1900 (Hashino 2012, pp. 32–33). Even though the exhibits had to be carefully produced if they were to achieve the prestige of winning an award and achieving a good reputation at such special events, the exhibitions also saw inferior-quality products being displayed.[3] The Competitive Exhibition of Silk and Cocoon, Textile, Ceramics and Lacquer-ware (hereafter 'the Competitive Exhibition'), held in 1885, is a good example of an exhibition where many inferior-quality products were presented. Therefore, it makes sense to examine the problems with the dyeing technology that was in use at that time by reviewing the evaluations of the exhibits and comments from the jurors (Tamura 2004, pp. 150–156).

In the Competitive Exhibition, which accepted textile exhibits from various weaving districts, most of the technical problems that were pointed out related to dyeing defects, unethical methods of inflating the weight of the yarn, and errors in the fabric dimensions and weight. In particular, it was recognized that the dyeing defects were more serious in the silk-weaving districts than in the cotton-weaving

[3] For diffusing innovations, promoting mainly indigenous and traditional industries, and reducing the reliance on Western technology, various kinds of expositions and competitive exhibitions were held. See Nicholas (2010, pp. 17–18) and Kiyokawa (1995, p. 241).

districts, and also more serious in Eastern rather than in Western Japan (Hashino 2007a, p. 115). Above all, the products from traditionally advanced weaving districts producing yarn-dyed fabrics received particularly harsh criticism. What kind of dyeing technology was actually used in these weaving districts? Hashino (2012) investigated *The Industrial Inspection Report* of 1896, which was a survey of major industrial districts involving the weaving industry conducted by the Ministry of Agriculture and Commerce. Interestingly, this document recorded how dyeing methods were misapplied. The report on the introduction and adoption of European synthetic dyestuffs provides critical evidence as to what happened in the weaving districts including Hachioji, Bushu, Isesaki, Ashikaga, Gifu, and Iyo, which were popular weaving districts before the Meiji period.[4] In particular, the document describes how European synthetic dyestuffs were used incorrectly. It seems that many weavers who had never engaged in the dyeing process before used Western synthetic dyestuffs in an attempt to obtain brighter colors and reduce their production costs without having appropriate knowledge of chemistry. After the cause of the inferior-quality problem became clear as a result of the Competitive Exhibition, the central government undertook activities to support improvement in the quality of products. The number of weaving districts where the Ministry of Agriculture and Commerce was involved in the technical improvement of the traditional weaving industry totaled 25 between 1885 and 1889 (Yui 1964, pp. 27–29).

9.3 Attempts by Local Producers, Trade Associations, and Local Governments to Solve Problems in the Domestic Market[5]

It was the institutes of training that provided technical guidance on dyeing-related issues. Local producers and traders in Tsuru, Wakayama, Ashikaga, Kiryu, Hachioji, Isesaki, and Matsuzaka, which were representative traditional weaving districts, established institutes or industrial research centers for training under the guidance of the Ministry of Agriculture and Commerce in the late 1880s. Many institutes and research centers applied to their local governments for subsidies for facilities and operating expenses. They also asked the Ministry of Agriculture and Commerce, through their local governments, to send specialists on dyestuffs to provide technical guidance (Yui 1964, p. 26). Considering that the inferior-quality problems had become a very serious issue by the late 1870s, the fact that the training institutes were only initiated a decade later suggests that the harsh criticism received at the Competitive Exhibition may have instigated such moves, albeit with a considerable time lag.

[4] For detailed information about the incorrect application of synthetic dyestuffs in each weaving district, see Hashino (2012, pp. 33–34).

[5] The description in this section is taken from Hashino (2012).

The Institute for Training in Dyeing in the Isesaki silk-weaving district, a prototype for other institutes, as well as one of the oldest training institutes in Japan, is a good example of cooperative attempts by local producers and local governments. At the beginning of the Meiji period, Isesaki textiles had lost their good reputation owing to an infestation of inferior-quality fabrics. Therefore, the local government's department of industrial promotion tried to recommend various measures for quality regulation. During the business downturn in the aftermath of the *Seinan War* or the riot by former *samurais* in 1877, the local producers and traders finally set up a trade association. In 1886, a year after receiving criticism at the Competitive Exhibition, the association organized a training institute for dyeing techniques. They asked Jiro Yamaoka, from the Ministry of Agriculture and Commerce, for guidance regarding the training of students, and invited Kin'ichiro Okamoto, who was one of the first graduates of the Tokyo School of Mechanics. The trade association also played an important role in introducing synthetic dyestuffs in an appropriate way. For example, the Isesaki weaving association selected specific sulfide dyestuffs, which every member of the association had to purchase and use. In addition, uniformity in the dyeing process and the materials that were used was important for maintaining homogeneous quality among all members under the district brand. Therefore, their yarns or woven fabrics had to be dyed using the selected dyestuffs in the cooperative dye factory that had been established by the association. Chemists or engineers from the dye-trading company visited the weaving districts to sell imported dyestuffs by providing demonstrations of the dyeing process and advising local producers on how to use the selected dyestuffs (Hashino 2007b, p. 39).

The establishment of these informal institutes of training can be understood as a collective action by local producers in the weaving district to improve the quality of their products. They recognized the need to acquire knowledge regarding the use of synthetic dyes to solve technical issues. Many institutes for training in different weaving districts also consulted engineers sent by the Ministry of Agriculture and Commerce and hired graduates of the Tokyo School of Mechanics as lecturers. These institutes certainly contributed to improvements in product quality (Uchida 1988, p. 165). As a result of the training provided by the institutes, the weaving districts recovered their good reputation and increased production through the diffusion of new knowledge in a number of cases.

The training institutes always suffered from a lack of funds, especially following the recession of 1890, but the local governments often supported their activities. Although most of the institutes were relieved of their functions during the recession, they formed the basis for the institutionalized technical schools that were later organized by the Ministry of Education, most of them becoming prefectural technical schools. This provided continuity of technical education through the technical schools, which continued to be set up until the mid-1890s in some districts. The success of the Fourth Exposition in 1896 was evident, as the jurors, in the course of providing positive evaluations of products from Kiryu, Ashikaga, and Hachioji, found that continuous education from the institutes/technical schools in those districts had a significant impact on improving product quality. This provided a significant stimulus for local producers in the Yonezawa silk-weaving district, where they did not yet have such schools, but could understand their benefits. For them, the establishment of a formal technical school became an important objective. As a result, improvement in the quality of products gradually spread throughout this district.

This improvement required the organized effort of local producers within the same district. In other words, joint action was needed to improve the quality of their products efficiently to enable the establishment of their own district brands. Trade associations played an important role in organizing local producers and traders within the same district to solve common problems. Thus, modern weaving districts were revitalized through the initiatives of the trade associations with respect to collective quality control, introduction of new technology, marketing, and even the establishment of large factories for preparation and finishing processes (Hashino and Kurosawa 2013).

As new products were developed incorporating new ideas and designs, the newly acquired technical knowledge had to be shared among the members of the district trade associations because the district brands became 'local public goods.' The associations attempted to eliminate free riders who produced and sold fake branded products. They also emphasized business ethics in trading throughout the weaving districts. According to *The Industrial Inspection Report*, 20 weaving districts with serious quality problems tried to solve them in three ways. First, 12 weaving districts set quality standards for producers. Second, nine weaving districts monitored the quality of fabrics and applied a quality proof seal to the finest fabrics. Finally, research meetings were held and institutes were established in nine districts (Hashino 2007a, p. 121).

The process of improving product quality led local producers to organize modern weaving districts with trade associations. Consequently, each weaving district was recognized as a single participant in the market for its unique weaving brand. More importantly, organized weaving districts or trade associations came to serve as a unified target for various government policies or as recipients of important information from government. In fact, the central government, through the Ministry of Agriculture and Commerce, strongly supported the organization of the new weaving districts.

9.4 Use of Consular Reports by Trade Associations and Local and Central Governments to Solve Problems in Export Markets[6]

As discussed in the previous section, the inferior-quality problems of Japanese manufactured goods occurred repeatedly during the industrialization process. In the case of export goods, including *habutae*, Consular Reports were sent from foreign markets to the producers in Japan. Some articles from the Consular Reports help us

[6]The description in this section is taken from Hashino (2010).

to understand how and to whom the information was transmitted.[7] The *habutae*-related article in the Consular Report from the 1900s can be roughly summarized in terms of three major problems: (1) inferior quality, (2) faults in the organization of inspections and the credibility of certificates, and (3) complaints about particular local brands or about the *habutae* produced in particular weaving districts. This section examines these problems and explores how weaving districts or trade associations and the local and central governments attempted to improve the quality of *habutae* in response to the Consular Report by focusing on the case of the Fukui weaving district.

First, regarding the inferior-quality problem, vague expressions such as 'coarse,' 'poor quality,' and 'flawed' can be found in the Consular Reports. However, the consul pointed out tangible quality problems. These can be roughly divided into two areas: those considered to have been generated during the weaving process, and those that occurred during the scouring and finishing processes. With regard to the former, the consul pointed out that Japanese *habutae* had the following problems: lack of uniformity in width, length, and selvage, unevenness caused by rough weft, different thicknesses in a single fabric, lack of weft and warp, and lack of uniformity in woven yarn. Regarding the latter coarse woven fabric, which was related to the scouring process, lack of washing, low-quality soap used in washing, and dirt and spots were identified, and an increase in weight due to starching was also regarded as problematic. The *habutae* was printed and finished at its destination, and in many cases, faults were concealed during negotiations and quality problems were not discovered until the *habutae* was dyed or printed. As the dyeing process required the removal of starch, *habutae* starching was greatly despised. Occasionally, starching increased the weight of the *habutae* by 20–30 %. According to a report entitled 'Demand Situation of Japanese Starched *Habutae* in New York' from the consul in New York in June 1904, "originally, *habutae* with starching was initiated by producers or brokers to produce or sell using a shortsighted policy. Local importers and dyeworks, however, never ordered such products." The consul reported that this was the fault of local traders and producers in Japan.

Turning to the problems regarding inspection and the issue of a certificate, the consul outlined the dissatisfaction with the current inspection system and suggested a better method of inspection. With regard to the dissatisfaction with the current inspection system, the consul indicated that certificates stamped in Japan were not credible. In short, even *habutae* of low quality was graded "A." For example, *habutae* with the following defects received a grade of A: lack of weaving uniformity; unevenness of weaving yarn, such as using both thick yarn and knotted silk; lack of warp or weft; adhesion of soap dregs in the scouring process; and yellow stains and wrinkles. The consul made it clear that this was a result of unfair inspection. Thus,

[7] Japanese consular staff played an important role in collecting market information in foreign countries for export promotion from the mid-Meiji period onwards (Tsunoyama 1986). The Consular Reports include a lot of information about Japanese exports other than *habutae*. See Ulbert and Prijac (2010) for an explanation of the role of the consular service in various countries including Japan.

there was a series of complaints regarding unreliable certificates issued by *habutae* districts as a result of inconsistent inspection.

The case of the Fukui district, where *habutae* production was most pronounced, as discussed in Chap. 4, provides a good example of this issue. There were repeated complaints about the *habutae* made in this particular weaving district. For example, *Echizen Habutae*, which was the *habutae* made in Fukui, was marked grade A and exported to France, but exhibited considerable variations in product quality. This resulted in a loss of credibility for the district's brand in the market. The Fukui district attempted to solve the problem in various ways under the leadership of the trade association in cooperation with the local government. In response to the Consular Reports, the Fukui district improved the weaving process and the scouring method, and tightened the inspection system to regain the market's trust in the district brand. In other words, the Fukui district responded to the Consular Reports by restructuring their institutions, as well as their organizations. One way they improved the scouring method involved strengthening their regulations, i.e., by monitoring the manufacturing process and undertaking strict inspections. By doing so, the local and central governments played a critical role in preventing 'the failure of community' in cases where the inspection function was not working well because of collusion between acquaintances.

In particular, the Consular Reports highlighted problems in the scouring process in Fukui. The first and most fundamental question was why they happened. In 1887, when *habutae* weaving started in Fukui City, there were no scouring factories at all. Therefore, the ordinary dye workers tried to scour the *habutae* in response to the demand, but they could not do it properly, so they asked scouring factories in Kyoto to scour their *habutae*. Because the process was time-consuming and expensive, the following year they decided to learn the scouring method from workers in the Kiryu district. With the growth of *habutae* exports, the number of scouring factories within the prefecture increased to 14 by 1893. However, this increase in the number of scouring factories caused another problem; a scramble for suitably trained workers. As a result, there was a reduction in scouring quality due to excessive competition among scouring factories.

To solve these problems and protect the interests of the factory owners, the scouring factories organized the Scouring Association, enacted agreements, and asked factories in the industry to join the organization. The Scouring Association contracted with the Traders' Association to inspect the scoured *habutae* every month in the presence of representatives of both organizations. If substandard *habutae* was discovered, the scouring factory concerned was dismissed from the Scouring Association, and a notice of 'purchase refusal' was displayed in front of shop of member of the Traders' Association. In this way, they tried to prevent fraud and to eliminate dishonest producers. Needless to say, monitoring must be effective if it is to prevent injustices such as increasing the weight by the addition of water or other substances, which took place between the scouring and weaving factories. The activities of the Scouring Association included sending delegations to Kyoto and Kiryu to learn the steam scouring method.

As the *habutae* price depended on weight, increases in weight through the addition of water by unscrupulous domestic merchants became a serious problem, particularly at the turn of the century. Therefore, the trade association attempted to measure the weight of *habutae* precisely. However, it was difficult to record the precise weight, mainly because the weight of *habutae* changes with the degree of drying. In addition, inaccurate inspection results were often obtained as due to increase in the weight of the *habutae* using various other substances prior to inspection by producers. In 1905, the Ministry of Agriculture and Commerce finally promulgated the Export *Habutae* Regulatory Rules. This law prohibited the use of magnesium, salt, sugar, or other substances specified by the Minister of Agriculture and Commerce to increase the weight. This action by the central government was needed to improve the quality of the *habutae*. In other words, joint action by the trade associations was insufficient to ensure that fine-quality *habutae* would be delivered to the export market.

Moreover, an approval system was introduced for scouring factories through the Export *Habutae* Scouring Method by the Ministry of Agriculture and Commerce in April 1906. Prior to that, crude scouring methods and equipment were used. Around the time of the Russo–Japanese War (1904–1905), overseas demand grew, particularly for thick *habutae* from Fukui. However, the scouring of thick *habutae* was difficult. To overcome the difficulties, the owner of a leading scouring company ordered a change from charcoal-fire drying to steam drying and introduced a new wringing machine from abroad. However, other scouring factories were arbitrarily equipped, and the *habutae* they produced was boiled in a Japanese basin and dried using a charcoal fire. Because they were apt to throw a large amount of *habutae* into a small basin, cracking and burning would occur. 'Cloud,' which the Consular Reports pointed out, was the same as face powder, was used on the surface of the scoured *habutae* when this happened, and these spots appeared more vivid after dyeing. To solve this problem, an industrial experiment station, which had been established by the local government, and the trade association attempted to organize joint research.

However, despite this measure being taken, as shown by the Consular Reports, the complaints from overseas about the scouring continued. Thus, to reduce excessive competition, improve technology, and create uniformity in the finished product, the local government proposed a merger of the scouring factories. To facilitate this, the local government sought the approval of representatives of the scouring factories, weaving factories, and merchants, respectively. Negotiations were conducted with the heads of the experimental station, the *habutae* inspection center, and a representative of the scouring factories. Thus, *Fukuiken Seiren Kabushiki Gaisha* (Fukui Prefecture Scouring Incorporated Company; now Seiren Co.) was established in 1911 with the merger of 14 scouring factories. Economies of both scale and scope were attained simultaneously because different kinds of fabrics were now able to be scoured separately.

Furthermore, in 1911, a trade association organized a research meeting regarding 'cloud spots' that was attended by the head of the Prefecture *Habutae* Inspection Center, the president of Fukui Prefecture Scouring Inc., and *habutae* traders and producers as committee members. They agreed to work towards removing *habutae* cloud spots by: (i) offering price competition, (ii) providing a method for substance analysis of the cloud to the Industrial Section, Ministry of Agriculture and Commerce, through their local government, (iii) asking the experiment station to confirm the weaving process without using wax and seaweed, and (iv) examining the liquid circulation scouring method.

As noted above, trade associations and the local and central governments focused on improvements in scouring, which was the main problem highlighted in the Consular Reports. The scouring technology was improved and the process was rearranged to solve the problem. Moreover, a close linkage between the private and public sectors, producers, traders, trade associations, inspection centers, experiment stations, prefectural governments, and the Ministry of Agriculture and Commerce was established to enhance the reputation of the *Echizen* (old name of Fukui) *Habutae* brand.

As noted above, the Consular Reports also required improvements in inspection standards and methods. One report expressed the complaint about *Echizen Habutae* as follows: "Even though their difference is apparent, the fact that pine grade (grade A) was given equally to them is enough proof that the inspection is not strict." The complaint that their certificate could not be trusted as a result of inadequate examination implies a loss of confidence in the district brand. It was therefore crucial for the *habutae* district to not only monitor the production process, but also to confirm the product quality before shipping.

In 1893, the trade association improved the grading system by introducing three grades that reflected the result of the association's product inspection process. Additionally, they forbade marketing of the product without a label from the association. The *Echizen Habutae* brand became common in the port of Yokohama in the late 1880s. Thus, the trade association succeeded in establishing a local weaving brand shortly after *habutae* production started. However, it was difficult for the trade association to maintain a good reputation for their brand, as evidenced by the fact that they repeatedly tried to reform the inspection process. For example, they defined 'standard goods' for comparison, and introduced a rotation system for inspectors to prevent collusion between producers and inspectors. In addition, the trade association introduced joint inspections by pairs of inspectors to maintain the objectivity of the inspection process in response to the complaints from abroad.

Despite these efforts by the trade association to achieve fair and credible inspections, the complaints from the export market never disappeared. Therefore, in 1909, responsibility for inspection was shifted from the trade associations to local governments. Finally, in 1911, the Ministry of Agriculture and Commerce established the Export Silk Fabric Inspection Regulation, which defined the inspection equipment and methods to be used. In addition, part of the inspection cost was met by the central government. Such support indicates that the central government regarded *habutae* as an important export product. This episode clearly shows that it was difficult for trade associations to carry out fair inspections and thereby maintain the good reputation of their brand in international markets.

9.5 Conclusion and Policy Implications

Although a model of the development of industrial clusters formulated by Sonobe and Otsuka (2006, 2011, 2014) does not mention these issues, inferior-quality products and fake products are serious problems in both the quantity expansion and quality improvement phases of industrial development. Rampant production of inferior-quality products led to a consumer boycott in industrial clusters in Zhejiang Province in China, which triggered a crisis, as will be discussed in Chap. 10. Similar inferior-quality product issues arose in the silk-weaving industrial district in Lyon, as discussed in Chap. 6. Furthermore, after establishing a high-quality apple brand, some producers in the district seem to have sold low-quality apples at high prices in Takedate Village in prewar Japan, as suggested in Chap. 7. Therefore, it seems clear that solving the inferior-quality product issue is universally important for the development of industrial districts.

Based on the case study of a silk-weaving district, this chapter found that key roles were played by trade associations, local governments, and the central government. First, trade associations must be formed through the collective action of producers to enable the introduction of new technologies, the provision of marketing information, and quality control of products through the use of grading systems. These associations are critically important, partly because technological knowledge and marketing information are local public goods, such that there will be underinvestment in their acquisition in the absence of collective actions, and partly because quality control cannot be implemented effectively without the cooperation of producers. Furthermore, to the extent that the root cause of the inferior-quality problem is a lack of technological knowledge, a trade association must solve this problem by disseminating the appropriate knowledge to its members. Second, local governments ought to play the role of a facilitator of the activities of trade associations. Being a voluntary organization, a trade association has limitations, as it is not equipped with the power to prevent uncooperative activities and dishonest conduct. Furthermore, some knowledge and information can be useful beyond the particular industrial district. Thus, local governments, which are well positioned to acquire knowledge about actual production and product quality, must support the trade associations. Third, there are some policies that can be most effectively implemented by the central government. This is particularly the case when products are exported. Thus, the central government in Japan collected information on the reputation of products exported by rural industrial districts consisting of small enterprises, informed their local associations, and undertook quality inspection of the products. Such a positive attitude of the central government toward promoting exports can be seen in relation to other important exported products in addition to *habutae* (Tsunoyama 1986).

In short, cooperation among trade associations, local governments, and the central government is the key to sustaining the growth momentum of export-oriented industrial districts consisting of small-scale enterprises in history and the developing world.

References

Abe T (1983) Meiji zenki ni okeru nihon no zairai sangyo (Indigenous industry in early Meiji Japan). In: Umemura M, Nakamura T (eds) Matsukata zaisei to shokusan kogyo seisaku (Matsukata finance and industrial-promotion policy). University of Tokyo Press, Tokyo, pp. 295–317

Abe T (2012) Sangyo shuseki, sangyo toshi, sangyo chiiki (Industrial cluster, industrial city, and industrial district). In: Society of socio-economic history (ed) Studies in socio-economic history. Yuhikaku, Tokyo, pp. 209–223

Hashino T (2007a) Keizaihatten to sanchi shijo seido (Economic development, industrial districts, markets, and institutions). Minerva, Kyoto

Hashino T (2007b) The rise of the Japanese synthetic dye industry during the First World War. Kobe Uni Econ Rev 53:35–55

Hashino T (2010) The importance of consular report for the export growth of Japanese silk fabric *habutae* in the late 19th century. In: Ulbert J, Prijac L (eds) Consulship in the 19th century. Dobu Verlag, Humberg

Hashino T (2012) Institutionalising technical education: the case of weaving districts in Meiji Japan. Aust Econ Hist Rev 52(1):25–42

Hashino T, Kurosawa T (2013) Beyond Marshallian agglomeration economies: the roles of the trade association in a weaving district. Bus His Rev 87(3):489–513

Hashino T, Otsuka K (2013) Expansion and transformation of the export-oriented silk weaving district: the case of Fukui in Japan from 1890 to 1919, Discussion Paper No. 1303. Graduate School of Economics, Kobe University, Kobe

Hashino T, Saito O (2004) Tradition and interaction: research trends in modern Japanese industrial history. Aust Econ Hist Rev 44(3):241–258

Kiyokawa Y (1995) Nihon no Keizai Hatten to Gijutsu Fukyu (Technological Diffusion and Economic Development in Japan). Toyo Keizai Shinposha, Tokyo

Kurosawa T, Hashino T (2012) From the non-European tradition to a variation on the Japanese competitiveness model: the modern Japanese paper industry since the 1970s. In: Lamberg JA, Ojala J, Peltoniemi M, Särkkä T (eds) The evolution of global paper industry 1800–2050: a comparative analysis. Springer, London

Nicholas T (2010) The origins of Japanese technological modernization. Explor Econ Hist 48(2):272–291

Saito O (2014) Was modern Japan a developmental state? In: Otsuka K, Shiraishi T (eds) State and development. Routledge, London, pp. 23–45

Sawai M (1999) The role of technical education and public research institutes in the development of small and medium enterprises: the case of Osaka between the wars. In: Odaka K, Sawai M (eds) Small firms, large concern: the development of small business in comparative perspective. Oxford University Press, Oxford, pp. 250–289

Sonobe T, Otsuka K (2006) Cluster-based industrial development: an East Asian model. Palgrave Macmillan, Hampshire

Sonobe T, Otsuka K (2011) Cluster-based industrial development: a comparative study of Asia and Africa. Palgrave Macmillan, Hampshire

Sonobe T, Otsuka K (2014) Cluster-based industrial development: kaizen management for MSE growth in developing countries. Palgrave Macmillan, Hampshire

Sugihara K (1994) The development of an informational infrastructure in Meiji Japan. In: Bud-Frierman L (ed) Information acumen: the understanding and use of knowledge in modern business. Routledge, London/New York, pp. 75–97

Sugiyama S (1988) Japan's industrialization in the world economy 1859–99: export trade and overseas competition. The Athlone Press, London

Tamura H (2004) Fasshon no shakaikeizaishi: zairai orimonogyo no gijutsu kakushin to ryuko shijo (A socio-economic history of the fashion market in Japan (1840–1880s)). Nihon Keizai Hyoronsha, Tokyo

Tsunoyama S (1986) Nihon ryouji hokoku no kenkyu (Studies in Japan's consular reports). Dobunkan, Tokyo

Uchida H (1988) Narrow cotton stripes and their substitutes: fashion change, technological progress, and manufacturing organizations in Japanese popular clothing 1850–1920. Text Hist 19(2):159–170

Ulbert J, Prijac L (eds) (2010) Consulship in the 19th century. Dobu Verlag, Humberg

Yamazaki H, Abe T (2012) Orimono kara apareru e (From textile industry to apparel industry). University of Osaka Press, Suita

Yui T (1964) Chusho kigyo seisaku no shiteki kenkyu (History of small business policy in Japan). Toyo Keizai Shinpo Sha, Tokyo

Chapter 10
Low-Quality Crisis and Quality Improvement: The Case of Industrial Clusters in Zhejiang Province

Jianqing Ruan and Xiaobo Zhang

Abstract Supporting institutions and policies are key in helping firms improve product quality. However, the emergence of quality-supporting institutions has not been well studied. Based on both qualitative and quantitative evidence from Chinese clusters, this chapter shows that quality-enhancing institutions and policies often emerge in response to crises. Crises such as consumer boycotts and impositions of export barriers can catalyze collective actions by entrepreneurs and local governments to improve product quality.

Keywords Crisis • Manufacturing industry • Industrial cluster • Quality upgrade • Local government • Zhejiang Province

10.1 Introduction

Although market competition stimulates entrepreneurs' creativity and ingenuity, it does not necessarily induce firms to innovate and develop high-quality products (Schumpeter 1934; Aghion and Howitt 1992; Hausmann and Rodrik 2003).[1] In the

[1] There is a large body of literature on the relationship between competition and innovation. However, the empirical findings are mixed. Using data from publicly traded manufacturing firms in the United States, Hashmi (2013) finds a mildly negative relationship between competition and innovation, offering support to the Schumpeterian view. In contrast, a few empirical studies based on UK data (Blundell et al. 1999; Bloom et al. 2011) reveal a positive correlation between competition and innovation. To reconcile the conflicting findings, Aghion et al. (2005) expanded the Schumpeterian model to allow an inverted-U shape relationship between competition and innovation. In their model, whether the relationship is positive or negative depends on a product's distance from the world technology frontier, which in turn may be determined by institutions and policies.

J. Ruan (✉)
China Academy for Rural Development, Zhejiang University, Zhejiang, China
e-mail: ruanjq@126.com

X. Zhang
International Food Policy Research Institute, Washington, DC, USA

T. Hashino, K. Otsuka (eds.), *Industrial Districts in History and the Developing World*, Studies in Economic History, DOI 10.1007/978-981-10-0182-6_10

wake of strong competition, firms are often reluctant to take the lead and invest in innovation for fear of competitors quickly entering the market and squeezing their profits. Considering the positive social effect of innovations by first movers, government policies to promote innovation are justified (Hausmann and Rodrik 2003). Empirical evidence suggests that competition plays a greater role in fostering quality upgrading, an important element of innovation, in countries with supporting institutions than those with weak institutions (Amiti and Khandelwal 2013).

Having recognized the importance of institutions and policies in determining the nexus of competition and innovation, a question arises: How does a country or region create an institutional environment that enables competition to promote quality improvement? This paper aims to answer this question using China as an example. The key message is that quality-supporting institutions and policies often emerge in response to crises.

The dramatic improvement of product quality in China makes it a good setting to answer the question of how to create an institutional environment that enables competition to promote quality improvement. Product quality in China has improved dramatically in the past three decades. During China's planned economy era (prior to 1977), the quality of its manufactured products was on par with other developing countries. As the following facts demonstrate, since the reforms of the late 1970s, the quality of China's manufactured goods has been quickly catching up with developed countries (Alvarez and Claro 2006). First, over the three-decade period of 1983–2013, the share of exports relative to China's GDP jumped from 7.4 to 24.2 %. Consequently, China's share of total world exports rose from 1.2 % in 1983 to 11.7 % in 2013, with the result that China became the largest exporter in the world.[2] Since exported goods are generally higher quality than those sold on the domestic market (Henn et al. 2013; Amiti and Khandelwal 2013), such a rapid increase in exports likely implies an improvement in Chinese product quality.

Second, the number of registered trademarks in China has experienced dramatic growth: starting from a mere 18,565 in 1982, applications for trademark registration in China exceeded 664,000 in 2005, the highest in the world, and further tripled to 1,881,546 by 2013 (China State Administration of Industry and Commerce 2014). This represents an increase of one-hundred times over three decades.

Third, since the 1990s, patent applications have also seen phenomenal growth in China, from 41,469 in 1990 to 2,377,061 in 2013, a 56-fold increase (China National Bureau of Statistics 2014a), and the fastest increase in the world during that period.[3] Finally, the proportion of merchandise sampled for quality inspection that passed the first grade or above has increased from 49.6 % in 1995 to 94.2 % in 2013 (China

[2] See http://stat.wto.org/CountryProfile/WSDBCountryPFView.aspx?Country=CN&. Export performance may not be a perfect measure of a country's product quality as a country can use "high-quality" versus "low-price" growth strategies (Hallak and Schott 2011). Nonetheless, as noted by Rodrik (2006) and Hausmann et al. (2007), China has comparable export quality to the most developed economies in the world.

[3] Strictly speaking, trademarks and patents are evidence of both innovation and upgraded quality. They do not necessarily represent only upgraded quality.

National Bureau of Statistics 2014a). Each of these facts indicates rapid improvement in the quality of Chinese manufactured products.

How has China so quickly upgraded its product quality? Foreign investment has been listed as a key to facilitating technology spillover and product quality improvement in the host country (Xu 2000; Cheung and Lin 2004; Hatani 2009). Processing trade is also considered a contributor to export sophistication (Amiti and Freund 2010). However, more than 70 % of China's economic growth in the past three decades has been driven by the domestic private sector (Wei and Zhang 2011). So the dramatic observed increase in quality cannot be solely attributed to foreign investment and trade. To understand the process of quality upgrading, it is essential to study the structure of production underlying most domestic private enterprises in China.

China's industrial production has become increasingly cluster-based in the past three decades (Li and Lu 2009; Lu and Tao 2009; Long and Zhang 2011). One-town/one-product has been a defining feature of China's industrialization. Clustering reduces transaction costs, through easier flow of information, labor pooling and proximity to product and input markets (Marshall 1920). Additionally, it can help reduce capital entry barriers by dividing an integrated production process into many incremental steps (vertical disintegration) (Ruan and Zhang 2009; Li and Lu 2009). Lower entry barriers enable more domestic small and medium enterprises, particularly private ones, to survive and thrive in clusters (Schmitz and Nadvi 1999; Long and Zhang 2011).

Thanks to low entry barriers, the number of firms in clusters expands quickly, resulting in intense competition. Firms often lack incentives to produce high-quality products because of easy imitation by others. Consequently, most firms choose instead to produce low-quality products. However, facing a downward-sloping demand curve, the market for low-end products may quickly become saturated as the production volume in clusters expands. After the low-end market is exhausted, firms must either exit or compete to improve their product quality and start to target the more lucrative high-end market. By synthesizing the experience of the East Asian economies, Sonobe and Otsuka (2006) hypothesize that cluster development often encompasses two phases: quantity expansion and quality upgrade.

However, few investigations have examined the process of transitioning from quantity expansion to quality improvement from the perspective of crisis. Rather than being smooth and automatic, this transition is often accompanied by crisis. Under fierce competition, producers in clusters operate on thin profit margins and have little if any opportunity to raise prices. Consequently, negative shocks seriously threaten the survival of many firms in a cluster. Under competitive pressure, some producers may choose to compromise product quality by using cheap or fake materials, which in turn can damage the reputation of a cluster and result in a cluster-wide quality crisis down the road. Simply put, the quantity expansion stage of cluster development is bound to result in a crisis. However, the timing of the crisis that accompanies quality upgrading has not been discussed in the literature.

When a shock strikes, both entrepreneurs and local governments are likely to have more incentives to act collectively to improve product quality than in normal times because failure to do so may result in the collapse of the whole cluster, bankrupting numerous small businesses and cutting off the revenue stream of local governments. Additionally, crises reshape the way in which different stakeholders perceive the benefits and costs of proposed reform measures. Even with these advantages, it is always challenging to coordinate the interests of different parties and take collective action amidst a crisis. Whether crises can provide an opportunity for a cluster to upgrade quality remains largely an empirical question.

This chapter examines the mechanism of quality upgrade in clusters and relates it to external shocks using China as an example. Although this study is based on Chinese data, the insights apply to other developing countries. For example, a ban imposed by developed countries on the import of low-quality surgical instruments produced in the surgical instruments industry cluster in Silakot, Pakistan compelled both local governments and business communities to take collective action and improve quality (Nadvi 1999).

Our study is also related to the literature on the emergence of regulations. The presence of information asymmetry has been argued to be one of the major drivers of the emergence of market regulations (Law 2003; Law and Kim 2005).[4] However, the literature largely ignores the timing of the enactment of regulations. Our paper complements this literature by linking it to crises. Information asymmetry often leads to poor production quality (Akerlof 1970). As consumers become fed up with the quality problem, they may boycott the product, creating a crisis for producers. Our point is that regulations are more likely to emerge after a crisis than in normal times.

This chapter is organized as follows: Section 10.2 discusses the general patterns of industrial clusters and relevant crises in Zhejiang Province. Section 10.3 presents several case studies to illustrate the role of crises in upgrading cluster quality. Section 10.4 develops a conceptual framework and tests the hypotheses. Section 10.5 concludes the study.

10.2 Industrial Clusters and Crises in Zhejiang Province

10.2.1 Cluster Development in Zhejiang

We selected Zhejiang as the focus of our empirical study for several reasons. First, Zhejiang ranks first among China's provinces for number of manufacturing enterprises. Second, Zhejiang's industrial development is cluster-based. In 2004, there were 839 industrial clusters in Zhejiang with total output exceeding 100 million Yuan (Zhejiang Manufacturing Cluster Empirical Research Group 2007).[5]

[4]The literature on regulations is too broad to comprehensively review (Coase 1959; Joskow and Rose 1987). Here we primarily mention a few works related to the emergence of regulations.

[5]The exchange rate in 2004 was about 0.13 USD:1 Yuan.

Located on the eastern coast of China, Zhejiang's natural resources are more limited than many other provinces in China. During China's planned economy era before 1978, the central government strategically invested less in Zhejiang than most other provinces, citing proximity to the front in the event of war with Taiwan as its reason for so doing. As a result, Zhejiang had a much lower share of state-owned enterprises than many other provinces. At the start of China's economic reforms in 1978, per capita gross domestic product (GDP) in Zhejiang was 331 Yuan (255 US Dollars), ranking 13th among 30 provinces. By 2013, Zhejiang's per capita GDP reached 68,462 Yuan (11,054 US Dollars), placing it among China's five richest provinces (China National Bureau of Statistics 2014a). Industrial development played a key role in Zhejiang's rapid economic growth. According to the China Economic Census, in 2004, Zhejiang had more industrial enterprises than any other province, totaling nearly 190,000. Also, more than 40,000 of these industrial enterprises had annual sales incomes exceeding five million Yuan, again more than in any other province in China (China National Bureau of Statistics 2006).

Zhejiang's industrial development is largely cluster-based (see Table 10.1). The phrases "one village, one product" and "one industry in one county" have been commonly used in the media to describe the concentration of industrial production in Zhejiang. In 2000, Zhejiang had 529 industrial clusters with an annual gross output of more than 100 million Yuan and 149 industrial clusters with annual output value exceeding 1 billion Yuan. On average each of these 149 larger clusters generated a gross output value of 3.3 billion Yuan, hired more than 20,000 workers and contained 1400 enterprises. By the end of 2004, the number of clusters that produced more than 100 million Yuan in industrial output increased to 839. These clusters included 156,500 enterprises, or 85.0 % of the total number in the province. The total industrial output value created by the clusters reached as high as 1.547 trillion Yuan (187 billion US Dollars), accounting for 78.6 % of total provincial industrial output, whereas total profit reached 79.4 billion Yuan (9.6 billion US Dollars), amounting to 76.5 % of total profit in the province's manufacturing sector. In 2007, the Chinese Academy of Social Sciences published a list of the top 100 industrial clusters in China, 36 of which were in Zhejiang (China Business Times 2007). In summary, in the past several decades, Zhejiang has followed a rather successful cluster-based industrialization path.

10.2.2 Quality Upgrade in Zhejiang

Zhejiang has witnessed not only a rapid expansion of industrial output but also an impressive improvement in quality. Table 10.2 shows the trends over time for the number of patents granted and the number of enterprises with quality certifications. As an important indicator of product quality and technological improvement, the number of patents granted in Zhejiang has jumped from 1328 in 1990 to more than 50,000 in 2008, and to 202,350 in 2013 (China National Bureau of Statistics 2014b).

Table 10.1 The distribution of industrial clusters in Zhejiang Province

Sector	Number of clusters	Gross industrial output value (in hundred Millions, Chinese yuan)	Ratio of gross industrial output value of all manufacturing clusters (%)
Processing of Food from Agricultural Products	25	281.8	1.8
Manufacture of Foods	6	50.5	0.3
Manufacture of Beverages	10	59.2	0.4
Manufacture of Textiles	56	2669.6	17.3
Manufacture of Furniture	11	90.7	0.6
Manufacture of Paper and Paper Products	45	396.6	2.6
Manufacture of Medicines	1	40.9	0.3
Manufacture of Chemical Fibers	4	306.8	2
Manufacture of Rubber	13	80	0.5
Manufacture of Plastics	58	854.2	5.5
Manufacture of Nonmetallic Mineral Products	58	624.4	4
Manufacture of Metal Products	57	748.9	4.8
Manufacture of General Purpose Machinery	68	1660.2	10.7
Manufacture of Special Purpose Machinery	47	474.4	3.1
Manufacture of Textile Wearing Apparel, Footwear, and Caps	44	760.1	4.9
Manufacture of Leather, Fur, Feather, and Related Products	20	680.8	4.4
Processing of Timber; Manufacture of Wood, Bamboo, Rattan, Palm, and Straw Products	18	165.6	1.1
Printing, Reproduction of Recording Media	32	184.1	1.2
Manufacture of Articles for Culture, Education, and Sports Activities	18	182.8	1.2
Manufacture of Raw Chemical Materials and Chemical Products	51	988.6	6.4
Smelting and Pressing of Ferrous Metals	6	93.5	0.6
Smelting and Pressing of Nonferrous Metals	15	293.6	1.9
Manufacture of Electrical Machinery and Equipment	51	1595	10.3
Manufacture of Communication Equipment, Computers, and Other Electronic Equipment	22	672	4.3

(continued)

Table 10.1 (continued)

Sector	Number of clusters	Gross industrial output value (in hundred Millions, Chinese yuan)	Ratio of gross industrial output value of all manufacturing clusters (%)
Manufacture of Measuring Instruments and Machinery for Cultural Activity and Office Work	18	181.4	1.2
Manufacture of Artwork and Other Manufacturing	36	323.8	2.1
Recycling and Disposal of Waste	3	28.9	0.2
Manufacture of Transport Equipment	46	986.3	6.4

Source: Zhejiang Manufacturing Cluster Empirical Research Group (2007)

Table 10.2 Number of approved patents and enterprises with quality certifications in Zhejiang Province

Year	Number of approved patents	Growth rate (%)	Number of enterprises with quality certifications	Growth rate (%)
1990	1328	–	0	–
1991	1928	45.18	0	–
1992	2513	30.34	0	–
1993	1868	–25.67	0	–
1994	2368	26.77	0	–
1995	2276	–3.89	0	–
1996	2632	15.64	0	–
1997	3393	28.91	1	–
1998	4341	27.94	5	400.00
1999	7172	65.22	5	0.00
2000	7495	4.50	31	520.00
2001	8355	11.47	89	187.10
2002	10,478	25.41	106	19.10
2003	14,402	37.45	330	211.32
2004	15,250	5.89	2181	560.91
2005	19,056	24.96	4255	95.09
2006	30,968	62.51	7994	87.87
2007	44,712	44.38	–	–
2008	52,924	18.37	–	–

Source: The numbers of approved patents after 2000 comes from the Zhejiang Intellectual Property Office (http://www.zjpat.gov.cn)
The numbers of approved patents before 1999 come from the National Intellectual Property Office (http://search.sipo.gov.cn/)
The numbers of enterprises with quality certifications come from the Zhejiang Quality and Technology Supervision Office

Zhejiang's first quality certification occurred in Wenzhou in 1997.[6] Since then, the number of quality-certified companies in the province has steadily increased, reaching 16,347 by 2013.[7]

In 1997, Zhejiang introduced the Zhejiang Famous Trademark Identification and Protection Regulations. In 2006, the province had 698 well-known trademarks. By the end of 2007, the number of registered trademarks in Zhejiang had reached 290,000, accounting for 10 % of the total registered trademarks in China. Zhejiang ranks first in the total number of overseas trademark registrations, well-known trademarks, agricultural trademarks, and trademark infringement cases investigated. Besides registered trademarks, the rapid growth in the number of quality certifications also reflects the overall quality improvement of manufactured goods from Zhejiang.

10.2.3 Crises in Zhejiang Clusters

The development of Zhejiang's industrial clusters has been associated with various crises. Because of a lack of comprehensive statistical data for all the clusters, we must select large and well-known clusters with publicly available information. *Zhejiang Yearbook* (China National Bureau of Statistics 2003) lists 149 clusters with gross output value exceeding one billion Yuan in 2000. Additionally, 36 clusters were included in the top 100 national clusters by the Chinese Academy of Social Sciences Survey in 2007. The Zhejiang Bureau of Small and Medium Business also published data on industrial clusters in Zhejiang in 2007. The three lists cover a total of 158 clusters. Some less developed counties lack large clusters, whereas some developed regions have more than three large industrial clusters. Because our analysis is at the county level and some counties have multiple clusters, in our main analyses, we limited the maximum number of clusters per county in our sampling survey. Among 76 counties, 16 have more than three clusters. Where a country has more than three clusters, we kept only the top three clusters. These trimming procedures resulted in the dropping of only 33 clusters. We randomly surveyed 85 of the 125 remaining clusters. To check the robustness of the results, we also used restricted samples in the main analyses by dropping counties with more than two clusters or more than one cluster. The results remain robust.

[6]People's Republic of China Product Quality Certification Regulations was introduced in 1991. China Quality Certification Centre (CQC) was created as a professional certification body to provide quality certifications. For a firm to apply for a quality certification is optional but costly (about 2000 US Dollars for each certification). CQC sends auditors to inspect factories and certify if their product quality complies with a certain standard. The most common standard is ISO 9001 drafted by the International Organization for Standardization. Certification is helpful for firms as a means to signal their product quality and increase exports.

[7]The information can be searched from the webpage of the Zhejiang Bureau of Quality and Technical Supervision (http://www.zjbts.gov.cn/search/cxzx.aspx).

We classified crises according to type into five categories: quality crisis, consumer boycott, export barriers, central government macro policy and regulations, cost price escalation (for example involving wages, as well as the prices of land, energy and other raw materials), and others (mainly accidents, such as fires and explosions). No official crisis-related statistical data records exist for industrial clusters. In the summer of 2012, we surveyed 85 clusters. By interviewing the major informants in the local government and business associations, we recorded the major milestones in the process of cluster development, such as major crises encountered and subsequent policy responses, if any. We also searched the internet and media reports to confirm the major crises and their timing.

Table 10.3 reports crises in the clusters by type and year. From 1990 to 2008, a total of 53 crises occurred in these clusters. Quality crises accounted for the largest share, followed by crises related to export barriers (10). All the crises in this category happened after 2004, probably reflecting China's fast export growth after joining the World Trade Organization (WTO). Some industries also occasionally encounter sudden and unfavorable policy changes. For instance, in 2004, China's National Development and Reform Commission announced a new regulation imposing an investment threshold for entry to the automobile and motorcycle industries, which struck a heavy blow to small automobile part suppliers in Wenling and Yuhuan. Overall, crises have become more frequent since 2000. Five crises can be categorized as accidents. For example, on October 21, 2006, the Zhili Children's

Table 10.3 Major crises in Zhejiang Clusters

	Shocks by type					
Year	Quality crisis	Export barriers	Macro policy	Factor price	Accidents and others	Total
1990	2	0	0	0	0	2
1992	0	0	1	0	0	1
1995	3	0	0	0	0	3
1996	1	0	0	0	0	1
1997	1	0	0	0	0	1
1998	1	0	0	1	0	2
1999	1	0	0	0	0	1
2001	2	0	0	0	0	2
2002	0	0	1	1	0	2
2003	0	0	0	1	1	2
2004	1	0	4	2	2	9
2005	3	6	3	3	0	15
2006	0	1	0	2	1	4
2007	0	1	1	1	1	4
2008	1	2	1	0	0	4
Total	16	10	11	11	5	53

The table reports the number of crises by type and year
The financial crisis in 2008 was not included as it affected all the clusters

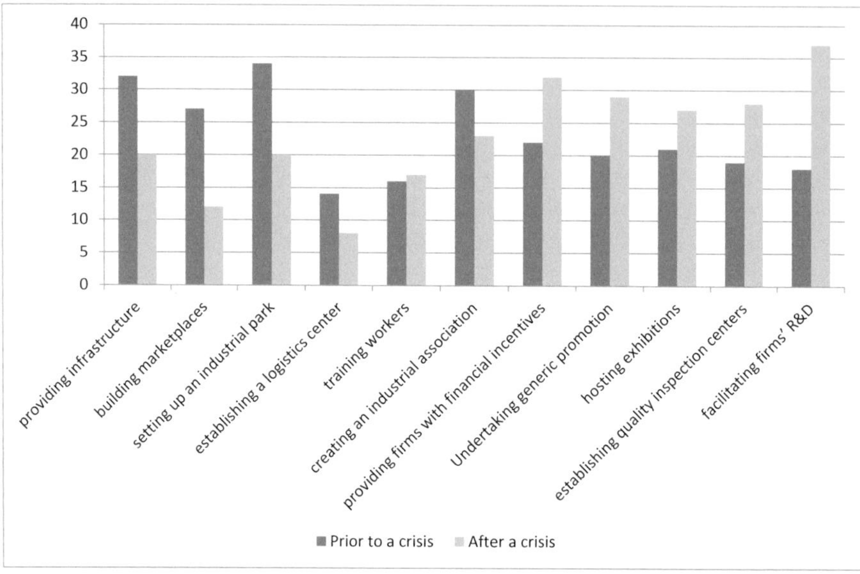

Fig. 10.1 Major local industrial polices before and after a crisis (Sources: Authors' surveys)

Garment cluster suffered an accidental fire, killing eight and injuring five. After the accident, the government imposed strong safety regulations, requiring all workshops to install fire exit stairs and separate production spaces from living areas.[8]

Figure 10.1 shows the number of major local government policies before and after a crisis. We consider 11 types of industrial policies: (1) providing infrastructure; (2) building marketplaces; (3) setting up industrial parks; (4) establishing logistics centers; (5) training workers; (6) creating industrial associations; (7) providing firms with financial incentives; (8) undertaking generic promotion; (9) hosting exhibitions; (10) establishing quality inspection centers; and (11) facilitating firms' research and development. Prior to a crisis, the first four types of policies in support of market expansion are more popular. After a crisis, policies (10)–(11), which are primarily conducive to quality upgrade, were more likely to be implemented. It seems that the menu of industrial policies differs before and after a crisis.

10.3 Case Studies

In this section, we use three case studies to illustrate the evolutionary process of industrial clusters amid crises.

[8] In many workshops, workers eat, live, and work in the same place. They are often called "three-in-one" workshops.

10.3.1 Burning Wenzhou Shoes at Wulin Gate in China

The city of Wenzhou is a major center of footwear production in China, renowned as "China's footwear capital." In 2004, the footwear cluster in Wenzhou produced 835 million pairs of shoes and employed 400,000 workers (Huang et al. 2008). However, the development process has not always been smooth. Particularly, a consumer boycott stemming from a quality crisis in 1987 almost devastated the cluster.

Wenzhou's footwear production cluster began in the late 1970s. The clustering mode of production lowers capital barriers to entry because production steps can be dispersed among different family workshops or firms (Huang et al. 2008). As a result, the number of enterprises soared, and total output expanded dramatically. Faced with price pressures, many enterprises adopted a low-quality and low-cost strategy. Some even started to use fake materials to reduce their production costs. This behavior damaged the reputation of the whole industry in Wenzhou because most producers lacked their own brands, and consumers, unable to differentiate producers, simply generalized that all the shoes made in Wenzhou were poor quality. Wenzhou shoes were called "day shoes," "week shoes," and "falling-heel shoes" and became synonymous with counterfeiting. Consumer dissatisfaction with Wenzhou shoes climaxed on August 8, 1987, when China's Hangzhou Industrial and Commercial Administration burned 5000 pairs of Wenzhou-made shoes in Wulin Plaza, Hangzhou during a televised broadcast. In April 1988, consumers destroyed a shop selling Wenzhou shoes in a large shopping center in Nanjing. Subsequently, consumers in other cities also protested Wenzhou shoes. Officials in Changsha, Harbin, and Zhuzhou also set fire to Wenzhou shoes in public. Subsequently, the Shanghai, Nanjing, Wuhan, Changchun, Shijiazhuang, and Dalian governments imposed bans on the sale of Wenzhou shoes. Even as far away as Russia, signs with messages such as "No Wenzhou goods" and "Wenzhou people out of Russia" were displayed on the streets (Chen 2006).

On the positive side, the crisis triggered an opportunity for enterprises and local government to work together to improve product quality. Facing an existential threat, local business communities cooperated with government on a series of collective actions to improve product quality and save the industry. The Wenzhou District Footwear Association, the first footwear association in Wenzhou, was established by a group of footwear industry veterans in June 1988 and initially included more than 370 enterprises. It called for all members to pay attention to product reputation and improve product quality (China Footwear Information Network 2007). The association established various regulations to curb vicious competition, punish producers of poor-quality products, and restore trust among members. For example, the association set up a new intellectual property rights committee to protect and promote the launch of new products and inhibit the spread of fake products. It blacklisted enterprises with bad reputations, shaming them before other members.

Furthermore, local governments took serious administrative actions. Led by the Lucheng district government of Wenzhou City, the Bureau of Quality and Technical

Supervision, the Administration of Industry and Commerce, and several other related agencies jointly established the Lucheng Footwear Quality Management Office. Since then, all shoes produced in Wenzhou have had to be certified by this office. The office began inspecting enterprises regularly and sampling their products. The office issues quality certificates to products that meet quality standards, and bans the sale of products that fail quality tests. To renew their production license with the Administration of Industry and Commerce, enterprises must provide the quality certifications for their products (Li 2006). In 1993, the Wenzhou municipal government implemented a strategy to create a regional brand, requiring all shoes shipped out of Wenzhou to carry the "Made in Wenzhou" label. The government also began providing incentives to encourage local enterprises to create brands. For example, if a firm earns the "China Famous Brand" title for its products from the State Administration of Industry and Commerce, the local government will award it 1 million Yuan (Li 2006). Moreover, the association and local governments worked together to regulate advertising. Enterprises that were blacklisted by the association for their bad reputation were also banned from posting any advertisements in Wenzhou. Given Wenzhou's status as the major shoe market and production center, this measure made it hard for the punished enterprises to gain business.

10.3.2 Quality Crisis in the Puyuan Sweater Industrial Cluster

Puyuan Township is located in northern Zhejiang Province, between Hangzhou and Shanghai. Historically, Puyuan was an important silk production center. In 1976, a collectively owned enterprise, the Puyuan Tanhua (Weaving) Production Cooperative, purchased three hand-loom weaving machines and began to produce cashmere sweaters. The cooperative's gross output value soared from 28,000 Yuan to 300,000 Yuan in just 1 year, prompting the group to devote its entire production capacity to cashmere sweaters by the end of 1977 (Chen 1996). Like the Wenzhou footwear cluster, the Puyuan sweater industrial cluster suffered a quality crisis between 1995 and 1996. In 1995, many merchants boycotted sweaters made in Puyuan because of their bad reputation. This greatly depressed demand for Puyuan sweaters. Subsequently, in late 1995 and in 1996, the entire textile industry fell into recession. Meanwhile, the Puyuan sweater market was plagued with serious management problems. The property rights of the market's multiple stakeholders were not clearly defined, and stakeholders had disputes about how to set rental rates, allocate revenues, and share maintenance costs. Owing to disagreements regarding these areas, the market lacked crucial public investment and performed poorly in many necessary services. Disgruntled with the poor service, some shops closed their doors, and some merchants voted with their feet by moving to another sweater market in nearby Honghe Township.

Realizing the seriousness of the problem, the local government and entrepreneurs responded to the crisis through a series of measures. One key initiative was to reform the management structure of the sweater market to provide better service to merchants. Another important strategy was to improve product quality. Similar to the Footwear Quality Management Office introduced to solve the Wenzhou shoe crisis, a quality control office was established to regularly inspect sweater quality. Also, the market added a new Quality Product Street, where only well-known brands could be sold while less well-known brands were excluded. Nowadays, having a brand for sale on Quality Product Street sends a strong signal of its premium quality. Through these measures Puyuan quickly reversed its reputation for bad quality.

The above two cases share some common features: First, each crisis damaged the reputation of the clusters and depressed demand for their products. Second, each crisis also provided an opportunity for the private and public sectors to cooperate to improve product quality. Together, these sectors took a series of actions such as establishing business associations, inspecting product quality, protecting brands, and punishing bad apples.

10.3.3 Shengzhou Necktie Cluster

Shengzhou is located in eastern Zhejiang, with Hangzhou to its north and Ningbao to its east. The Shengzhou necktie cluster started in 1984 when a Shengzhou local returned home from a successful business career in Hong Kong to set up a necktie plant. In less than three decades, Shengzhou became one of the largest necktie clusters in the world, developing a comprehensive supply chain that involves dying, weaving, sewing and marketing. Shengzhou's necktie marketplace has the grand name "China Necktie City," and boasts of being the largest in China. In 2010, more than 1300 enterprises were engaged in tie production and the cluster employed more than 50,000 workers. The cluster sold over 300 million ties worth USD 1.5 billion to more than 100 countries, accounting for 90 % and 40 % of the Chinese and global markets, respectively.

Besides the rapid expansion in the quantity of neckties produced by the cluster, there has also been rapid improvement in quality. To better control quality in the cluster, the Shengzhou government set up a "China Necktie Quality Inspection Center," the most authoritative of such centers in China. Five Shengzhou brands earned the title of "China famous trademark" and 11 brands enjoyed export exemption status (eliminating the need for quality inspection). The government also named "Shengzhou Necktie" a regional brand.

These developments did not simply occur as part of a smooth process. The industry only reached this glamorous stage by overcoming numerous challenges. The most salient was the rise of raw materials prices in 2005. Silk is the major material used in necktie production. The cluster consumed 7000 t of silk, 95 % of which originated elsewhere. The wholesale price of silk started at 170,000 Yuan/t in 2005, soared to 260,000 Yuan/t by the end of the year, and reached 344,000 yuan/t by February of 2006. Each 10,000 Yuan/t increase in the price of silk adds 0.4 Yuan to the production cost of a necktie. This means that the rise in the silk price over 14 months during 2005–2006 increased the cost of each necktie by 7 Yuan (about 1 US Dollar). The industry runs on thin margins. As the silk price increased, profits were squeezed and the industry fell into the red during 2005–2006.

In response to rising silk prices, the local government and firms came up with a series of collective actions. First, the industrial association persuaded 33 of its large members to collectively pledge to raise necktie prices by 10 %. To ensure this pledge was kept, the association collected a security deposit from each firm based on its number of sewing machines. Any firm that independently lowered product prices was to forfeit its deposit.

The second strategy was to lower the transaction cost of buying silk and expand the silkworm cocoon production base. The local government earmarked 2 million Yuan annually to support a logistics company that purchased raw materials on behalf of local necktie companies. Thanks to its greater bargaining power, the logistics company could obtain lower prices for the firms it represented than any single firm acting alone could. Meanwhile, supported by the Shengzhou government, some big firms signed agreements with silkworm cocoon producers in western China to secure a stable supply.

Third, the local government and necktie producer industry association helped a few big firms establish a digital necktie design library, which was open to all the firms in the cluster. The availability of a large variety of historical designs gave firms a fertile ground to create innovative designs.

Fourth, the local government encouraged firms to establish their own brands. Specifically, it earmarked a fund to subsidize firms that exported neckties under their own brands, purchased international brands, or registered their brands overseas. This policy quickly paid off. For example, one local firm purchased an Italian necktie company well known for its designs, while another company set up a design studio in Milan.

Thanks to these efforts, and despite rising silk prices, the Shengzhou tie cluster has thrived and steadily moved up the quality ladder.

10.4 Empirical Analyses

In this section, having presented the case studies, we describe how we empirically tested the impact of crises on quality improvement in clusters. To do this, we used county-level data from Zhejiang for the period 1990–2008 following the specification below:

$$Q_{it} = \alpha * Crisis_{it} + \beta X_{it} + Year_t + County_i + \epsilon_{it} \tag{10.1}$$

where Q_{ij} stands for quality measurement in county i at year t. It would have been ideal to use the quality measurements at the cluster level. However, such data were not systematically available and instead we based our analysis at the county level. We considered three outcome variables: patents per capita, quality certifications per capita, and share of professional and technical personnel in total population. These three variables are incorporated into a logarithm. The patent data since 2000 come from the Zhejiang Intellectual Property Office, while data prior to 2000 are obtained from the website of the China Intellectual Property Office. The number of firms with quality certification is obtained from the Zhejiang Bureau of Quality and Technical Supervision.

$Crisis_{it}$ is defined as the total number of accumulative crises that county i has encountered by time t. In regressions, we also used lagged crisis variables to check robustness. Among the 85 clusters in our sample, most were at the county level in Zhejiang, but some were at the township level (one level below the county). However, because the cluster-level data were not systematically available, we used the county-level data to measure variables related to clusters in our analysis. If a county had multiple clusters, we defined the crisis variable as the total number of crises that had occurred at time t (or t-1, t-2, and t-3) in all the clusters sampled in a county. As a result, the value of crisis can exceed 1.

X_{jt} is a set of control variables at the county level in year t, such as per capita GDP, population density, per capita foreign direct investment, and share of industrial GDP. Initial conditions at the world technology frontier have been found to be mitigating factors in the upgrade decision (Verhoogen 2008; Amiti and Khandelwal 2013). We controlled for per capita GDP and share of industrial GDP to proxy the distance to the world technology frontier. Since foreign direct investment has been listed as a driver of China's quality upgrade in the literature, we included per capita foreign direct investment. Innovation behavior may differ between private firms and state-owned enterprises.

All data are gathered from the *Zhejiang Statistical Yearbook* (National Bureau of Statistics 1991–2009). Some data were missing, and in such cases we tried as much as possible to replace the missing values with figures from local statistical yearbooks or government documents. However, we still had to interpolate a few variables. From 1990 to 1992, the provincial yearbook did not report industrial sector GDP. We used the ratio of gross industrial output value to total gross output value to total GDP to estimate the missing GDP in the industrial sector. In 1992, gross industrial output values in a few counties were missing. We interpolated these missing values with the average values in 1991 and 1993. Additionally, we included year fixed effects ($Year_t$) and county fixed effects ($County_t$) in all the regressions.

10.4.1 Regression Analyses

We first regressed the number of patents per capita in the logarithm on the crisis variable and other control variables according to Eq. (10.1). The first regression (R1) in Table 10.4 reports the estimation results using the crisis variable in the

Table 10.4 Crises and number of patents

	Patents per capita in logarithm			
	R1	R2	R3	R4
	Current crisis	Crisis lagged by 1 year	Crisis lagged by 2 years	Crisis lagged by 3 years
Crisis	0.445***	0.422***	0.397***	0.374**
	(3.716)	(3.443)	(2.931)	(2.453)
Per capita GDP (log)	0.255	0.223	0.149	0.101
	(1.084)	(0.987)	(0.700)	(0.521)
Population density	−9.760***	−10.672***	−12.354***	−12.638***
	(−3.811)	(−4.243)	(−4.717)	(−4.524)
Per capita foreign direct investment (log)	0.040*	0.04	0.031	0.036
	(1.817)	(1.662)	(1.221)	(1.366)
% of industrial GDP	−0.046	−0.083	−0.561	−0.431
	(−0.181)	(−0.304)	(−0.741)	(−0.416)
Adj-R^2	0.834	0.83	0.827	0.828
AIC	2332	2186	2076	1949
Number of observations	1387	1314	1241	1168

Both county and year fixed effects are included in all the regressions
AIC stands for Akaike information criterion
The numbers in parentheses are *t*-statistics
*, **, and *** indicate significance at 10, 5, and 1 %, respectively

current year.[9] The coefficient for the patent variable is 0.445, and is statistically significant and positive. This means that one incidence of crisis results in a 56 % (=exp(0.445)*100–100) increase in the number of patents per capita. The coefficient for foreign direct investment (FDI) is 0.040, and is positive and significant at 10 %, indicating that a 1 % increase in FDI is associated with a 0.04 % of increase in the number of patents, a rather small impact.

Because it takes time for a crisis to develop, we also ran a set of regressions (R2-R4) by lagging the crisis variable for one, two, and three years, respectively. All the main results remained robust. The lagged crisis positively impacts the number of patents per capita across the three specifications. The magnitude of the coefficient declines slightly with lag length. The coefficient for the crisis variable lagged by three years is 0.374, compared to 0.445 estimated using the current crisis variable in R1. The coefficients for other variables across the four specifications are robust and consistent.

[9] Here we mainly examined the correlations between crises and quality upgrade. One should be cautious in drawing any strong inferences on causality.

Table 10.5 Crises and number of quality certifications

	Number of enterprises with quality certifications in logarithm			
	R1	R2	R3	R4
	Current crisis	Crisis lagged by 1 year	Crisis lagged by 2 years	Crisis lagged by 3 years
Crisis	0.417***	0.328***	0.205	0.047
	(4.023)	(3.221)	(1.356)	(0.164)
Per capita GDP (log)	1.907***	1.898***	1.774***	1.444***
	(5.260)	(4.598)	(3.818)	(2.705)
Population density	27.360***	27.541***	27.115***	28.130**
	−2.811	−2.963	−3.048	−2.38
Per capita foreign direct investment (log)	−0.037	−0.042	−0.049	−0.072
	(−1.287)	(−1.216)	(−1.243)	(−1.586)
% of industrial GDP	−6.631***	−7.021***	−6.884***	−5.876***
	(−4.825)	(−5.008)	(−4.376)	(−3.348)
Adj-R^2	0.885	0.882	0.883	0.885
AIC	1181	1096	980	845
Number of observations	730	657	584	511

Both county and year fixed effects are included in all the regressions
AIC stands for Akaike information criterion
The numbers in parentheses are *t*-statistics
*, **, and *** indicate significance at 10, 5, and 1 %, respectively

Table 10.5 reports the estimation results with the number of quality certifications as an outcome variable. Since quality certification did not occur until 1997, we restricted our sample to 1997–2006 in regressions on this variable. As shown in R1 and R2, the current and previous year crises are positively associated with the number of quality certifications. However, when the crisis variable is lagged by two or three years, it becomes insignificant. It seems the response of quality certification to crisis is instantaneous but not lasting. Per capita GDP is positively related to number of quality certifications. Interestingly, the share of industrial GDP to total GDP is strongly negative, probably due to its high collinearity with per capita GDP. The coefficient for FDI is insignificant in any of the regressions on the number of quality certifications.

Table 10.6 repeats Table 10.4 but replaces the dependent variable with the share of professional and technical personnel relative to the total population. Because the provincial yearbook did not report this variable until 1995, the regressions in this table are for 1995–2008. The findings for the crisis variable still hold up. Both current and lagged crises are positively correlated with number of technical staff. The coefficient peaks in R3 when the crisis variable is lagged by two years. This means that a crisis this year is followed by a 28 % (=exp(0.245)*100–100) increase in the share of professional and technical staff in the total population 2 years later. This

Table 10.6 Crises and the share of professional and technical personnel relative to the total population

	Share of professional and technical personnel in total population (logarithm)			
	R1	R2	R3	R4
	Current crisis	Crisis lagged by 1 year	Crisis lagged by 2 years	Crisis lagged by 3 years
Crisis	0.230***	0.236***	0.245***	0.232***
	(2.805)	(3.035)	(3.351)	(3.061)
Per capita GDP (log)	0.705***	0.678**	0.741**	0.820***
	(3.091)	(2.582)	(2.608)	(2.653)
Population density	−4.881***	−4.768***	−4.077**	−3.582
	(−3.183)	(−2.744)	(−2.157)	(−1.658)
Per capita foreign direct investment (log)	0.01	0.008	0.011	0.009
	(0.706)	(0.560)	(0.695)	(0.555)
% of industrial GDP	−2.516***	−2.730***	−2.999***	−3.255***
	(−3.975)	(−4.031)	(−4.199)	(−4.115)
Adj-R^2	0.727	0.718	0.712	0.705
AIC	636	587	554	532
Number of observations	1021	948	875	802

Both county and year fixed effects are included in all the regressions
AIC stands for Akaike information criterion
The numbers in parentheses are *t*-statistics
*, **, and *** indicate significance at 10, 5, and 1 %, respectively

suggests that crises may induce firms to hire more highly skilled laborers to upgrade their product quality. Coefficients for GDP and share of industrial GDP have the same signs as in Table 10.5. Total FDI has little to do with the proportion of professional and technical staff relative to the total population.

Tables 10.4, 10.5, and 10.6 examine the impact of shocks on quality improvement without distinguishing their type. In principle, it is possible that different types of shocks may differently affect the outcome of quality upgrade. To address this concern, Table 10.7 presents the estimates of the five types of shocks listed in Table 10.3 on three measures of quality upgrade. For the crisis variable, we used the current value in the regressions. The regressions based on lagged crisis values are similar and are not reported here. Four of five shocks positively and significantly impact the three outcome variables.

10.5 Conclusion

The quality of products manufactured in China has improved significantly in the past several decades. In this study we aimed to understand the mechanism of the quality upgrade process. Crises reshape both entrepreneurs' and local governments'

Table 10.7 Impact of different types of shock on quality upgrade

Types of shock	Number of patents	Number of certifications	Number of professional and technical staff
Quality Crisis	0.408*	0.138	−0.007
	(1.967)	(0.979)	(−0.082)
Export Barriers	0.446***	0.750***	0.274**
	(2.834)	(4.496)	(2.263)
Macro Policy	0.478**	0.345**	0.281**
	(2.534)	(2.359)	(2.213)
Factor price	0.399***	0.449***	0.299**
	(3.057)	(4.871)	(2.294)
Others	0.437	0.607*	0.480**
	(1.466)	(1.798)	(2.228)

The crisis variable is defined as the accumulative number of crises by year t
The three dependent variables are in the logarithm. Per capita GDP (log), population density, per capita foreign direct investment (log), share of industrial GDP, county fixed effects, and year effects are included in all the regressions, but not reported here
The numbers in parentheses are *t*-statistics
*, **, and *** indicate significance at 10, 5, and 1 %, respectively

perceptions of the payoffs and costs involved in proposed reform measures. When facing a harsh external environment, the public and private sectors are more likely to take collective action to improve product quality. Using data from 85 industrial clusters in Zhejiang, we empirically examined the impact of crises on the quality upgrade process. We found that number of patents, number of enterprises with quality certification, and share of professional and technical staff in the clusters all increase significantly post-crisis. Therefore, crises imply an opportunity for clusters to upgrade product quality.

However, the positive correlation between crises and quality upgrade does not mean one can expect crises to automatically solve all quality problems. Only when crises are successfully addressed can they become a catalyst for institutional change.

References

Aghion P, Howitt P (1992) A model of growth through creative destruction. Econometrica 60(2):323–351

Aghion P, Bloom N, Blundell R, Griffith R, Howitt P (2005) Competition and innovation: an inverted-U relationship. Q J Econ 120(2):701–728

Akerlof GA (1970) The market for "Lemons": quality uncertainty and the market mechanism. Q J Econ 84(3):488–500

Alvarez R, Claro S (2006) The China phenomenon: price, quality or variety? Working paper No. 411. Central Bank of Chile, Santiago

Amiti M, Freund C (2010) An anatomy of China's export growth. In: Wei S-j, Freenstra R (eds) China's growing role in world trade. University of Chicago Press, Chicago

Amiti M, Khandelwal AK (2013) Import competition and quality upgrading. Rev Econ Stat 95(2):476–490
Bloom N, Draca M, Reenen JV (2011) Trade induced technical change? the impact of Chinese imports on innovation, IT and productivity, NBER working papers 16717. National Bureau of Economic Research, Inc, Buxton
Blundell R, Griffith R, Reenen JV (1999) Market share, market value and innovation in a panel of British manufacturing firms. Rev Econ Stud 66(3):529–554
Chen X (1996) Puyuan Zhenzhi. Bookstore Publishing House, Shanghai
Chen W (2006) Siwei de Zuji: Zhongguo Jingji Shehui Qianyan Baogao. Economic Science Press, Beijing
Cheung KY, Lin P (2004) Spillover effects of FDI on innovation in China: evidence from the provincial data. China Econ Rev 15(1):25–44
China Business Times (2007) Zhongguo Shekeyuan Fabu Zhongguo Baijia Chanye Jiqun
China Footwear Information Network (2007) Wenzhou Xieye Ershi Nian Dashi Ji. <http://www.shoelib.com/xwh/xyjs/200709/t20070920_44179.html>. (In Chinese)
China National Bureau of Statistics (2003) Zhejiang yearbook (2003). China Statistics Press, Beijing
China National Bureau of Statistics (2006) China economic census (2004). China Statistics Press, Beijing
China National Bureau of Statistics (2014a) China statistical yearbook. China Statistics Press, Beijing
China National Bureau of Statistics (2014b) Zhejiang statistical yearbook. China Statistics Press, Beijing
China State Administration of Industry and Commerce (2014) China trademark strategy report in 2013. Available from http://sbj.saic.gov.cn/tjxx/201405/P020140504399619464010.pdf
Coase R (1959) The federal communications commission. J Law Econ 2:1–40
Hallak JC, Schott P (2011) Estimating cross-country differences in product quality. Q J Econ 126(1):417–474
Hashmi AR (2013) Competition and innovation: the inverted-U relationship revisited. Rev Econ Stat 95(5):1653–1668
Hatani F (2009) The logic of spillover interception: the impact of global supply chains in China. J World Bus 44(2):158–166
Hausmann R, Rodrik D (2003) Economic development as self-discovery. J Dev Econ 72(2):603–633
Hausmann R, Hwang J, Rodrik D (2007) What you export matters. J Econ Growth 12(1):1–25
Henn C, Papageorgiou C, Spatafora N (2013) Export quality in developing countries. International Monetary Fund working paper No. 13/108
Huang Z, Zhang X, Zhu Y (2008) The role of clustering in rural industrialization: a case study of Wenzhou's Footwear Industry. China Econ Rev 19(3):409–420
Joskow PL, Rose NL (1987) The effects of regulation, Working paper No. 447. Department of Economics, Massachusetts Institute of Technology, Boston
Law M (2003) The origins of state pure food regulation. J Econ Hist 63(4):1103–1130
Law M, Kim S (2005) Specialization and regulation: the rise of professionals and the emergence of occupational licensing regulation. J Econ Hist 65(3):723–756
Li J (2006) Kankan Renjia Wenzhouren. Jinghua Press, Beijing
Li B, Lu Y (2009) Geographic concentration and vertical disintegration: evidence from China. J Urban Econ 65(3):294–304
Long C, Zhang X (2011) Cluster-Based industrialization in China: financing and performance. J Int Econ 84(1):112–123
Lu J, Tao Z (2009) Trends and determinants of China's industrial agglomeration. J Urban Econ 65(2):167–180
Marshall A (1920) Principles of economics. Macmillan and Co. Ltd, London
Nadvi K (1999) Collective efficiency and collective failure: the response of the Sialkot surgical instrument cluster to global quality pressures. World Dev 27(9):1605–1626
Rodrik D (2006) What's so special about China's exports? China World Econ 14(5):1–19

Ruan J, Zhang X (2009) Finance and cluster-based industrial development in China. Econ Dev Cult Chang 58(1):143–164
Schmitz H, Nadvi K (1999) Clustering and industrialization: introduction. World Dev 27(9):1503–1514
Schumpeter JA (1934) The theory of economic development. Harvard University Press, Cambridge, MA
Sonobe T, Otsuka K (2006) Cluster-based industrial development: an East Asia model. Palgrave MacMillan, New York
Verhoogen E (2008) Trade, quality upgrading and wage inequality in the Mexican manufacturing sector. Q J Econ 123(2):489–530
Wei S-j, Zhang X (2011) Sex ratios, entrepreneurship, and economic growth in the people's republic of China. National Bureau of Economic Research working paper No. 16800
World Trade Organization (2007) World Trade Developments in 2006. WTO Press, Geneve <http://www.wto.org/english/res_e/statis_e/its2007_e/its07_world_trade_dev_e.htm>
Xu B (2000) Multinational enterprises, technology diffusion, and host country productivity growth. J Dev Econ 62(2):477–493
Zhejiang Manufacturing Cluster Empirical Research Group (2007) The empirical research on Zhejiang manufacturing industrial cluster. Zhejiang Statistics Bureau. (In Chinese)

Index

T. Hashino, K. Otsuka (eds.), *Industrial Districts in History and the Developing World*, Studies in Economic History, DOI 10.1007/978-981-10-0182-6

MIX
Papier aus verantwortungsvollen Quellen
Paper from responsible sources
FSC® C105338

If you have any concerns about our products,
you can contact us on
ProductSafety@springernature.com

In case Publisher is established outside the EU,
the EU authorized representative is:
Springer Nature Customer Service Center GmbH
Europaplatz 3, 69115 Heidelberg, Germany

Printed by Libri Plureos GmbH
in Hamburg, Germany